Praise for *The Wisdom of Failure*

"*The Wisdom of Failure* is an epiphany. From the very first chapter, Weinzimmer and McConoughey shift the reader's focus beyond short-term accolades and trade-offs to a horizon where a leader can find true success and accomplishment. In their well-researched book, the authors give leaders the tough love they need to learn from their mistakes before their mistakes become costly. A must-read for aspiring, new, and seasoned leaders."

—Jennifer Robin, Ph.D., author, *The Great Workplace*

"The importance of understanding failure's lessons cannot be overstated in today's fast-moving business environment, and *The Wisdom of Failure* offers a smart research-based guide to navigating these tough leadership lessons. You'll be engaged from the very first page."

—Amy C. Edmondson, Novartis Professor of Leadership and Management, Harvard Business School; author, *Teaming*

"*The Wisdom of Failure* allows you to benefit from the inevitable growth that comes from failure without having to experience it first-hand. An invaluable read for anyone striving to move themselves and their business forward."

—Dan Schawbel, founder, Millennial Branding; author, *Me 2.0*

"Never before has learning from failure been more important—to innovation, to learning, to strategy under uncertainty, and to the development of the next generation of leaders. Ironically, in many organizations the attitude towards failure virtually guarantees not only that people won't learn its valuable lessons but that they will also suffer the brunt of its downsides. This well-researched and accessible book is a timely summary of how failure can be useful, even essential, and serves as a welcome reminder of the importance of 'failing forward.'"

—Rita Gunther McGrath, strategy and innovation advisor, Columbia Business School Professor; coauthor, *Discovery-Driven Growth*

"Having worked with hundreds of emerging companies, I have seen failure in all flavors! Finally we have, in one well-written book, the lessons learned from such experiences. *The Wisdom of Failure* is an instant business classic destined for the tablets and shelves of our innovation economy's leaders."

—**Larry Weber**, chairman and CEO, W2 Group

"Leaders become great only when they have overcome adversity. We learn how to grow from our setbacks. Weinzimmer and McConoughey have created a simple framework and practical methodology to develop an organizational culture that encourages productive innovation. *The Wisdom of Failure* provides us with the research, case studies, and tools to transform our failures into our biggest successes."

—**Jeff DeGraff**, professor, Ross School of Business, University of Michigan; author, *Innovation You, Leading Innovation,* and *Creativity at Work*

"Every truly great leader has experienced failure and (more important) learned from it. Organizations that support 'smart' failure are more innovative, adaptable, resilient, and profitable. In *The Wisdom of Failure*, Weinzimmer and McConoughey have distilled the key factors that are most likely to push every one of us off track, and outlined the practices that leaders, teams, and entire organizations can use to navigate around those hazards. If you aren't pushing yourself to the point where failure is a possibility, you are not coming close to your potential as a leader. But in today's times, where acceleration is the new normal, you'll need this book as your guide."

—**Eric McNulty**, editor, Harvard School of Public Health; coauthor, *You're It! Lessons from Crisis Meta-Leadership*

The
WISDOM
of
FAILURE

The
WISDOM
of
FAILURE

HOW TO LEARN THE TOUGH LEADERSHIP LESSONS
WITHOUT PAYING THE PRICE

Laurence G. Weinzimmer
Jim McConoughey

JOSSEY-BASS
A Wiley Imprint
www.josseybass.com

Published by Jossey-Bass
A Wiley Imprint
One Montgomery Street, Suite 1200, San Francisco, CA 94104-4594
www.josseybass.com

Jossey-Bass books and products are available through most bookstores. To contact Jossey-Bass directly call our Customer Care Department within the U.S. at 800-956-7739, outside the U.S. at 317-572-3986, or fax 317-572-4002.

Wiley also publishes its books in a variety of electronic formats and by print-on-demand. Some material included with standard print versions of this book may not be included in e-books or in print-on-demand. If the version of this book that you purchased references media such as CD or DVD that was not included in your purchase, you may download this material at http://booksupport.wiley.com. For more information about Wiley products, visit www.wiley.com.

Library of Congress Cataloging-in-Publication Data

Weinzimmer, Laurence G.
  The wisdom of failure : how to learn the tough leadership lessons without paying the price / Laurence G. Weinzimmer, Jim McConoughey. – 1st ed.
     p. cm.
  Includes bibliographical references and index.
  ISBN 978-1-118-13501-3 (cloth), ISBN 978-1-118-22529-5 (pdf),
  ISBN 978-1-118-23872-1 (epub), ISBN 978-1-118-26333-4 (emobi)
  1. Leadership.   2. Success in business.   3. Business failures.   I. McConoughey, Jim, 1961–   II. Title.
  HD57.7.W4513 2013
  658.4'092–dc23

                                        2012027907

Printed in the United States of America
FIRST EDITION
HB Printing   10   9   8   7   6   5   4   3   2   1

CONTENTS

PART THREE
Personality Issues

The
WISDOM
of
FAILURE

ONE

Flawless Leadership
Learning the Lessons Without Paying the Price

He was lauded as one of America's greatest business leaders after he transformed a small, unremarkable regional company into one of the nation's most prominent organizations. Under his leadership, his company became a Wall Street superstar. He became one of the highest paid CEOs in the United States. He owned lavish homes across the country. In February 2001, *Fortune* magazine's ranking of America's most admired companies listed his company as number one for "innovativeness" and number two for "quality of management." Moreover, *Fortune* rated his company as "America's Most Innovative Company" for six consecutive years. He became personal friends with the president of the United States and was an advisor to world leaders.

What added to his aura was his rags-to-riches story. He became the poster child for living the American dream. He had a less than modest childhood, growing up in poverty. Even though his father worked multiple jobs, the family did not have running water in their house. He, too, had to work multiple jobs to help his family survive—even though he was just a child. But he always dreamed of having a better life. He once told a reporter that spending hours performing manual labor gave him time to think about that life, about how he would get into business rather than create a future similar to his past.

As a young man, he obtained the support of a local university professor, who described him as an "outstanding student," based on the strong work ethic he had learned out of necessity as a child. This same professor figured out a way to fund him to earn a master's degree in economics.

After serving four years in the U.S. military, he took a job with the U.S. government to learn how policies were made. He then decided to continue his education and received a Ph.D. in economics. Armed with a solid work ethic and a good education, he was on his way. Shortly after entering industry, he quickly realized success beyond his wildest dreams, ultimately attaining celebrity status as one of the greatest leaders in industry. Some even called him a hero.

As an individual, he was described as an extraordinarily giving man. What was most unique was his ability to support issues without having an obvious personal agenda. He supported numerous charities, including everything from ballets and museums to the Urban League. He also funded numerous scholarships and provided millions of dollars to political campaigns for *both* Republicans and Democrats. And most impressive—even with all of his successes and recognition—he donated a considerable amount of his time, serving as chair for numerous worthy causes.

Leadership gurus described him with terms like "cutting edge," "trustworthy," and "supportive." His leadership philosophy was to hire the brightest people possible and then have them "push the business envelope."[1]

His confidence was one of his greatest sources of strength. His employees described him as mild-mannered and quiet, but stern and demanding when necessary. In fact, the views of his employees were so strong that his company was ranked by *Fortune* as a Best Company to Work For from 1999 to 2001. He had a knack for picking the best employees and then giving them freedom to do their jobs without micromanaging.

Ultimately, his leadership approach was profiled in newspapers, magazines, and leadership books. We became enamored with his success story. We read about him and we admired him. And when "leadership experts" said that to become a great leader, all you need to do is mimic great leaders, we even sent our aspiring managers to executive-development forums to hear about him.

But have you ever noticed that many "successful" leaders profiled in leadership books have failed when faced with challenging situations?

The leader we just profiled was Ken Lay, the former chair and CEO of Enron—the man at the center of the largest business scandal in the United States in its time. In the final years at Enron, President Jeffery Skilling and CFO Andrew Fastow used accounting loopholes and unethical financial reporting to hide billions of dollars in debt incurred through failed ventures. When mistakes—failed deals and failed projects—were brought to Lay's attention, he had two choices: (1) admit the mistakes, move on, and try to learn from them in order to improve performance on future ventures; or (2) hide the mistakes and look the other way. He chose the latter path—the way that meant he wouldn't have to admit failure. Subsequently, Lay not only approved the unethical actions of Fastow and Skilling, but he also refused to know the details. Not only did Lay fail to learn from his mistakes and the mistakes of others, but he also misled Enron's board of directors by using misrepresented earnings and falsified financial statements to show inflated performance. Ultimately the company went bankrupt, bilking shareholders of $11 billion.

In the end, Ken Lay's leadership style became synonymous with lying, disgrace, and humiliation. The same man that so many aspired to be today is profiled in books like *The Book of Bastards: 101 Worst Scoundrels and Scandals from the World of Politics and Power.*

Following convictions on fraud and conspiracy, Lay died of a heart attack in 2006, a few months before he would have been sentenced to prison for the rest of his life. Lay's example of how *not* to be a leader resulted in fundamental changes in how U.S. companies view leadership, governance, and accountability.

Lay's path is a spectacular example of the fact that there are two sides to every story: it was the best of times, it was the worst of times; you take the bitter with the sweet; every rose has its thorn. But when it comes to great leadership, we tend to tell ourselves only half of the story—there is a discernible gap in our fundamental understanding of what it takes to be an effective leader. There are thousands of books written about leadership success, books that want us to believe the sky above the great leader's head is always blue and her road is always smooth. These books make us feel good. Unfortunately, they also lull us into a false understanding of what it means to be a great leader. What about the flip side? Great leaders *don't* always have blue skies or smooth paths—not by a long shot. The reality is that we don't— and can't—learn how to be great leaders by just imitating great leaders' accomplishments. It's not that easy. Being a great leader isn't exclusively about making the "right" decisions; often, as illustrated by the case of Ken Lay, it is about how to proactively avoid making the wrong decisions. He made plenty of right ones. And then he was seemingly unable to avoid making some catastrophically wrong ones. Why?

TWO LEADERS, TWO STORIES

In terms of their backgrounds, the similarities between Ken Lay and Jim Owens, former CEO of Caterpillar Inc., are remarkable. Lay and Owens were born less than two years apart, grew up in households where money was scarce, went to public schools, worked numerous jobs to help their families, went to state universities, and ultimately earned their Ph.D.s in economics before becoming CEOs of Fortune 50 companies. They both developed as leaders during the same period of American management reform. Business, both financial and manufacturing, was growing a greater footprint in the world's economy. Big companies were aggressively getting bigger by selling to an increasingly larger number of consumers and countries.

Although the similarities of background, position, education, and opportunity are remarkable, in terms of their leadership stories, the differences are distinct. Specifically, Owens achieved numerous successes in large part by learning from his own mistakes as well as the mistakes of others, and became the "smartest guy who's ever been in the job."[2] In 2001, Lay attempted to hide his mistakes and those of others and as a consequence went from the top of the charts to ending as one of the most catastrophically flawed leaders in U.S. business history.

Owens earned a tremendous reputation in the business community by successfully navigating one of the largest companies in the world through some of the stormiest economic conditions known to business. In an interview, Owens told us, "Black swan events [global structural failures] have given us invaluable learning opportunities. Leaders need to use these learning opportunities in ways we have historically never done." And it was his ability to observe and learn from these failures, not only his own but those of others, that helped make him such an effective leader.

In the early 1980s, Owens was a mid-level manager at the construction-equipment company Caterpillar. He recalls, "I started paying close attention to the whats and whys of the company's mistakes." At one point in an '80s recession, Caterpillar was losing up to $1 million a day. As the domestic market was spiraling downward, other issues, such as labor costs and union issues, were consuming the attention of Caterpillar's leaders. While the industry as a whole was evolving into global outsourcing, Caterpillar leaders were looking inward and stubbornly hanging on to strategies that had worked in the past. Owens paid particular attention to these errors, and he thought about what he would do differently if given the chance.

This story isn't just about the evolution of the construction-equipment industry. It's about what Owens observed early in his career and his resulting actions as a CEO. The attention he paid to mistakes made by others in the '80s created the foundation for his strategies during the 2008–2011 world recession—strategies that proved remarkably successful and put Caterpillar in a very select group of companies that were celebrated by Wall Street as weathering the recession relatively unscathed.[3]

In the 1980s, Owens experienced the innovation block common in big corporate bureaucracies—a focus on maintaining the status quo. At that time, most of the Caterpillar management team had operated in the boom years of the 1970s. Leaders at Caterpillar assumed that the secret to their success was that they ensured quality by "making everything" rather than outsourcing certain processes. Owens recalls how leaders were "stubbornly attached" to the way they had always done business. When he tried to challenge the status quo, namely by suggesting the company reduce costs by outsourcing products, he hit brick wall after brick wall. But he wouldn't back down. Once he was even warned by a senior executive, "Jim, you can be an officer at Cat someday, but you may get fired first!"

What Owens was learning throughout this period was that pushing for change in a conservative company—without data to back up the idea—did not work, even when it was a "good idea." One important lesson he learned at that time would become invaluable decades later—the fact that change in the form of out-sourcing could create flexibility in a downturned economy, allowing the company to limit losses from idle equipment and labor.

Years later, when he became CEO, Owens and his management team regularly studied the data and reports on world economic conditions. He also met throughout the prerecession year with world leaders from government and business. Management weighed the impact of indicators predicting the decline of economic conditions. Some Wall Street analysts have suggested Owens and his management team had great intuition. Owens' take is more concrete: "Our management team recognized a pattern from past experience and previous mistakes."

When the Great Recession hit in 2008, Owens and his team had developed a playbook to preserve cash and maintain relationships with outsourcing partners. Everything had to be cut to just the right size. Major equipment buyers had huge orders on the books and would be financially hurt for years to come if they were forced to honor their purchases. To maintain these relationships, Cat allowed the orders to be cancelled without penalty. Owens made hundreds of huge high-stakes decisions—decisions that were influenced by the mistakes he observed as a young manager in the early '80s.

In 1982, Owens had observed that leaders at Caterpillar had maintained the status quo when the world around them was changing. So when the recession hit in 2008, instead of focusing on trying to maintain the status quo, Owens aggressively pursued data-based change. "Corporations are bureaucratic," he said. "In crisis times, executing strategy quickly often prevents the bureaucracy from stagnating implementation." And although many of his decisions were not popular, Owens decided that he needed to be transparent.

At the other end of the spectrum, Ken Lay buried information. He was caught up in a perceived "hot streak" of successes that corrupted his decision making. Rather than learning from his company's mistakes when things started to unravel, Lay decided to cover them up. In contrast, Jim Owens used his company's previous mistakes to unwind Caterpillar's stubborn attachment to existing practices. He then leveraged this knowledge gleaned from mistakes to create a new reality for Cat, based on what he and his management team saw as evolutionary changes in the market.

GREAT LEADERSHIP: SHAPED BY
OPPOSING FORCES

We have found a common theme among industry's greatest leaders: Their most important lessons have come from trial and error. Unfortunately, yet understandably, many of us don't pursue the trial because we are fearful of making the error.

In a recent interview with the *Harvard Business Review,* A. G. Lafley, former CEO of Procter & Gamble, was asked "Can leaders learn as much from success [as they can from failure]?" His response was, of course, "No." He went on to say: "My experience is that we learn much more from failure than we do from success. Look at great politicians and successful sports teams. Their biggest lessons come from their toughest losses. The same is true for any kind of leader. And it was certainly true for me."[4] Lafley refers to his failures as "gifts," because they have given him tremendous growth opportunities as a leader.

Mistakes are part of taking healthy risks. They provide us with new ways of thinking and give us new insights into how we can improve as leaders. Real failure doesn't come from making mistakes; rather, it comes from avoiding errors at all possible cost, from the fear of taking risks to the inability to grow. Being mistake-free is not success—in fact, it's not even possible. Still, we often avoid risks and ignore (and sometimes even hide) our mistakes. We don't like to talk about our mistakes and bring attention to them. It feels safer to look the other way or sweep them under the rug. But doing so stifles growth and dooms us to repeat our mistakes—it's why so many leaders have the same struggles over and over again.

So why is it that we don't embrace challenges and become accepting of mistakes, learning from them and ultimately growing from them? And if learning from mistakes has so much value, why is it taboo to even talk about mistakes in the context of business and leadership? The answers aren't hard to find.

The Performance Review Trap

We are all evaluated on how well we perform our jobs. Companies pay their employees to succeed, not to fail. The better the performance review, the better we are compensated. However, performance reviews tend to reward us for our short-term success and penalize us for our short-term mistakes. Rarely does someone receive a performance review spanning several years. And personal growth from mistakes is an evolutionary process. It takes time. Mistakes made today usually hurt our performance evaluations in the short term. So we avoid them.

Consider Thomas Edison's remark: "I have not failed. I've just found ten thousand ways that won't work." Do you think he would have lasted in today's corporate environment? We have created an evaluation platform on which successes are celebrated and failures are not. Remember, "failure is not an option." To be a fast-track leader in this environment, you can't afford to make mistakes. If you do, you may feel pressured to bury the evidence or blame someone else in order to avoid any negative consequences.

A Culture of Perfectionism

Fear of failure isn't limited to performance reviews. Our entire culture values perfection. As children, we were told "practice makes perfect." We learned that making mistakes was bad, that we needed to always color inside the lines. We learned that to succeed we needed to strive for perfection. Perfectionism is one of the biggest deterrents to learning from mistakes. We become so fixated on not failing that we never move forward. We focus on the upside risk associated with failing, rather than the downside risk of not trying.

Losing Balance Between "What" and "How"

We are also a very goal-oriented culture in which status and success are paramount. We're proud when we're at the top of our game and when others see we're there. But we probably don't spend enough time considering how we got there. Jennifer Robin, coauthor of *The Great Workplace: How to Build It, How to Keep It, and Why It Matters* and research fellow with the Great Place to Work Institute, tells us that in great workplaces, rather than focusing exclusively on goals—the "what" of success—leaders also take time to focus on process—the "how." Like management and leadership, or tactics and strategy, both are necessary, and so is paying attention to both. Attending to how goals are achieved, rather than the goals themselves, builds strong relationships and solid business acumen—and knowing how we achieved what we achieved (or failed to) can educate us about the real basis of our success.

THE FAILURE PARADOX

While every great leader makes mistakes, it's just as true that there are only a limited number of mistakes you can make before proving yourself an unworthy leader—you can fall off the corporate ladder only so many times before your climb is finished. And the higher you get, the more severe the fall; the more failure becomes unthinkable. This is where the downward spiral of "winning" at all costs can begin—even if it means hiding mistakes, blaming subordinates, and even lying, as in the case of Ken Lay. Simply put, at a certain level, failure is not an option. Yet in order to succeed, we need to know failure. This is the failure paradox. In this book, we are going to talk frankly and instructively about the things that are hard to talk about.

There is a way around the problem, and it's right in front of us. We'll all make our own mistakes, true, and ideally we will learn from them. But the real opportunity comes when we are able to learn from others' mistakes before we are confronted with similar challenges ourselves; we can actually learn the lessons without paying the price. And this perspective is starting to gain significant momentum.

There is an increasing awareness of the fact that what makes leaders effective is their ability to learn from mistakes—their own mistakes as well as others'. In 2011, *Harvard Business Review* devoted the entire April issue to the importance of learning from mistakes and failure. And a substantive body of academic research has demonstrated the considerable value of looking at how leaders react to mistakes, especially when they result in undesirable consequences.[5] Recently, Max Bazerman and Ann Tenbrunsel completed a study illustrating that over the last twenty-five years there has been a dramatic increase in our preference to learn from failures rather than from successes. They argue, "How much do we talk about learning from failure? How much about learning from success? The gap between them is growing—which suggests we prefer to learn from flops."[6]

A PERFECT STORM: EMPIRICAL RESEARCH, UNFORESEEN TIMING, AND UNTOLD STORIES

Business leaders have strived for years to find the secret to business success. Unfortunately there is no one secret, no 100-percent rule, no list of the right things to do. To become great leaders, we need to develop disciplined leadership acumen, which often is crafted from lessons hard learned. Great leaders embrace the learning they get from mistakes (both their own and others'). As best-selling author Stephen M.R. Covey puts it, smart people have the ability to "see mistakes as feedback that will help them improve, and they become expert in learning how to learn from mistakes."[7]

We built the foundation for this book on the results of a seven-year-long study in which we surveyed almost a thousand managers. Although it is grounded in data-driven research that we have already published in academic journals, we qualitatively confirmed results through subsequent interviews with some of the country's most well-known business leaders. And the timing of our interviews happened at a most interesting time—the global economic downturn. This gave us an unusual opportunity to hear untold stories of mistakes and failures that had been buried under prosperity for decades—revenue growth hides a lot of mistakes. The recession stripped away the cover-ups to reveal the unvarnished truths necessary to be an effective leader. As with a tide that has gone out unusually far, we were able to see a part of the ocean floor that is rarely seen. Rather than sweeping mistakes under the rug, the leaders in our interviews were unusually candid in sharing stories and insights, not only into the mistakes you need to avoid but, more important, into how to avoid them.

In the end, we were able to leverage a perfect storm, starting out with empirical research that verified the importance of learning from mistakes, and then digging deeper to hear the untold stories that numbers alone couldn't tell.

The research for this book can be broken down into three distinct phases:

- Investigating the efficacy of learning from mistakes
- Identifying the most damning mistakes
- Verification, takeaways, and insights

We detail these in the following sections.

Phase One: Investigating the Efficacy of Learning from Mistakes
In the first phase of our research, we set out to determine whether learning from mistakes was as effective as we suspected. The key research question we were trying to answer was whether learning from mistakes actually improved performance— both at the individual level as well as financial performance at the firm level.

We asked 857 managers across 21 industries—including man-ufacturing, service, retail, professional, and not-for-profit—to agree or disagree with thirty-five statements, broadly focusing on cultural attributes such as their sense of the value of mistakes, their acceptance of mistakes as part of doing their job, and their ability to create a safe environment in which employees were not afraid to make mistakes as a result of taking healthy risks. Anonymity and confidentiality were ensured for all respondents because mistakes in business are such a sensitive issue.

The results of our research provided strong statistical evi-dence that the ability to embrace mistakes can lead to improved individual performance. Specifically, we found that leaders who learn from mistakes:

- Proactively deflect potential problems
- Have a higher level of confidence when taking action and making decisions
- Possess a more accurate understanding of their environments
- Think more strategically
- Are more creative

These traits and capabilities also translated to higher levels of financial performance for the organizations, such as increased revenue growth and increased profit growth. To study the impact of learning from mistakes on various aspects of performance, we lagged performance over a five-year period; our reasoning was that when a leader learns from mistakes, the benefits may take several years to be realized.

Phase Two: Identifying the Most Damning Mistakes

In the second phase of our research, we ran thirteen focus groups, recruiting and meeting with 115 leaders, from CEOs to frontline managers from numerous industries and functions—human resources, IT, sales, engineering, and so on—and from around the country.

The focus groups were designed to validate the significance of the original research findings and identify the most damning mistakes. They were also designed to help us see firsthand how people deal with these important issues. Our hope was to capture some of the intense emotions that leaders express about failure and what they do to cope with the frustration of not seeing their people and their companies work most effectively.

The meetings were originally scheduled for ninety minutes, but sometimes they went on for hours. At times we felt like we were leading group therapy. Leaders shared with each other stories that made us think, "I wonder how your company actually survived with all these mistakes?" Other times the discussion was very pointed and direct, as if we were in the middle of a high-stakes sporting event. Participants would bark out observations. Occasionally one of the leaders (usually a CEO) would say, "How could you not see that coming?" It was our intent in these groups to keep the conversation civil and constructive, so we'd rein them back in and get refocused on how common the mistake was or how detrimental (measurable) the negative action was.

One of the major findings was how much leaders struggle, and how much time they invest in this topic. When we asked the groups how much time each day they spent working on "fixes" for the company, the response was dramatic. Some said "I spend most of my time," whereas others said "I have people who focus on that; I focus on strategy." When we probed more deeply with the "I have people" leaders, all of them admitted to devoting a tremendous amount of intellectual energy to thinking about how to avoid failure.

After the focus group portion of our research was concluded, we had a great inventory of stories, processes, and validation, which served as the next step of our research. We now knew what the most common, hidden, and expensive mistakes were. And we heard hundreds of ways to proactively avoid or deliberately eliminate them. All the participants recognize that mistakes are going to happen in any organization. We were ready to move on to the C-level interview phase of the project.

Phase Three: Verification, Takeaways, and Insights

For the final phase of our research, we conducted personal interviews with dozens of industry's most experienced leaders to flesh out our statistical findings and results from our focus groups. Sitting CEOs confirmed the important lessons from our original research; still, the topic of our conversations was a hard one. The CEOs were often uncomfortable, and sometimes they asked to remain anonymous. Some would say, "You know, this may help people, but don't make me look bad." After several of our interviews, we got calls from the interviewee saying, "Hey, I just don't feel comfortable talking about this. Don't put me in the book."

To overcome this problem, we started interviewing retired CEOs—the true sages of business—with very different results. The retired CEOs shared great insights with almost no reservations. Typically, these leaders' roles have shifted from day-to-day management to sitting on national and international boards. They have evolved a keen ability to help other leaders learn from their experiences and observations and a willingness to share invaluable stories, of themselves and of others, that hold key takeaways and lessons.

The one thing we found in common across all of our interviews was this: learning from mistakes, whether you made them yourself or you observed them in others, is invaluable in becoming a great leader—whether you are a retired CEO of a Fortune 100 company, an aspiring leader, or a small-business owner.

Putting It All Together

We wanted to make the results of our research useful for you and your managers. Having said that, you may find the results of our research a bit thorny and controversial. Our findings challenge the traditional paradigm established by conventional leadership wisdom—that to become a great leader, you need to simply imitate great leaders' successes. But there is a duality to effective leadership that is seldom discussed in leadership books—that although there are paths you should follow in order to be an effective leader, there are also paths you should *not* follow in order to be an effective leader.

Leadership ability actually results from two distinct practices—following patterns of successes *and* developing skills to avoid failures. An apt comparison is the study of history, wherein we take note of what has worked in the past in order to replicate successes *and also* consider challenges and failures in order to avoid making the same mistakes over and over again. We need to understand what has worked in the past—and why; we also need to understand what has not worked in the past—and why. And we need to learn both through our own direct experience and through clearsighted analysis of others' failures. Although great leaders will still make mistakes, they only make "original" mistakes—they are not doomed to repeat the lessons they've already learned, whether directly or indirectly.

A TAXONOMY OF LEADERSHIP MISTAKES

The remaining nine chapters of this book explore the most common leadership mistakes by groups—at the organizational, team, and individual levels. But before we delve in, it's important to note that not all leaders' mistakes are created equally. There are small, inconsequential challenges that have little effect on a leader's career, and then there are the big ones—the high-visibility, devastating challenges that can destroy careers. And the higher up you go in an organization, the bigger the mistakes can become.

Consider rock climbing as an analogy. Beginning rock climbers, like beginning leaders in business, start with skill development and technique. They practice tying knots. Mistakes result in scrapes and bruises. Even a long fall, although possibly more serious, is almost always recoverable. As climbers mature, teams or "ropes" start to form. Now climbers literally depend on one another for survival. A single misplaced piton could result in the death of a team member.

Ultimately, the leader of the rope team develops even more specialized skills. Through experience—trial and error—rope leaders can develop a recognizable "sense of path" up a mountain. To an outsider, this sense of path may seem like instinct, but experienced climbers know that it comes from the wisdom accrued from a set of successes and, more important, from valuable lessons learned from failures. The rope leader keeps the mission and progress—the path to the top—identifiable and achievable. But if the rope leader makes a mistake, the entire team could perish.

In business, the same relationships exist. Many young leaders, like young rock climbers, are consumed with attaining technical skills. Their amount of resource responsibility is usually limited, and so are the impacts of their actions beyond their individual success or failure. At the other end of the spectrum, senior-level leaders have much more responsibility and greater reach, and consequently their failures are magnified—even multiplied.

Based on our interviews with business leaders—from small-venture entrepreneurs to Fortune 500 CEOs—we have identified three critical areas in which aspiring leaders fail. These funda-mental categories of mistakes reveal significant opportunities for effective leaders to observe and learn in order to continuously improve. Because these categories represent the material causes of wrong direction, wrong decisions, and wrong behaviors, rather than just symptoms, they travel well—once you understand the underlying error, you can identify it in almost any setting. The categories are:

- *Unbalanced orchestration* at the *organizational* level—misuse of talent and resources in the short term coupled with inability to focus on the future vision.

- *Drama management* at the *team* level—lack of discipline, pace, and appropriate communication, leading to dysfunctional teams.
- *Personality issues* at the *individual* level—personality faults and disconnects with reality that inhibit the ability to lead effectively.

Leaders from both our focus groups and our interviews contended that mistakes in these three categories are responsible for numerous leadership failures. Notably, the categories are equally important sources of leadership error. For example, if you have a great vision but can't effectively manage your top management team, failure will usually result. Any one of these weaknesses can lead to failure, even if you are doing everything else right.

Unbalanced Orchestration

Effective leaders guide companies—it's their most critical responsibility. That's why they are the ones at the top of the organizational chart. Failure to effectively orchestrate a strategy can sink the ship, whereas successful orchestration of a strategy can create the resilience to prosper in both good times and bad. It is the leader who creates and holds onto the vision, the strategy, and ultimately the roadmap to move a company forward. Without balanced, sustained, engaged strategic direction from a leader, a company can drift like a boat without a rudder, changing direction as the tides change, never getting anywhere—except perhaps washed up on the rocks. Unbalanced strategic orchestration exposes companies to considerable risk, and our research and analysis shows it arises from three particular leadership errors:

- Trying to be all things to all people
- Roaming outside the box
- Putting efficiencies before effectiveness

Each of these is described briefly in the following section, and then treated in depth in one of the chapters that follow.

All Things to All People

Often, ineffective leaders lack the disciplined business acumen to say "no." They start giving in to requests from potential customers that don't fit with their strategic direction. Why? Because there is an opportunity to generate revenue—in the short term. As they start chasing these alluring dollars, their strategic direction slowly erodes. The truth is, saying no to money is hard.

Dick Blaudow—chairman and CEO of ATS Corp., an industry leader in managing manufacturing processes—knows this very well. He has had to turn down potential new business because the company was expanding too fast. "It's awfully hard to say no to new customers sitting on your doorstep wanting to give you money," says Blaudow. "But if we continued trying to be all things to all people, we would have lost our sight on our purpose—and eventually it would have buried us." Chasing dollars may work in the short run, but in the long run it can destroy your ability to lead strategically. Fortunately for Blaudow, he recognized the point where his company was starting down the wrong path and he made the right (tough) call before it was too late.

Roaming Outside the Box

Failing leaders are tempted to start "thinking outside the box." Invariably they find that business dictums about boxes and creative thinking are cheap, but randomness in leadership is expensive. The received wisdom of thinking outside the box is entrenched. When we address audiences, inevitably an attendee asks something like, "To be a good leader, don't you need to think outside the box?" Everyone else in the room nods in approval as if they have just heard the gospel truth. It's been written about in books, everybody talks about it, so it must be correct—right?

We usually respond to the question by asking: "What box?" And usually the audience is silent.

Although the idea of thinking outside the box sounds provocative, it is in most circumstances without substance. To begin with, how can you think outside the box if you don't know what the box is? It could represent your current product line, your company's boundaries, maybe even your industry's boundaries—all essentially arbitrary designations. When a leader commits to thinking outside the box, it leads to unbalanced orchestration—often involving innovation for the sake of innovation, a situation in which the innovation hammer is searching for new nails. A leader needs to have a vision and a strategic direction, and thinking outside the box slowly erodes that direction every bit as much as trying to be all things to all people does. It also violates the leadership principle of valuing effectiveness in all endeavors.

Efficiencies Before Effectiveness

Another harbinger of unbalanced orchestration is a focus on efficiency rather than effectiveness. Efficiency involves "doing things right"—trying to improve on something you already do. It is internally focused and has little to do with growth. In contrast, effectiveness involves "doing the right things." It is strategically focused. It considers an organization in the context of its markets, rather than in the context of itself. Stated differently, a company may be very efficient at making a product, but if it's the wrong product to meet customer needs, the company fails to be effective, and risks failing altogether.

Consider the debacle of Circuit City. Casual observers might blame Circuit City's demise on a bad economy. But on closer inspection, it's clear that failure was caused by an unbalanced focus on efficiency over effectiveness.

"Circuit City was successful in the 1980s and 1990s, but they never changed after that," says David Schick, an analyst at Stifel Nicolaus.[8] Circuit City was successful in the '80s and '90s by operating effectively (doing the right things); in the 2000s this focus was replaced with an overemphasis on efficiencies (doing things right). Phillip Schoonhover, CEO of Circuit City, became so concerned with cost management that he lost sight of the company's sources of competitive advantage. While Best Buy was securing prime real estate in locations convenient to customers, Circuit City acquired real estate in stressed shopping centers— based on price. Similarly, when Best Buy and even Wal-Mart moved aggressively into gaming, Schoonhover took his eye off the ball. But Schoonhover's biggest mistake was his "transformation work" initiative. In March of 2007, he cut 3,400 knowledgeable sales people to decrease costs, ignoring the fact that customers want knowledgeable sales people when making an electronics purchase. Moreover, this move ultimately helped Best Buy, by giving them ready access to a large pool of knowledgeable sales associates. In each case, Schoonhover literally gave away his competitive advantages to focus on efficiencies.

The result? Circuit City saw a significant decline in sales that year, whereas Best Buy easily surpassed all of its sales and profit projections. If Schoonhover had continued to focus on *doing the right thing*, like Best Buy did, the company could still be in business today. Instead, it collapsed, and Herb Greenberg of the *Wall Street Journal* picked Schoonhover as the worst CEO of 2008.

Drama Mismanagement

If unbalanced orchestration is the source of a leader's failures in managing an entire organization, drama mismanagement derails a leader's ability to manage teams. Leaders who experience failure in this category literally manufacture unnecessary drama for their employees. And although drama is great for movies, it is not an effective tool to motivate most employees. According to our interviews, unnecessary drama is prevalent in industry, and it has the effect of driving people away, be they good employees or reliable customers.

Our research identified three key leadership failures that contribute to overly dramatic atmospheres in organizations:

- Bullying management
- Dysfunctional harmony
- Distracted purpose

Bullying Management

High school is full of bully drama. Remember the teacher who used to throw erasers at students during class? Or the big kid who picked on smaller kids on the playground? Bullying management isn't much different. It's a leadership style that creates a highly dramatic work environment. Bully leaders abuse their authority by using fear to motivate employees rather than using real leadership techniques based on empowerment, appropriate accountability, and respect. Bullying is a corrosive force inside organizations, and unfortunately it is more common than you may think. As you will see in the following chapters, bullying takes on many forms, from overt intimidation tactics like yelling to covert tactics such as subliminally demeaning comments.

Dysfunctional Harmony

It's lonely at the top. Not everyone will like you. As a matter of fact, there are countless examples of great leaders who are not liked much at all—Jack Welch, for example. But some people will try to be liked at any cost, and that spells disaster for leadership. Being an effective leader means that sometimes you will not make the most popular decisions. By doing what is necessary, you will sometimes make some people angry. That's okay. It's part of the job. If you are in a leadership role and you try to be liked by everyone all of the time, you will inevitably create drama and undercut your own authority and effectiveness. You are pursuing dysfunctional harmony—harmony at the cost of business effectiveness.

It gets worse. The biggest mistake that leaders make regarding dysfunctional harmony is the desire to have everyone like *each other* all of the time—to be "one big happy family." An insistence on a "happy family" leads to passive-aggressive behaviors because there's no healthy, up-front way to resolve normal conflicts. On the surface, everyone appears to get along, but behind closed doors, things can get downright ugly—much, much uglier than they need to. And leaders who desire an appearance of harmony above all else not only enable passive-aggressive behavior, they encourage it. If you have ever worked in such an environment, you know what we mean by drama.

Distracted Purpose

A leader can create unnecessary drama by losing sight of the fact that a team is more than a collection of individuals. Although there are advocates of intrateam competition, mismanaged competition within teams—a form of distracted purpose—can create divisiveness and ultimately destroy well-functioning work units. There is a wealth of research that supports this. Other failures involving distracted purpose include playing favorites and overreliance on individual talents instead of leveraging synergies of the team.

Personality Issues

Some leaders have personality attributes that lead to highly visible failure. These failures stem from personal traits that, in less extreme forms, can serve a leader well. Young leaders often show attributes of courage, confidence, and a bit of company celebrity that factor into their risk taking and their rise. When these attributes become exaggerated and distorted, they create leadership failure. Three types of failure can be attributed to personality issues:

- Hoarding
- Disengagement
- Self-absorption

Hoarding

Have you ever known a leader unable to delegate to her or his employees? When a leader has such a sense of superiority that letting go of responsibility becomes difficult, if not impossible, it is the team—and the organization—that suffers. Leaders who hoard responsibility fail in three different ways. First, they don't give employees a chance to develop the necessary skills to be effective team members, resulting in long-term stagnation. Second, what may work when an organization is small doesn't work when an organization grows, and entrepreneurial leaders who cannot delegate responsibility hold back their own organizations from opportunities to grow. Finally, for organizations of any size, when leaders hoard responsibility, they tend to micromanage. Rather than giving responsibility to their team, they become involved in every minor decision. Because they are constantly looking over the shoulders of their employees, they are unable to lead their organizations, and at the same time they alienate their team.

Disengagement

Burnouts who stay on the payroll too long, bosses who have no interest in their jobs, and celebrity CEOs all have one thing in common: all are disengaged from their company's culture. They become lost in their own world, unable to communicate with key stakeholders in their own organizations or to effectively lead.

Rod Blagojevich was elected governor of Illinois by overwhelming popular support. Over the following six years, he slowly created his own reality. He lost sight of his responsibilities, alienated his own staff, and ultimately became incapable of communicating with the public. He eventually made irreparable mistakes that not only cost him his job but also led to his being sentenced to federal prison.

Celebrity is often part of a leader's experience; however, when you let it get too big, it can lead to disengagement from your real work, which in turn leads to leadership failure.

Self-Absorption

Ego can get in the way of a lot of things, including effective leadership. Sometimes successes can actually lead to failures, especially if leaders feel as though they are on a roll. Business acumen and a sense of reality take a back seat.

Some people are narcissistic by nature, and their leadership style will reflect that. But others, without even realizing what is happening, slowly fall into the trap of self-absorption. For a variety of reasons, their egos get out of check, and they start to feel invincible.

Isaiah Thomas, former point guard for the Detroit Pistons and a Hall of Fame basketball legend, let his past success give him a feeling of infallibility. For several years he was the general manager of the New York Knicks basketball franchise. During that time he made some of the worst investments in NBA history. He slowly assembled a team of all point guards. His sense of infallibility led him to believe that because he was so successful as a point guard, five players similar to him would be five times as good. Needless to say, this strategy was unsuccessful, and he was soon fired. A self-absorbed leader will make bad decisions most of the time, simply because he can't see past himself.

NEW DISCOVERIES

We have been speaking to audiences for the last several years, sharing our research and analysis with thousands of executives all over the world. Now we want to share it with you. You are not going to find the "correct answer" at the end of this book. What you will find is an array of stories, examples, analyses, and step-by-step guidelines that demonstrate the qualities of both great leaders and failed ones. Learning from others' mistakes works, and it is a necessary part of the journey of leadership. It's our belief that you will walk away from reading this book armed with action-based tactics, a sense of the benefits of a balanced approach to leadership, and new insights on the most potent leadership virtues and vices (which, as we'll see, can sometimes be hard to distinguish from one another).

The research that underpins this book was broad-based, so we do not limit our examples to stories of Fortune 500 companies (clearly, though, there are some classics that would have to make it into any book on leadership failure). We also include many examples of leaders in mid-sized and entrepreneurial businesses. While leaders in entrepreneurial firms can learn from leaders in large multinationals, the reverse is true as well.

Certain ideas in this book will appear to be common sense—which doesn't mean, of course, that many or even most leaders may act accordingly. We'll also introduce some ideas that you may find controversial, even radical. We hope that these ideas will provoke you to challenge your current thoughts on leadership growth.

THE REST OF THE STORY

Leadership success doesn't just happen. It takes a lot of the right kind of work. As previously discussed, we have identified three major categories of leadership lessons emerging from our research: unbalanced orchestration (leadership failures at the organizational level), drama management (leadership failures at the team level), and personality issues (leadership failures at the individual level). The rest of the book takes these lessons in turn, with three chapters each on specific lessons in unbalanced orchestration, drama management, and personal issues. Each chapter concludes with practical ideas and key takeaways to help you identify the potential for failure and proactively avoid mistakes.

It doesn't matter what kind of business you are in—large or small, public or private, manufacturing or service, profit or not-for-profit. These insights were carefully developed by studying thousands of executives in hundreds of varied companies. This rich pool of experience doesn't yield cut-and-dried answers about leadership success and failure, but it can allow you to learn from others' failures *without* having to experience those mistakes and thereby risk the survival of your organization or your career.

We've seen "how-to" business books for years. This book provides the rest of the story. It's the "how-not-to" business book—with stories every bit as compelling and no less important in ensuring the success of any leader.

PART ONE

Unbalanced Orchestration

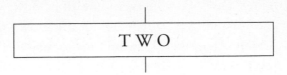

TWO

Seduced by Yes

Trying to Be All Things to All People

Throughout time and industry, leaders have made some pretty huge errors in spending—errors that we spectators love to mock as moments of insanity or, at the very least, idiocy. Why would a leader spend resources in a way that actively destroys his company? Assuming the leader is thoughtful, paying attention, and not *trying* to sabotage anything, why would he push the "spend" button so eagerly, when it seems so clear it was the wrong call? Chances are that he is neither insane nor an idiot. Rather, leaders drive companies—and their own careers—into the ground because they have a problem with the word "yes." They suffer from an inability to step back, get off the treadmill, and say "no" to opportunities when that's exactly what they should be saying.

Jim Owens, whom we met in the last chapter, described the consequences of the "yes" problem as "having a long tail." It can take months, or even years, to assess whether the outcomes of many leadership decisions were right or wrong. With the benefit of 20/20 hindsight, we followed several of these "yes" mistakes all the way back to the decision's origin in order to identify the underlying causes. When you look closely at where all the trouble began, the lessons inspire an edifying mix of "Aha, I should have seen that coming" and "Wow, I never knew that." Intel CEO Craig Barrett diagnosed the "yes" problem in this way: "Companies have to invest to make money. It's when my managers one, speculate; two, overcommit; and three, try to be heroes that we run into real trouble." As it turns out, Barrett's list aligns closely with the three major catalysts identified in our research: irrational greed, escalation of commitment, and trying to be all things to all people.

By *irrational greed* we mean chasing dollars for the sake of chasing dollars. It is characterized by the inability to say no to new opportunities—even if they don't fit within the strategic context of the organization. *Escalation of commitment* occurs when a leader cannot admit failure. She makes a poor strategic move, and instead of saying "no more" and conceding the battle, she commits even more resources, throwing good money after bad and sinking costs into a bottomless black hole.

Finally, leaders falter when they try to *be all things to all people.* This behavior stems from the attitude, "Why would we intentionally exclude a customer segment?"

These three catalysts are responsible for destroying careers and destroying companies. In this chapter, we will discuss each one, provide examples of otherwise good leaders who fell into common traps, and offer tools to help you steer clear of these mistakes yourself.

IRRATIONAL GREED: CHASING PENNIES WITH DOLLARS

You are a pretty good leader. Your track record is solid, and you've accomplished some short-term victories as you've led a successful organization. Most of your decisions have been effective. Now you are faced with a new opportunity—an opportunity that has the potential to generate significant revenue, but that doesn't fit strategically with the scope of your organization. Nevertheless, your eyes open wider when you discover that the revenue potential is bigger than you originally anticipated. You are very tempted. What do you do?

If you take the leap, you're not alone. Many leaders don't have the discipline to say "no" to money-making opportunities, even those that fall outside of the firm's scope. And many times, that's when a downward spiral begins. The company jumps in with both feet and starts chasing dollars without critically assessing whether the opportunity is strategically appropriate. The leader becomes so enamored with the idea of the new opportunity that he sacrifices his strategic direction. Once that's gone or compromised, the company may lose focus altogether. The leader starts leading opportunistically rather than strategically, like a shark attacking anything that moves.

This sort of thing happens all the time because, very simply, it's hard to say no to money, and sticking to a plan is challenging when alluring opportunities arise. Leaders don't realize they are making a mistake, because making money is their job. So *following* money seems like a sensible strategy. It isn't. It's a substitute for strategy, and it can be a costly mistake.

When we interviewed Jeff Hoffman, a founder of Priceline .com, he admitted as much. "It's hard to say no to money," he told us, then added, "A good leader needs to know when to leave the money on the table." Hoffman explained how he and his partners were able to do exactly that in order to succeed. While the dot-com bubble was bursting and many entrepreneurs were finding themselves the victims of dollar chasing, Hoffman refrained. "When Priceline became good at airline tickets," he said, "others wanted us to sell their things on our website. Our business was built around airlines and hotels. We had to decide if we were going to expand through other products or new geographies. We had a chance to sell suitcases. Is there money in selling suitcases? Absolutely, but we have decided we are not going to get into luggage. Rather, we are going to expand the business that we already do better than anyone else."

When a leader starts chasing dollars, she runs the risk of losing strategic direction and misallocating resources. Unbalanced orchestration, or unfocused leadership, is virtually guaranteed. Chasing after dollars is like taking "strategy spaghetti" and throwing it against the wall: whatever sticks becomes your next opportunity. There is no cohesive direction, no firm control. The leader has a problem that stems from irrational greed. She makes decisions without constraints—but a leader needs to work within constraints while avoiding constriction. Constraints set up parameters that represent your strategic direction—a leader's responsibility. If the direction is too narrow, it constricts the flexibility you need to grow; if it's too broad, it offers no guidance for decision making.

Imagine you are driving down an expressway in a large city. There are six lanes going in your direction. To the left of the six lanes, there is a large concrete median; to the right there is a shoulder. You cannot cross over the concrete median to the left nor drive over the shoulder to the right. These are your parameters, your constraints or boundaries. However, they are not so constricting that you have to stay in one lane. You are free to change lanes as much as you want to get where you're going, as long as you don't cross over the boundaries. Leaders who engage in chasing dollars *have* no boundaries—they jump the concrete median (or at least they try to). As long as they think they can make money, they pursue it, without rhyme or reason, and with predictable consequences.

Consider the story of L.A. Gear. Robert Greenberg, founder and former CEO of L.A. Gear, spent his early professional days as a hairdresser and wig salesman. From these experiences he developed a deep understanding of women's fashion. He then started to rent and sell roller skates to patrons in the Venice Beach area of California. With his keen fashion sense, Greenberg started marketing E.T. shoelaces (based on the movie *E.T.*) as a way to accessorize the skates, and ultimately opened up a hip women's fashion shop: L.A. Gear.

While selling women's clothes, Greenberg noticed that his daughter's friends wore boys' high-top basketball shoes because none were designed specifically for girls. He soon discovered that only 20 percent of athletic shoes were actually used for athletic activities, and he came up with a fantastic idea: Why not design trendy high-top shoes for girls—not as athletic gear, but as a fashion accessory? He closed his retail shop and started importing Korean-made fashion sneakers under the same name. He designed shoes in bright flashy colors like pink and turquoise, and he started to "bedazzle" the sneakers with sequins, palm trees, and other California-inspired bling. Greenberg even redesigned the high-top shoe, stopping the eyelets at the ankle—a design effort to improve style, not performance, as removing the eyelets made it anything but a performance shoe. Additionally, each pair of shoes was sold with multiple pairs of shoelaces, to further help the purchaser accessorize. L.A. Gear even developed its own type of "slouch" sock to be worn with its shoes, further targeting young women.

Greenberg knew his market. L.A. Gear became an instant success. In 1984, Greenberg launched a national advertising campaign, promoting his shoes as the "Los Angeles lifestyle." Sales skyrocketed from approximately $11 million in 1985 to more than $820 million in 1989.[1]

To position his fashionable shoes as a high-end brand, Greenberg sold them only in stores such as Macy's and Nordstrom. By 1989, L.A. Gear was the top-performing stock in the shoe industry, becoming a national brand known for cutting-edge accessorized girls' and women's shoes, and promoted with risqué ads featuring beautiful California women. Greenberg's company was named Company of the Year by *Footwear News* magazine and ranked third on *Business Week*'s list of the 100 Best Small Corporations.

Everything was going great. But things slowly started to unravel in the 1990s when Greenberg and the leadership team at L.A. Gear apparently became greedy and started to chase dollars. Three devastating strategic mistakes put the "Company of the Year" into bankruptcy.

○ *Strike one.* In 1990, Greenberg made the decision to sell L.A. Gear's excess inventory though deep discount outlet stores. This antagonized the retail distributors that sold L.A. Gear products at full price, as it diminished the high-end brand perception of the shoes. It was the beginning of the end for Greenberg's company.

○ *Strike two.* Also in 1990, Greenberg threw the metaphorical strategy spaghetti against the wall—and where did it stick? Men's high-performance athletic shoes. Nike was making millions with its Air Jordan line of basketball shoes, so why not L.A. Gear? The allure was too great; the potential payoff was so tempting. But Greenberg was in the business of women's fashion, right? Regardless, given his tremendous success in marketing and retailing women's fashion shoes, he decided to chase dollars in men's high-performance basketball shoes. Up until this point, the company had been heading down the proverbial expressway quite well, changing lanes when necessary to offer new and exciting styles of women's shoes. But now Greenberg consciously decided to jump the concrete median to chase dollars in the highly competitive performance-athletic shoe market.

Greenberg started investing significant resources in men's athletic shoes, paying top dollar for high-visibility endorsers, including L.A. Lakers basketball great Kareem Abdul-Jabbar and San Francisco 49ers football great Joe Montana.[2] Greenberg decided to massively market his Catapult line of shoes to compete directly with Nike's Air Jordans. Unfortunately, for a company that was known for selling the California lifestyle to young girls, jumping the median was difficult, as consumers were not very receptive to the marketing campaign. To make matters worse, in a nationally televised college basketball game between Kansas and Marquette in December of 1990, one of the pairs of L.A. Gear high-performance basketball shoes literally fell apart during the game, causing a player to trip and fall. It's no surprise that the national media picked up this story, and it was all over national television.

Greenberg learned the painful way that competing in the men's high-performance basketball shoe industry is different from retailing trendy shoes to young girls. The college basketball game blunder caused L.A. Gear to report its first quarterly financial loss in early 1991. The death spiral continued in the second quarter. Bank of America lowered L.A. Gear's credit line. The company was in financial trouble. In January 1991, L.A. Gear was acquired by Trefoil Capital Investors L.P. Two weeks later, Trefoil replaced Greenberg as CEO with Mark Goldston, a former Reebok marketing executive. In 1994, L.A. Gear decided to abandon their men's high-performance athletic shoe lines and began refocusing on lifestyle brands to women and young girls. Goldston tried to acquire the Ryka brand of women's shoes, but the deal fell through, as Ryka was in about as much financial trouble as L.A. Gear.

○ *Strike three.* The allure of chasing dollars became too great again in 1995, when leaders at L.A. Gear chased an opportunity to sell large volumes of shoes through the biggest retailer in the world—Wal-Mart. They agreed to a three-year contract, whereby L.A. Gear committed to rolling out a new line of lower-priced shoes targeted toward Wal-Mart customers. The potential to partner with Wal-Mart was such a large opportunity to chase dollars that leaders at L.A. Gear believed they couldn't afford to pass it up—even though it didn't support the brand image. Unfortunately, sales declined and the brand was ruined.

○ *You're out!* The leaders at L.A. Gear had jumped the median yet again to chase dollars, and this time there was no going back. By 1998, the company filed for Chapter 11 bankruptcy. The company's stock, once valued at over $1 billion, was now worth absolutely nothing. A company that had been known for its tremendous rise to success now became even more famous for its leadership mistakes. In 2000, an article in the *New York Times* described L.A. Gear as one of the industry's "most spectacular collapses."[3]

Lest this cautionary tale scare leaders into staying solely on the straight and narrow, note that if you insist on sticking to just one lane, results are similarly poor. Leaders must create some constraints, but that simply means they must establish parameters to help keep their business on track. Businesses that too strictly constrain their products often are negatively affected by new competition and environmental changes such as recession. One of the CEOs we spoke with explained, "I got on a way of doing business that was producing okay revenue. I was in my space making brass washers and springs. I limited my focus to only these narrow products. I didn't see China coming into the market as fast as my customers did." He lost his entire business.

Our research has shown that when leaders abandon their strategic direction to chase after opportunities outside the scope of their business, bad things happen. In contrast, when leaders hold on too tight and don't let go—or worse, *can't* let go—bad things happen, too. It's a phenomenon known as *escalation of commitment*.

ESCALATION OF COMMITMENT: KNOWING WHEN TO SAY WHEN

The gambler's paradox is a phenomenon you can sadly, and clearly, see in any casino on any given day. Someone decides to play the slots and starts burning through his life's savings in hours. He convinces himself that "the next time I pull the handle on the slot machine, I will win everything back. I just need to keep playing to finally get a win." The voice inside his head says, "I can't quit now, I am already in too deep." Obsession is driven by his escalating commitment.

The term "escalation of commitment" was first coined by Barry Staw, a business professor at the University of California, Berkeley.[4] It's defined as a decision-making pattern in which a person—for our purposes, a business leader—continues to support or believe in a strategy even after it has continually failed. Escalation of commitment is often described as the inability to let go, or as an obsessive need to try to succeed even when failure is inevitable. And as we discussed in Chapter One, it can stem from perfectionism, which prevents people from accepting failure as an option. Escalation of commitment is also described as an irrational decision-making approach that arises when a significant emotional, psychological, or financial investment has been made, resulting in a significant sunk cost. And this sunk cost is so great that the leader keeps on pouring more and more resources into the project to justify what has already been invested. She continues to support the venture even though there is data that argues otherwise. Ultimately the leader starts throwing good money after bad. It is yet another scenario in which a leader needs the discipline to say no, to realize that enough is enough, to be able to raise the white flag. This discipline is hard to come by, and as a result, escalation of commitment is more common than you may think.

Escalation of commitment is almost inevitable in failing entrepreneurial ventures. An entrepreneur invests his life's saving to start a small business. Markets may turn out to be worse than anticipated, resulting in low demand. The company has not been able to develop any sources of competitive advantage, and other competitors are taking away what little market share he already has. Cash is running out. So what does he do? Instead of admitting failure, he doubles down; he throws more money into the business and ultimately loses everything. As the expression says, you have to "know when to hold 'em, know when to fold 'em." Unfortunately, many leaders aren't able to figure this out. It is extremely hard to admit to strategic failure, because it means resources have been invested, money has been spent, and neither is coming back—they're gone for good. Prior investments are now nothing more than water under the bridge. Emotionally, this is difficult to admit, so many leaders make the mistake of increasing investments when the writing is on the wall, even when logic says they should walk away. As with many other leadership mistakes, the decision is one to defy logic. Leaders get caught in the trap of "We've already come this far, might as well see it to the end." These leaders have become less like CEOs and more like pit bulls. Once a pit bull bites something, it will not let go, even when holding on is detrimental to its well-being. It has been bred to ignore pain and not let go.

Priceline.com's Hoffman has a metaphor for escalation of commitment: the "Thanksgiving Test." Imagine a scenario in which someone shows up to Thanksgiving dinner and proudly tells everyone at the table about a magnificent venture he is going to pursue over the next year. During that year, things start going wrong. As the venture starts to fail, he realizes he can't show his face at the next Thanksgiving dinner, because he'd hyped things up the year before. People might ask how things are going. What would he say? What could he say? Rather than be forced to admit his failure at Thanksgiving dinner, he keeps trying, throwing good resources after bad resources. As Hoffman puts it, people in this situation "just keep on beating the dead horse bloody." So a leader should be able to ask himself, "Am I continuing to chase a losing proposition in order to save face and avoid the shame of failure? Am I too worried about showing up at Thanksgiving dinner this year?"

Leaders fall into this trap over and over because they let emotion influence their decisions. Our research shows that the three most common emotional motivators for beating that dead horse are:

Eternal Hope—The belief that somehow more investment in a dead-end project will turn things around.

Pride—The inability to admit defeat when the inevitable has occurred.

Ownership—The more ownership a leader feels when it comes to a failing effort, the higher the probability for escalation of commitment.

None of these qualities, in and of themselves, are bad. Hope can be a good thing; leaders *should* motivate their employees and inspire them in the face of challenges. And pride is an admirable quality in any leader, or in any follower for that matter. Similarly, we encourage leaders and their workers to take ownership of their actions—that makes for strong and healthy organizations. But when these three emotional motivators take over from logic and rational decision making—when the writing is on the wall and the strategy either has already failed or is doomed to fail—they can end careers and ruin companies.

We can also look at escalation of commitment in terms of overt versus covert investment. Overt investment is the actual dollars that you spend. Overt investment is measurable and tangible. Often it can be rationalized as an effective use of resources to "save" an investment. In contrast, covert investment is the time that you have invested, the emotional energy, and the psychological commitment to the project. Although overt investment is easier to discern, covert investment can be the more costly of the two. It's hard to put a dollar figure on emotional investment, which is another reason why escalation of commitment is such a critical mistake: we never actually know the total cost. Whenever a leader is backed into a corner, needing to justify his decision, or whenever ego trumps pride, irrational decisions are made and resources—both tangible and intangible—are allocated poorly.

A classic business example of escalation of commitment is that of Motorola's Iridium project. In the 1980s, the business community was demanding a new way to make phone calls. In 1985, Barry Bertiger, an engineer working at Motorola, created the concept for Iridium, ultimately resulting in a network of sixty-six low-orbiting satellites to allow users to make calls directly from anywhere in the world. At the time of inception, the idea had a lot of promise, so Motorola spun off Iridium. Given the complexity of the technologies necessary to make the network functional, it took over fifteen years from inception to commercialize the idea. Unfortunately for Iridium, during that span of fifteen years, the cell phone industry developed rapidly. By the late 1980s many of the problems with cell phones had been resolved. But how did the leaders at Iridium respond? With escalation of commitment— they said, in essence, "Well, we have already gone this far, so let's continue to move forward." But how could they move forward with the initial idea when the cell phone industry had virtually eliminated the need for Iridium's low satellite network? When Iridium finally got their product to market, the phone cost around $3,000 and was relatively large. Also, given that the phones relied on satellite technology, they could only be used outdoors. The company filed for bankruptcy in 1999 and was sold for an estimated $25 million, but it had invested $5 *billion* over the fifteen years it spent developing the network. At a certain point during the development period, the writing was on the wall and it was time to pull the plug, yet Iridium continued to plod ahead.

Although Iridium is considered a classic example of escalation of commitment, a classic-in-the-making is emerging now. News Corp., the second largest media giant in the United States (behind Disney Corporation), bought the social networking company MySpace for $580 million in 2005. However, shortly after the acquisition, MySpace fell from its position as the dominant player in social networking to one of a company in danger of becoming obsolete. Consumers had moved on. Yet given the large initial investment, News Corp. kept pouring resources into their fallen icon.

Founder Tom Anderson had built MySpace in June of 2003, and, prior to the News Corp. acquisition in 2005, MySpace was the most popular social networking site in the world. However, by early 2008, Facebook had overtaken MySpace. The site's downward spiral started to accelerate. Facebook had a more user-friendly platform, a brand that appealed to adults rather than the thirteen-to-fifteen-year-old demographic that MySpace had targeted, and, quite frankly, Facebook had the coolness factor working in its favor. Anderson tried several redesigns of MySpace, even changing the site's color palette to appear more like Facebook. However, these efforts were in vain. Anderson's company was too slow to integrate technologies that allowed users to send messages—especially direct messages—more easily.

By 2009, the verdict was in, and Facebook had won. Still, leaders at News Corp. continued to pour investment dollars into MySpace, including opening extravagant new offices around the world. Facebook, in contrast, had no such plans and continued to successfully attract new users from all over the world. But escalation of commitment won again, as News Corp. had to try to recoup its $580 million price tag.

In April 2009, Rupert Murdoch, chairman and CEO of News Corp., changed the leadership team at MySpace. Anderson stepped down as president, and Owen Van Natta, former Facebook COO, was hired to turn things around. After reducing his workforce by 40 percent, Van Natta restructured the company at a cost of $180 million; the hope was that MySpace would be positioned to rebound with a new purpose. But it was too little too late, and the company continued to fail. Van Natta left after less than a year on the job, at which point he lamented that MySpace was no longer even a social networking site, but was now only a media site[5]—a far cry from being the world's preferred social network, which it had been just years earlier.

In March 2010, under the leadership of copresidents Mike Jones and Jason Hirshchorn, MySpace developers added recommendation engines to suggest games, videos, and music based on a user's previous search behaviors. Developers also invested considerable resources to make the site more secure, added a new photo option, and developed a new photo app. Then in September 2010, MySpace developers enabled users to integrate MySpace with Twitter and Facebook. Wait a minute—integrate with Facebook? Wasn't this an admission of defeat? Yet development continued to increase. Specifically, in November 2010, MySpace announced that it had created a platform to fully integrate with Facebook Connect. Developers referred to this as an effort to "Mash up with Facebook." This mash-up seemed to represent the raising of the white flag, as MySpace recognized that Facebook had won.[6]

Despite all of the investments and changes, the downward spiral of MySpace continued to spin out of control. Specifically, even as MySpace was developing several new mobile apps, market research figures released by comScore uncovered that MySpace had lost ten million users between January and February 2011, and traffic was down 44 percent from the previous year.[7] Advertisers (MySpace's source of revenue) were no longer interested in working with MySpace. Finally, News Corp. officially admitted defeat and put MySpace up for sale.

After investing $580 million in 2005 and throwing additional undisclosed millions into MySpace for the six years that followed, News Corp. sold MySpace to Specific Media on June 29, 2011, for a mere $35 million. The MySpace debacle is destined to be a classic in the category of escalation of commitment. There was a point when each of the leaders at MySpace could have said "enough!" But Anderson, Van Natta, Jones, and Hirshchorn all said "more." If these leaders had seen the writing on the wall rather than continuing to invest in a losing proposition, careers could have been saved, as well as millions of dollars.

Although the inability to quit is as common as the inability to avoid money-making opportunities, there is a third mistake, one that is the most common of all: the inability to turn down a customer.

BEING ALL THINGS TO ALL PEOPLE

Our interviews with executives illuminated the third common mistake affecting a leader's ability to say *no:* fear of exclusion, or trying to be all things to all people. Whereas the actions driven by irrational greed are akin to throwing a whole bowlful of strategy spaghetti against the wall and seeing what sticks, fear of exclusion has an effect akin to throwing multiple bowls against the wall and trying to do everything—pursuing the spaghetti that sticks to the wall as well as the spaghetti that falls on the floor. This fear spurs a leader to cast his net as wide as he possibly can to ensure that no one is excluded. The outcomes of trying to be all things to all people are similar to those we saw with chasing dollars earlier in this chapter; the result is a loss of strategic direction. But the underlying catalysts that drive leaders to pursue this strategic choice are diametrically opposed. Whereas chasing dollars is based on irrational greed, being all things to all people is based on fear of failure and lack of decision-making confidence.

It is very common in entrepreneurial ventures to want to be all things to all people—especially before a leader has identified a strategic direction. Often in entrepreneurial ventures, the owner is pulled in multiple directions simultaneously. He needs to encourage talented people to join his not-so-profitable company. Investors need to be reassured that their investment will return. Suppliers need to know their invoices will get paid. The leader is so busy trying to please everyone that he has no semblance of strategic direction.

But leaders who want to be all things to all people appear at larger companies too. Recently, numerous automotive blog sites—such as autoevolution.com, autoblog.com, and benzinsider .com—have posted articles that question Mercedes-Benz USA introduction of the Mercedes B-class hatchback and a new two-door C-class coupe.[8] These critics are concerned that these new models will dilute the Mercedes-Benz brand. Up until the introduction of the C-class, only the ultra-rich could afford to buy a Mercedes. Unfortunately for Mercedes, these articles have been accurate. The new model alienated a segment of Mercedes' core customer base. Owning a Mercedes historically correlated with prestige, exclusivity, success. The brand has long appealed, to some extent, to an elitist market segment. Bottom line, the brand represented a specific image—an image for which customers were willing to pay a premium.

With the new models, Mercedes made it possible for customers to buy a new Mercedes for around $30,000. What once was a car that exuded prestige can now be purchased by a recent college graduate. The leaders at Mercedes have diluted the brand because they want to be all things to all people. Trying to be a luxury car company and simultaneously selling cheaper cars using the same brand? Well, it didn't work for Mercedes. The result? For the first time in history, Audi outsold Mercedes in the first three months of 2011. According to Bloomberg, Audi is on its way to being the top luxury car manufacturer in the world, as the company expects to sell 1.5 million vehicles per year by 2015.[9]

The process of sticking your flag in the sand, taking a position, and following your strategic direction by nature will exclude potential customers. Some customers will feel left out, but that's okay. Trying to please everyone will ultimately lead to not pleasing anyone. Strategic focus actually requires exclusion.

If you are still not convinced that trying to be all things to all people is a bad idea, ask Charles Conaway, former CEO of Kmart. At one time, Kmart was one of the most respected brands in the United States. What led to its demise? Trying to be all things to all people. Kmart tried to be chic and yet known for its low prices, resulting in lost strategic direction and confused customers.

As the first real national discount retail chain, Kmart was a brand known for great prices. Then in the 1980s, under the leadership of Bernard Fauber, Kmart decided to be all things to all people. It started to develop designer brands—Jaclyn Smith, Kathy Ireland, Joe Boxer, and later, Martha Stewart—to attract a wealthier clientele. At the same time Fauber didn't forget about price-conscious shoppers: Kmart still relied on its weekly fliers offering huge discounts and the famous "blue light specials" in its stores.

Harvard Business School professor Michael Porter, credited as the "father of strategic management," identified two categories of strategic focus. At one end of the spectrum, firms compete on price; at the other, they compete on being unique or differentiated. He defined firms that try to do both strategies simultaneously as "stuck in the middle." And there is significant data to show that firms that are stuck in the middle will likely fail.[10] Kmart was straddling this proverbial fence.

Then, as market conditions changed in the early 2000s, the choice for large national retailers became especially stark. H. Lee Scott Jr., CEO of Wal-Mart, decided to continue on the path of competing on price. Scott knew that his stores would not appeal to urban shoppers looking for high-end designer names. Robert Ulrich, CEO of Target, decided to follow the path of competing on differentiation. He knew that he would alienate shoppers who cared only about price, but his stores were going to be more upscale and carry more designer brands. Charles Conaway, CEO of Kmart, decided that Kmart should continue to try to serve everyone. Kmart pursued both paths and succeeded at neither. In January 2002, Conaway's Kmart had to file for bankruptcy.

How can trying to be all things to all people be so damaging? First: brand dilution. When Mercedes and Kmart tried to be all things to all people, their respective brands became diluted. And once a brand becomes diluted, customers become confused (Kmart) or disgruntled (Mercedes). Second: sunk costs. When trying to be all things to all people, you will incur additional development costs—beyond what is necessary—resulting from a more complex business model of serving multiple markets. Trying to recoup those sunk costs can lead to an escalation of commitment.

Olli-Pekka Kallasvuo, former CEO of Nokia, provides an apt example of the sunk cost consequence of trying to be all things to all people. In 2007, Nokia appeared at number 3 on *Fortune's* Top 10 Companies for Leaders. By 2010, what was once the world's largest cell phone manufacturer was quickly deteriorating. A cursory look at their website in 2010 revealed that they had *forty-four phone models* available on their "short list." Apple offered two. Too many choices resulted in excess product-development costs and very confused customers. Then Stephen Elop, Kallasvuo's successor as CEO of Nokia, announced that the company would not compete in the smartphone market. How could the world's leader in cell phones miss a fundamental shift in their own market? They were actually already too busy being all things to all people. Not only had Nokia invested in a plethora of models, but its leaders also had fallen victim to escalating commitment with its own operating system (Symbian). As a result, Nokia has gone from the world leader in cell phones to struggling giant. The company's escalation of commitment combined with trying to be all things to all people created a scenario for the perfect storm. On June 22, 2011, Nokia made *24/7 Wall Street's* list of the "Ten Brands That Will Disappear in 2012."[11]

Story after story emerges of huge, well-established companies that lose their way trying to be all things to all people. Perhaps Alan Lacy, CEO of Sears, said it most poignantly: "We've had some lack of clarity and focus . . . And I think at the end of the day we had just not—in some shape or form—been able to get the right kind of relevance to customers in this category."[12]

JUST SAY NO: AVOIDING THE MISTAKE OF YES

So far in this chapter we have talked about three critical—and common—mistakes that leaders make when they are not able to say "no"—"no" to chasing dollars, "no" to escalation of commitment, and "no" to being all things to all people. How can a leader develop a mind-set of saying "no" instead of "yes" when necessary?

There are four tactics leaders can use to avoid making these types of mistakes, which we will go into at length. First, explicitly define your perception of your organization based on its value. When you look in the mirror, what do you see? One way to avoid saying yes to any of these temptations is to define your organization based on the value your company provides rather than the products or services it offers. Second, relentlessly pursue an inventory of potential opportunities. The larger the inventory, the less likely a leader will jump at the first opportunity that presents itself. Comparing opportunities over the long term can help you know when to say no, whereas forcing growth opportunities is a primary manifestation of chasing dollars and trying to be all things to all people. Third, establish and use a repeatable framework that enables you to assess whether or not a potential strategy falls within the strategic scope of the organization. Finally, know where your market segments are, and, more important, know where they are not.

Perceive Your Organization's Value Proposition

If leaders really challenge themselves to seek it out, they will find that every organization has some unique value proposition. If you develop a fundamental understanding of how your markets *define* value, and you couple that with a fundamental understanding of how your organization *delivers* value, you'll better know which opportunities to pursue and which to avoid. The primary question a leader needs to consider is, what are the underlying reasons for the company's existence (other than maximizing shareholder wealth)? Defining why the company exists can be the difference between pursuing the right opportunity and making a huge mistake. To define why your company exists, you have basically two choices:

1. Define your organization based on your products or services.
2. Define your organization based on the value you provide to customers.

Products and services are the outcome of business activity; value is the reason for those products and services to exist in the marketplace. Focusing on value can help you avoid a lot of strategic blunders. Every company is in business to fulfill a need, plain and simple. At Mercedes, they saw their company as an automobile manufacturer—they focused on product. And in this light, it seemed to make a lot of sense to create a new, relatively affordable line of cars. What Mercedes didn't take into account was the value that its brand portrayed and the need it fulfilled. The brand portrayed an image of success and prestige. That was a key value driver for Mercedes, but they missed it. If they had kept their eye on protecting and building their value proposition, they would not have made this blunder.

As human beings, we are constantly trying to fulfill our needs. Every successful product or service fulfills a need. As leaders, when we focus our attention on the "needs" our products or service fulfill, rather than on the actual product or service itself, we can gain the vision needed to avoid saying "yes" when we should be saying "no."

Relentlessly Pursue Potential

Some leaders have the false belief that opportunities for strategic growth emerge periodically, when the time is right. They see growth opportunity as a reliable—if irregularly scheduled—train.

But we've all heard the expression "window of opportunity," and, in reality, that's how an opportunity presents itself—as a window that's open briefly, and not according to any sort of schedule. There is only a small window of time when a leader can seize an opportunity. Many executives told us that in order to find the "right" growth opportunities, a leader needs to relentlessly persist, making opportunity identification an ongoing process. This is how to be ready when the window opens. Our leaders told us that almost every opportunity they've successfully leveraged was by design. The concept of blind luck does not exist in their world. Priceline.com's Jeff Hoffman puts it succinctly: "Great leaders create their own luck."

SRC Holding Company CEO Jack Stack (also author of *The Great Game of Business*) has shown some remarkable persistence in his career. During the height of the 2008 recession, Stack and his leadership team relentlessly pursued opportunities through some bold, contrarian moves. They borrowed at long-term fixed rates when banks were collapsing. They hired top people while other companies in their competitive space were "right sizing." They redefined their strategic mission from fast growth to a focus on "clear roles, clear goals, clear communications and complete ESOP objectives." One of Stack's great formulations for this approach was to "use pessimism to our advantage and lead with optimism." While many leaders saw the recession as a threat, Stack saw it as a potential opportunity.

Also consider Sir Richard Branson, president of the Virgin Group and one of the richest people in the world. He sees opportunities that most of us would never see, and he writes them down in notebooks. He carries around a collection of these notebooks wherever he goes, making entries on a daily basis. He states, "I can't believe when I see people not writing things down. You know they're not going to remember everything." At last count, he had over 125 black ledger notebooks containing years and years of ideas. His observations turn into opportunities, totaling over four hundred business ventures associated with the Virgin Group. Hundreds more, obviously, were never operationalized, but Branson has never had to wait around for opportunity to knock on his door.

A persistent leader is constantly learning, thinking of new opportunities, like Branson. The problem with many leaders is that they don't have an inventory of opportunities to assess, so when one presents itself, they are vulnerable to putting significant resources behind it without thinking it through and determining whether it is even strategically appropriate.

Determine Strategic Appropriateness

Often, when a leader considers pursuing a new opportunity, he spends a lot of time looking at financials. Metrics such as expected rates of return, payback periods, and cost of capital are all important considerations. Financial metrics like these are commonly used because they are hard numbers—relatively easy to generate and relatively easy to justify. But what about some of the soft-side criteria, such as strategic fit and leadership skill sets? By looking at the soft-side criteria, a leader can decrease his probability of falling into the trap of saying "yes" when he should be saying "no." Here are three basic questions to ask in this regard:

1. *Does the strategy support the current overall strategic position of the organization?* If a company is pursuing cost leadership, as in the case of Kmart, does it make sense to start pursuing a strategy that focuses on differentiation? If the answer is no (and it probably is), then saying "yes" to the new strategy may indicate that the company is trying to be all things to all people. When the leadership at Mercedes decided to offer its C-class automobiles, did this support the strategic position of the organization? The answer is clearly no, as leadership diluted the Mercedes brand.

2. *Is the strategy appropriate, given the current competitive environment?* Given what competitors are doing, or the changing value

propositions for customers, does the opportunity still have merit? Consider Motorola's Iridium project. Several years into the project, competitors in the cell phone industry came up with new solutions to the problems Iridium was trying to solve. If leaders at Iridium had continually assessed the market, they could have saved billions instead of escalating commitment to a project that the marketplace had already doomed. When the cell phone market's next big product was the smartphone, did it make sense for Nokia to shrug it off, even though every other major competitor was developing a smartphone?

3. *Is the strategy consistent with the skills and competencies of our organization?* A leader should make sure that a strategy is not spreading the company too thin. When considering skills and competencies, this could include areas such as sufficient operations, valuable intellectual property, effective distribution channels, and a leadership team with the skills to pull it off. When L.A. Gear's Greenberg decided to get into men's high-performance basketball shoes, the company did not have the skills to succeed. The demands that a customer puts on a high-performance shoe are different from the demands a customer puts on a stylish shoe. The technologies are different; the products are different. Considering skills and competencies can help keep you from chasing dollars for the sake of chasing dollars.

Although these questions may seem like common sense, it is easy to overlook them. The companies we profile in this chapter were all leaders in their respective industries at one time. When their leaders said "yes" at a time when they should have said "no," it cost these companies millions, even billions, and weakened or even destroyed the company. By asking—and thoughtfully, honestly answering—these fundamental soft-side questions before embarking on new ventures, these leaders could have avoided the critical mistakes of chasing dollars, escalating commitment, or trying to be all things to all people.

Use Segmentation

Segmentation is a final technique that can help leaders avoid strategic mistakes. Segmenting markets involves dividing customers into different groups based on their unique values and needs. Every market, regardless of customer needs, can be segmented. Segmentation requires breaking a market down into its definable parts, and the more tightly you segment markets, the greater the number of potential customers that you will not serve. However, the benefit of segmenting markets is that you will avoid trying to be all things to all people. An astute leader will realize that excluding customers doesn't mean less business; often it means *more* business. There are many examples of leaders who have entered slow-growth markets by discovering underserved segments.

Consider the airline industry. For decades, the passenger airline industry was considered low- to no-growth. However, Herb Kelleher, founder of Southwest Airlines, understood that there was an underserved segment of customers who wanted a no-frills airline with an exceptional on-time track record, at a low price. So Herb Kelleher created a totally new business in this seemingly impenetrable industry.

Honda Motor Co. has successfully segmented markets in different parts of the world, without diluting its brand as Mercedes did. In the United States, Honda is perceived primarily as an automobile manufacturer, with a smaller ancillary business in motorcycles. In Japan, Honda is perceived primarily as a motorcycle manufacturer, with a smaller ancillary business in cars. Even though Honda is a world leader in both automobiles and motorcycles, each market has its own perception of what the Honda brand means to them. Honda figured out that trying to cover multiple product categories in the same market with the same brand would not work.

Consider taking a look at the characteristics of customers in your markets. Do different types of customers have different value drivers? Does each type of customer have different needs? If the answer is yes, then approaching your markets as an aggregation of smaller, thoughtfully defined segments may help you avoid making many of the mistakes discussed in this chapter.

The content of this chapter may have appeared somewhat eclectic. We discussed leadership mistakes resulting from irrational greed, escalation of commitment, and the fear of exclusion (and resulting attempts to be all things to all people). However, all three of these mistakes have one critical catalyst in common: the inability to say "no" when, as a leader, you should be. And developing the ability to say "no" is often tricky to navigate. What seems like a good idea at the moment may in hindsight have you asking yourself "What was I thinking?!" However, armed with the ability to see your company through a different lens—fulfilling needs rather than products—combined with tools to build an inventory and mind-set of potential opportunities, assess strategic appropriateness, and pursue effective segmentation, you can bolster your ability to say "no" and minimize if not eliminate many of the perils that result when you allow yourself to be seduced by "yes."

KEY TAKEAWAYS

Lessons Learned from Mistakes

- The inability to say "no" brings a risk of misallocating resources and destroying strategic direction.
- Chasing dollars at the cost of strategic coherence—being driven by irrational greed—can devastate a company.
- When things are going badly and failure is imminent, escalating commitment (continuing to allocate resources to a project out of emotion, of hope, pride, or a feeling of responsibility) is a common and destructive mistake.
- Trying to be all things to all people (through fear of exclusion from a perceived market) leads to brand dilution and loss of the ability to reach any market segment.

Successful Navigation

- Define your organization based on needs and value rather than products. This provides insight that will diminish the chance of saying "yes" when you should be saying "no."

- Relentlessly pursue opportunities. This will provide you with a large inventory from which to draw, decreasing the possibility that you'll pursue a wrong strategy simply because it's the only one in front of you.

- Assess strategic appropriateness of any potential opportunity. Doing this consistently and rigorously can reduce or virtually eliminate mistakes associated with pursuing the wrong strategy.

- Segment your markets effectively, understanding which segments you can or cannot offer value to. This can reduce the potential for brand dilution and create new growth opportunities.

THREE

Businesses You Have No Business Being In

Roaming Outside the Box

A train can be heading along a track, deliberate and steady, for hundreds of miles. All of a sudden something happens, and the train derails and flies off the track. The "something" might be a break in the tracks, excessive speed, mechanical problems, human error, or a combination. The Federal Railroad Administration reported that in 2008, nearly two thousand derailments occurred in the United States.[1] Among those incidents, nearly one third were caused by human factors. Human factors are usually a result of going too fast. The cliché "falling asleep at the switch" is rarely a cause. It's not that the people in charge aren't paying attention; they are. They're just making bad decisions.

What does train derailment have to do with thinking outside the box? Just as a train can be heading quite steadily down the tracks and suddenly derail, so can a company be making good money, moving along steadily and methodically for years, even decades, and suddenly be derailed, leaving the leaders scratching their heads, wondering how this could have happened. And according to our survey of executives, the number one cause of business derailment is thinking outside the box. It can derail even the most successful companies in no time at all.

"Thinking outside the box" has become one of the most common buzz phrases in business. We read about it in books and hear about it from some of the leading management gurus. Thinking outside the box is billed as innovative and exciting, and many blue-sky business books tell you that you must do it in order to succeed. But is that true? Have you ever really thought about whether or not it is a good idea when a leader is trying to sustain performance? Thinking outside the box has its place, but that place is a limited one—and it only rarely has anything to do with good strategic leadership.

In practice, it is often a reactionary position, taken in a misguided effort to keep the new-product pipeline full—truly, there are better, more effective ways to keep a pipeline full. In British novelist Sir Terry Pratchett's pointed words: "I'll be more enthusiastic about encouraging thinking outside the box when there's evidence of any thinking going on inside it!"[2] In this chapter, we will show you how thinking outside the box is, contrary to popular perception, one of the most common—and most destructive—mistakes that leaders make. We'll discuss why some leaders pursue out-of-the-box thinking when they should not, and tell you how avoid this mistake.

BOXES AND STRATEGIC DIRECTION

Outside-the-box thinking—let's call it the "box paradigm"—can lead to pursuing new ideas simply for the sake of pursuing new ideas. This can be particularly dangerous when applied to the strategic direction of the organization—the underlying reason why the company exists. New ideas, whether or not they are achieved as a result of having a box paradigm, aren't necessarily bad ideas, but often they are shinier and get a lot more attention than older ways of doing business, regardless of their merit. When leaders use the box paradigm to define the strategic direction of their organizations, it can lead to strategic ambiguity, blurring the company's direction. And although free-form thinking may be an interesting exercise in creativity, when applied to strategic direction it can lead to random actions, and randomness in leadership can be very costly at many levels—and even lethal.

As appealing as thinking outside the box sounds—conjuring images of brainstorming sessions in roller skates, or promising inspired, creative innovations—the entire concept has no objective reality. The conceptual "box" could be anything, and there can be many of them. They may represent any aspect of your business from your current customer base to your company structure, or maybe even your markets—yet all of these definitions are subjective, lacking true substantive boundaries. And the big peril of the box paradigm is in clinging to it as a business nostrum without ever thinking through its terms. As media entrepreneur and writer Kirk Cheyfitz argues in his book *Thinking Inside the Box*, "We can't think outside the box . . . unless we have a precise idea of what the box is."[3]

So how can you expect to think outside the box if you have no way of accurately defining it? Or, for the sake of argument, let's say that you are brighter than everyone else and you have figured out a way to define the boundaries of the box. Here is when it gets dangerous. The concept of thinking outside the box provides no direction regarding where you need to focus your efforts. According to our interviews, rather than following a well-thought-out strategy, thinking outside the box leads to (1) creativity for the sake of creativity rather than for the sake of progress, and (2) situations in which a "solution" is identified first, and it goes in search of problems to fix. As a form of unbalanced orchestration, not only is the box paradigm expensive in terms of resources and time, but often it gets in the way of what a leader needs to be focusing on. Author Seth Godin warns, "Don't think outside the box, because outside the box there's a vacuum. Outside of the box there are no rules, there is no reality."

Moreover, he contends, "If you set out to do something way outside of the box . . . then you'll never be able to do the real work."[4]

Many of the successful leaders we interviewed referenced the box paradigm as "aimlessly wandering," "lost," and "dabbling." George Ruebenson, former president of Allstate Property and Casualty, told us that the box paradigm "can cause a leader to dabble. When you dabble, you make mistakes." Dabbling is needlessly risky, especially when, as in Ruebenson's case, you are managing the futures of millions of customers, over seventy thousand employees, and one of the biggest brands in the United States. "Allstate decided to dabble in hotels," he told us. "There was a Holiday Inn near our corporate headquarters in Northbrook, IL. We were sending numerous visitors there all of the time. So we decided to get into the hotel business. Even though we booked the hotel to capacity every night, we ran it into bankruptcy. We didn't know how to run a hotel. We got involved in a business that we knew nothing about."

In the moment, getting into the hotel business probably seemed like a fine idea for Allstate. But in retrospect, it was a business they had no business being in.

THE LURE OF THE EXCITING AND THE NEW

Most leaders with whom we spoke were very open about times they'd learned from others' mistakes. However, several of these same executives found it embarrassing to talk about mistakes they themselves had made, and they did not want us to disclose their names. Their stories and the underlying messages are powerful, so we still opted to tell them (but, in accordance with their wishes, without disclosing their names and the names of their companies). One such story involves a large, well-known real-estate developer.

This organization represents a classic success story. Started as a small land-development firm in the 1970s, by 2005 the company had become one of the largest retail developers in the central United States. They would purchase undeveloped land, then improve it to make it sellable to others. They also started partnering with others to build retail space on the newly improved land. Business was great. The company grew from a small family start-up to a multifaceted development firm with several locations and employing hundreds of people. Their scope had grown from improving land to financing, construction, brokerage, and leasing.

When the founder retired in 1997, his son took over as CEO. The son successfully led the company for eight years, but then decided it was time to start thinking outside the box. He started looking for new growth opportunities. Up to this point, the company had successfully developed numerous retail outlets, many in the form of large strip malls. Most strip malls have a large "anchor" store—a nationally recognized brand that attracts customers to the location with the idea that customers will also shop at smaller stores in the mall. Specifically, most of the strip malls that this particular real-estate developer built used a regional or national grocery store as the anchor.

And then came the big mistake. An outside-the-box idea that caused the company to lose its strategic direction, sending it into a devastating tailspin in less than eighteen months. The CEO decided to reinvent the company to not only develop retail space but also manage the retail operations. After all, who better to manage a grocery store than the company that built the facility? According to the son, "Managing a grocery store seemed like a good idea, a cash cow. And quite honestly, it sounded exciting compared to the doldrums of real estate development. Can you think of any other business where multiple cash registers are ringing all day long? I completely convinced myself that the grocery store business was just the real estate business at a faster pace. I mean, companies have to lease shelf space from the chain groceries." So off he went, investing significant capital in his new outside-the-box idea.

Unfortunately, no one at the company knew anything about managing a grocery business. Everything was different. Rather than working in a business-to-business environment, they were now working in a business-to-consumer market. Supply chains were different, employees were different, and operations were different. Instead of working with timelines focusing on months or even years, the company now had timelines that focused on days. Inventory such as steel beams sitting on a job site for months was a far cry from perishable inventory that had to be turned over in a week.

The company was in over its head. Management started throwing more and more capital into the grocery stores to cover up day-to-day mistakes. It became so bad that they started pulling money out of their construction projects to cover the grocery stores. In less than a year, the company was running out of cash and had started borrowing money against the real-estate development business—the business that had been so successful for decades.

After almost two years of burning through cash, wrong turns, and sleepless nights, the CEO finally realized that going into retail had been a big mistake. As the CEO told us his story, he began to slump in his chair, shake his head, and avoid eye contact with us. As he got to end of his story, he stared despondently out the window. "What the heck was I thinking?" he said. "I thought, as a leader of this company, I needed to think outside the box to take my company forward. If I would have just focused on what we did well, we would still be in business today. Thinking outside the box killed my company."

In 2007, the company retrenched to focus on real-estate development. Unfortunately, in 2008, when the real-estate market began to unravel, the company had very little cash. As the market began to slip away, so did the CEO's company. In 2009 he closed all but one office, laying off hundreds of employees. In 2010, he closed his doors for good. In contrast, most of his direct competitors were in a good cash position when the recession hit; they weathered the storm and today are rebounding quite well.

How could this happen? Why would the CEO of a successful company suddenly decide to change course and get into a business that he had no business being in? As Seth Godin suggested, when you start thinking outside the box, you can't do the real work. For this company, the real work wasn't in reinventing itself but in continuing down its established path. It wasn't broken and didn't need fixing. Because of his attraction to the box paradigm, the CEO destroyed the family business and also affected creditors, suppliers, and hundreds of families. He chased something that he thought was exciting. And it was. Unfortunately, exciting doesn't always make the best business sense.

LETTING COMPETITORS DEFINE THE BOX

Another mistake leaders make is looking over the fence into someone else's backyard—presumably a competitor's—and letting that someone else define the box. This can happen even if the company on the other side of the fence hasn't proven itself yet. It seems beyond reason that a market leader would decide to change the course of what their company has done so well in the past in order to follow a follower. Even worse, in some cases companies will collect data to justify changing course, only to find out in the end that the data was bad—or at least badly used—and the decision was a big mistake. Mistakes of this nature are not reserved for small start-ups; they happen to Fortune 100 companies as well. What many pundits dubbed the most notorious business blunder in history was Coca-Cola's roll-out of New Coke. Let's examine the thought process that went into this debacle.

In early 1985, rumors started circulating that Coca-Cola's chairman Roberto C. Goizueta and president Donald Keough had been working on a secret plan called "Project Kansas," named for a photograph of a Kansas journalist, William Allen White, drinking a Coke—a photo that Coke had used in many advertising campaigns. Project Kansas—headed by the president of Coca-Cola USA, Brian Dyson, and marketing vice president Sergio Zyman—charged its team with inventing a new kind of Coke. The company was very adept at keeping things under wraps; they ran taste tests and conducted research for over two years prior to the announcement of New Coke.

Coca-Cola was about as American as hot dogs and apple pie. It was part of U.S. history. What would motivate the leaders of a company with literally the highest-rated brand in the world to try to change everything up? Simply, they looked over the fence. Project Kansas was a reaction to an aggressive marketing campaign initiated by PepsiCo, the Pepsi Challenge, wherein Pepsi was cast as the choice of the "new generation," and Coke was portrayed as old and stuffy. The leadership at Coca-Cola looked over the fence, got caught up in what they saw, and started playing by new rules—rules established by Pepsi—even though Coke still had the vast majority of worldwide market share. Up to this point, Coke had never thought about changing the formula that gave the company the number one brand in the world. But PepsiCo decided to make the debate about taste, not about nostalgia. Alas, so did Coke.

After Coca-Cola took the bait of PepsiCo's marketing campaign, on April 23, 1985, New Coke was distributed to the masses. Goizueta decreed New Coke a "smoother, rounder yet bolder" experience. He spoke of New Coke being "more like a fine wine than a carbonated treat."[5] And it got worse. Not only did Zyman and Dyson attempt to change one of the greatest brands in world history, but they decided to take the original Coke off the market in order to change the company's focus.

Within days, New Coke became one of the biggest business disasters industry had ever seen.[6] The backlash was unprecedented.

Consumers were nothing short of outraged that their beloved original Coke was being taken away from them. How dare the leadership at Coca-Cola do this!

Over the following few weeks, Coca-Cola Company received over four hundred thousand phone calls and letters from disgruntled customers. Bob Greene, nationally syndicated writer for the *Chicago Tribune*, dedicated his column to ridiculing the new flavor and directly chastised the leaders at Coca-Cola Company for making such a significant mistake. Even Fidel Castro (incidentally, the man who had created the environment that caused Goizueta's family to flee Cuba) chimed in, saying that American capitalism was damaging relationships with customers; he was a loyal Coke drinker, too.

The weekend after Goizueta's big announcement, Roger Enrico, director of PepsiCo North American operations (who ultimately became Chairman and CEO in 1996), took out a full-page ad in the *New York Times* declaring that Pepsi had officially won the cola war, and he actually instituted a company-wide holiday to celebrate. The momentum kept growing. Pepsi ran television commercials ridiculing Coke for its decision to play by PepsiCo's rules—namely, the rule that taste was more important than brand. One ad featured a first-time Pepsi drinker stating, "Now I know why Coke did it." There was also a commercial featuring an elderly man sitting on a park bench, despondently questioning how leadership at Coke could take his drink away.

It was only seventy-seven days before Goizueta announced that the original Coke would soon be back on the shelves, but the damage to Coca-Cola and its brand was already done.

This debacle begs the question: How could leadership at the company with the number one brand in the world be so convinced that this was the correct decision, when it so clearly was not? Bad data. Armed with the same approach that Pepsi used against them, Coca-Cola marketing experts had performed taste tests to prove that New Coke tasted better than Pepsi. They spent millions on these tests, focus groups, interviews, and surveys. Results were overwhelming, justifying that New Coke did indeed taste better than Pepsi. Leadership at Coca-Cola then determined that if they kept two brands of Coke on the market, they'd cannibalize each other, so they decided to pull old Coke off. The strategy, according to Goizueta, was "New Coke or no Coke."[7]

After the dust had settled, leadership at Coke spent a lot of effort (and resources) trying to figure out what had gone wrong. The company had forgotten one of the most important value drivers for customers: emotional attachment. They had missed the fact that people were emotionally attached to Coke, as if it were a family member. Years later, author Malcolm Gladwell delved into the debacle in his book *Blink*. He argued that much of Coke's success is based on "sensation transference," wherein the packaging of the product subconsciously affects drinkers' reactions to a beverage.[8] For example, when 7-Up drinkers were offered a sample from a bottle with a yellowish label, they stated that the drink tasted more lemony, although in reality the flavor was not changed. Further, Gladwell asserted that taste tests are flawed at the core—sipping a beverage and drinking a larger quantity are two totally different experiences, especially when researching flavor. Coca-Cola had ventured outside the box with nothing to lead them but flawed information.

When the original Coke was reintroduced (rebranded as "Coca-Cola Classic"), millions of customers were relieved. The protests stopped, the lawsuits from disgruntled customers stopped, the lobbying interest groups disbanded. Years and years later, in 2009, Coke finished its long retreat from New Coke, announcing it would drop the word "Classic" and revert back to plain Coca-Cola.

Some believe that the New Coke debacle was an intentional publicity stunt to lure customers back. "Some critics will say Coca-Cola made a marketing mistake," Keough said in response. "Some cynics will say that we planned the whole thing. The truth is we are not that dumb, and we are not that smart."[9]

The truth was, leaders at the number one brand in the world had missed the big picture. They had focused on flavor (and used a flawed methodology to do so) when flavor was only one factor in a long chain of characteristics motivating customers to buy Coke. But the bottom line of the New Coke episode—the fundamental takeaway—is that the way to make buying into the box paradigm an even worse mistake is letting your competitors define the box. As Earl Nightingale observed in his 1950s bestseller *Lead the Field*, "It's been said that if the other guy's pasture appears to be greener than ours, it's quite possible that it's getting better care. Besides, while we're looking at other pastures, other people are looking at ours!"[10]

THINKING INSIDE THE BOX

As we have seen, over and over again, trying to be a visionary leader by using the box paradigm can make you blind. So how can you, as a leader, effectively avoid the mistakes associated with a box paradigm and still identify growth opportunities? By thinking "inside the box"—being very aware of what business you are in and what value propositions your company and your brand offer. You can still do critical, analytical, and creative thinking within the context of your own business environment. But you will need to pay attention at times when it is tempting to take a quick peek over the fence into someone else's. Effective leaders know what businesses to be in, and know what businesses they have no business being in. Although many pundits credit Apple's successes to outside-the-box thinking, closer inspection reveals that Steve Jobs was a master at using technology, not for the sake of making things more complicated but to make things more simple. Did Apple develop the first personal computer, the digital music player, the smartphone, or even the tablet computer? No! Jobs was able to take the ideas of others and use technology to make usable products like the Mac, iPod, iPhone, and iPad. That was his business model.

Can thinking inside the box provide us with enough possibilities to fill our pipelines and lead our organizations successfully? Yes! Effective leaders can avoid veering off course and still find numerous ways to effectively navigate their organizations, by what's come to be known as "diamond mining."

The concept of diamond mining was popularized in the late 1950s by Earl Nightingale. It is based on a true story of a young African farmer. He worked long hours out in his fields all day, with little to show for his efforts. He began to hear stories, fascinating tales of other African farmers getting rich beyond their wildest dreams by discovering diamond mines. These get-rich-quick stories consumed the farmer to the extent that he decided to sell his farm (a difficult decision, given this farm had been in his family for many generations), and he set out in search of his own diamond mine. He aimlessly wandered around the African continent for several years in search of his own fortune. Eventually he ran out of money and had nothing to show for his efforts. As the story goes, he became so despondent and humiliated after selling his family farm and failing to find diamonds that he threw himself into a river and drowned.

Meanwhile, the man who bought his farm was wandering around the property one day, and as he was crossing a small stream he saw a brilliant flash of blue and white light coming from the bottom of the stream. He bent down, reached into the stream, and picked up one of the stones. When he got back to his house, he placed it up on his fireplace mantel. A few weeks later, when a friend came over to visit the man, he noticed the brilliant stone on the mantel, and after carefully looking at the stone, he had trouble catching his breath. He asked the farmer if he had any idea what he had found. The farmer said he assumed it was just a beautiful piece of crystal. The friend told the farmer that what he had found was not crystal at all, but a diamond in its rough form. This piece of "beautiful crystal" was one of the biggest diamonds ever discovered. The farmer was amazed; he couldn't believe what was happening. The farmer told his friend that the creek was full of these stones—maybe not as big as the one he had put up on his mantel, but there in abundance.

This same piece of land that the first farmer had eagerly sold to someone else so he could go off in search of diamonds became the most productive diamond mine on the entire continent of Africa. The first farmer had owned literally acres of diamonds, free and clear, and the land had been in his family for generations. But instead of considering the value of what he already had, he had sold his fortune for almost nothing in order to look for it somewhere else. If the first farmer had only taken the time to understand how a diamond appeared in its rough form, he would have achieved everything he ever wanted. Bottom line, he should have explored the value of his own farm before aimlessly wandering off to look elsewhere. Leaders will—and should—continually explore in an effort to find new ideas and opportunities. However, where they look for those opportunities and, more important, *how* they look can be the difference between leading their organizations effectively or putting them out of business.

Mike Delazzer, a founding member of Redbox, told us that "the difference between effective leaders and those that fail is that effective leaders have the ability to see opportunities that don't expose the company to undesirable risk. They have the innate ability to perceive their markets in different ways. Average leaders may take a look at a market and think it is stagnant, whereas a successful leader will effectively explore the market, looking for opportunities that most others cannot see." Only through awareness and persistence can an effective leader avoid the pitfalls of the box paradigm and instead identify new opportunities that may have gone unnoticed by most. Effective leaders are constantly learning, educating themselves regarding what their diamonds look like in rough form, rather than wandering off in search of diamonds on someone else's land.

Netscape's leaders made the mistake of the first farmer. The company got too far ahead of itself on numerous occasions, trying to identify new and creative opportunities, when the diamond mine was sitting under their feet the entire time, waiting to be discovered. Instead of realizing the value that Netscape had already created as an internet browser, leaders at Netscape were peeking over the fence to try to figure out what opportunities lay outside the box. At that same time, however, Bill Gates, CEO of Microsoft, was already lurking in Netscape's backyard with his own internet browser, Internet Explorer. Instead of developing new features for Netscape's successful internet browser, cofounder Marc Andreessen invested significant resources in developing a new Java-based language from scratch, only to come to the realization that the language he was fueling was still too underdeveloped to meet the needs of Netscape. Andreessen's decision paralyzed the company. Netscape was unable to add any new features for three years. So, while Gates's Internet Explorer was evolving to meet the changing requirements in the market, Netscape had to sit on the sidelines while Gates took away their market share. By thinking outside the box, Andreessen overlooked significant diamond mining opportunities in his own backyard—namely, to focus on providing the most cost-effective solutions for internet browser services. In an interview, Andreessen confessed that he'd overlooked an obvious opportunity that had been staring him in the face the entire time, admitting, "I thought [using our website] was a distraction. It's kind of funny to think about how many people have had the opportunity to make billion-dollar mistakes. I absolutely thought we were a software company—we build software and put it in boxes, and we sell it. Oops. Wrong."[11] He was so busy focusing on technology for the sake of technology that he never saw the obvious opportunity to develop Netscape's web browsing business.

Any seasoned leader will tell you that the pressure to find new opportunities can become extremely intense. Proactive leaders will make mistakes—more mistakes than leaders who are never willing to take risks. Correctly anticipating change is extremely difficult—and occasionally impossible. This is why successful leaders tend to look closely at what they are already doing well and consider how they can leverage and build on existing strengths, rather than jumping into something way out in left field.

Are you using a box paradigm to generate new ideas for the strategic direction of your organization, or are you exploring your own acre of diamonds? Take inventory of what is already around you; there's probably a very good rationale for being in the business you are already in. Identify it and take a good look at it. At some point your predecessors decided to do what you are currently doing. What have you previously done that has created success for your people and your organization? How can you leverage previous successes and current strengths?

Before you decide to wander outside of the box into totally new areas (like the real-estate developer getting into the grocery store business), or feel forced to look into someone else's backyard, as Goizueta did with PepsiCo, make sure that you have looked in your own backyard first and have taken the time to understand what a diamond looks like in its rough form. Make sure that you truly understand the underlying reasons for your previous successes.

INSIDE-THE-BOX LEADERS

There are many industry leaders who have applied "diamond mining" principles to avoid the box paradigm—leaders who have understood the importance of strategic direction and have created multibillion-dollar opportunities without ever having to wander outside.

We profiled Jim Owens' Caterpillar in the first chapter; one of his predecessors there, George Schaefer, was a master at thinking *inside* the box to identify new growth opportunities. In the early 1980s, Caterpillar lost considerable market share to Komatsu. Schaefer could have looked to expand into a different sector, like the real-estate developer we profiled earlier in this chapter, but he didn't. Schaefer could have panicked, like Coke's Goizueta, and looked at reinventing the company—even though Caterpillar, like Coke, had the number one brand in their industry—but he didn't. Instead, he decided to look inward to discover new opportunities.

Because Caterpillar was the world leader in manufacturing earthmoving equipment, they had become very skilled at getting the right part to the right place at the right time—anywhere in the world. They had to do this to maintain their competitive presence. Caterpillar had developed processes and put systems in place to improve their logistics management capabilities. They had become so good at managing parts and manufacturing logistics for their own company that other companies had started asking them questions about how they did it. Caterpillar recognized an opportunity to leverage the world-class logistics management processes they had already developed for themselves, without having to think outside the box.

Schaefer decided to create a new logistics management organization. Founded in 1987, the new organization was called Caterpillar Logistics Services and when Caterpillar ultimately decided to sell off part of the business in 2012, it boasted 130 facilities in 25 countries, employing over 12,000 people. This organization provides considerable value to other companies, using the same expertise Cat developed for itself. The opportunity was right in front of Schaefer, and he saw it and successfully operationalized it.

Michael Eisner, former CEO of Disney Corporation, also found numerous opportunities that had been staring previous leadership in the face for decades. Immediately after Eisner took over in 1984, he discovered many of Walt Disney's old films (e.g., *Fantasia, Bambi,* and *Cinderella*) locked up in a vault. He cleaned them up and started releasing them on video for limited periods. He would then take the videos off the market in order to be able to rerelease them in the future. These films had been sitting in Disney's own vault for years doing nothing. Under Eisner's leadership, they netted the company billions of dollars in revenues. It was low-hanging fruit, just waiting to be picked.

Another great example of how Eisner understood the concept of diamond mining was the development of the Disney Institute. Over many years, Disney Company had developed an outstanding corporate culture. Considerable effort was made to socialize all of its new employees to the "Disney Way." To accomplish this, Eisner built a world-class executive development training facility called Disney University. Everyone from senior vice presidents to college interns had to receive training in the Disney Way. Disney became so good at training its own employees that soon other companies asked if they could send their executives to the facility to receive the same training. So Eisner built the Disney Institute. Since its inception in 1987, the Disney Institute's Disney Approach Business and Management Program has attracted millions of leaders from over thirty countries to learn about the Disney Way. In 2009, the Disney Institute was recognized as one of the top three brands in executive development and was awarded a ranking in the Top 20 Training and Development firms from 2009 to 2011. Rather than thinking outside the box, Eisner saw an opportunity to leverage something that the Disney Company was already doing for itself. There was no outside-the-box thinking for this venture, just the ability to see what was right in front of him already.

Eisner and Schaefer were being innovative and creative—qualities usually attributed to outside-the-box leadership. But how does a leader know when she is innovating in her backyard and when she is roaming outside of the box? First, note the differences between the actions of leaders at Caterpillar and Disney compared to the grocery store example earlier in the chapter. At Caterpillar, they had already built up a strong logistics knowledge base. Cat had been doing this for itself for years. For Schaefer, it was just a matter of taking something that the organization was already doing and commercializing it for others. He was leveraging, not leaping. Similarly, at Disney, the company had already developed an outstanding executive development model for itself. Eisner had the sense to see this and to start offering these same services for executives at other companies. He used resources appropriate to the task, starting a side venture that did not distract him from the business of running a media company— which is what Disney was and remained.

Unlike Caterpillar and Disney, the real-estate developer had no knowledge of or experience in the grocery store business. He didn't understand the supply chain, retailing, or advertising to general consumers. The owner of the real-estate development firm wasn't already in the grocery business, and his core business was nothing like his new venture. He was truly thinking outside the box, and he failed. Schaefer and Eisner were thinking inside the box, and they succeeded.

Does this mean that no one has ever succeeded by thinking outside the box? And that no one has ever failed by thinking inside the box? Of course not. Yet the probability of success is much higher when you leverage something you are already doing compared to venturing into a new landscape where you have no experience or business knowledge.

The French novelist and critic Marcel Proust wrote, "The real voyage of discovery consists not in seeking new landscapes, but in having new eyes."[12] It's the low-hanging fruit, the low-risk opportunities, the things you are already doing. So before you go off half-cocked in search of new business, make sure that you're not overlooking the obvious. It's just common sense, not a thrilling exploit or exciting adventure, but it works.

THE POWER OF COMMON SENSE

"Common sense" may be one of the biggest oxymorons in leadership. Although common sense has tremendous power and provides critical insights, it's actually not all that common. However, a leader can improve his chances of benefiting from common sense if he hits a metaphorical "pause button." When you're at the point of pursuing an opportunity that sounds like a good idea, stop. Think about why you are pursuing the opportunity. Start with the basic question, "Does this meet face validity?" *Face validity* refers to whether an idea makes sense; whether we are actually doing what we intend to do. It is the idea of taking something at face value. It means taking the time to kick the tires to make sure they're sound—and this is a more basic assessment than making sure the numbers look good. In all of the leadership mistakes we've profiled here, outside-the-box ideas seemed like great ideas in the moment. The leaders had gathered data to back their ideas up, and felt the numbers looked good. If they'd hit the pause button and looked more closely, they probably would have seen that their ideas did not have face validity; the tires were flat.

There is a specific approach that leaders can use to check face validity. It is the ability to understand synergy. "Understanding synergy" sounds like a standard consulting phrase or material for a Dilbert cartoon (guilty on both counts), but there is tremendous value for leaders in the approach.

One of the best ways to proactively avoid blunders like the ones in this chapter is to ask yourself whether you are leveraging your assets synergistically. Are you recognizing true expertise in one area and leveraging that expertise in another area? Consider a basic example of synergy. A child wants an apple from a tree. She is not tall enough to reach it on her own. So she gets a friend to stand on her shoulders. They can now reach the apple. Alone, she couldn't accomplish her goal. By leveraging (literally and figuratively) her height with her friend's height, she could. Working together they could succeed; independently, they would fail. So next time you are considering an outside-the-box idea, ask yourself what you are leveraging. If the answer is nothing, as in the case of Allstate getting into the hotel business and the real-estate developer getting into the grocery store business, is it really something you should do?

■■■

A final thought: Note the similarities between the takeaways in Chapter Two and the takeaways in this chapter. For you as a leader, the ability to keep a strong focus on how you deliver value, combined with the ability to assess whether a new idea is strategically sound, not only decreases the chances of your chasing dollars for the sake of chasing dollars (as discussed in Chapter Two), but can also minimize the ill effects of using a box paradigm.

KEY TAKEAWAYS

Lessons Learned from Mistakes
- Thinking outside the box has creative uses, but it can be disastrous when applied to strategic direction.
- Making a mistake in defining strategic direction can completely derail a company.
- Letting competitors define the box can lead to poor orchestration of resources.

Successful Navigation
- Think inside the box by evaluating your existing activities—look first in your own backyard.
- Hit the pause button before pursuing outside-the-box ideas, and look for synergy.
- Check face validity—does this idea make sense strategically?

FOUR

Entrenched in Efficiency

Forgetting to Put Effectiveness First

The great management guru Peter Drucker once said, "There is nothing more wasteful than becoming highly efficient at doing the wrong thing." Another noted management expert, Kenichi Ohmae, put it this way: "Rowing harder doesn't help the boat if it is headed in the wrong direction." Not only are the quotations on the topic of foolish efficiency endless, but so are the examples.

Former professional cyclist Robert Millar would almost certainly agree. Consider the heartbreak the Scottish athlete experienced—an outcome of being highly efficient while doing the wrong thing. Among his many impressive accomplishments, Millar won the "King of the Mountains" title in the Tour de France in 1984. This title is given to the winner of the mountain competition stage of the race. It was the first time a cyclist representing Great Britain had ever won any major tour classification. In 1988, Millar had a chance to make racing history by becoming one of a select few to win the "King of the Mountains" title for a second time. It was late in the race in Guzet-Neige. He had separated himself from the pack. Millar seemed destined to win the title again. He was in a superb aerodynamic position, that familiar crouched posture elite racers use to minimize drag. His pedal strokes were perfect; as one foot pushed down, the other foot pulled up, both legs working in perfect unison. At that moment, he was the most efficient racer in the world. Unfortunately, he had misunderstood one of the racing official's signals and taken a wrong turn right off the race course. He literally gave the title to Massimo Ghirotto.

Was Millar efficient? Absolutely. His technique was perfect. Unfortunately, he was efficient on a path that was not part of the race. It's not good enough to be efficient; you must be effective, and you must be effective *first*.

The same rule applies to leadership. Misguided efficiency— being efficient at the expense of being effective, or being efficient at doing the wrong thing—is a common mistake among leaders. They get so entrenched in efficiency that they fail to consider whether they are even on the right path.

UNDERSTANDING EFFECTIVENESS

Losing your way between effectiveness and efficiency is at the heart of unbalanced orchestration, and understanding the difference is a critical foundation for effective leadership. Simply stated, efficiency and effectiveness are two different ways of defining your work. With a focus on efficiency, a leader often disregards the outside environment, and the primary concern becomes the operation of the firm itself. Conversely, when a leader focuses on effectiveness, she views her organization as a part of a greater whole, as a single piece of the puzzle. The competitive environment—rather than the organization—becomes the unit of analysis.

Efficiency focuses on "doing things right." It usually emphasizes processes to improve something you currently do, frequently in the area of operations. Questions relating to efficiency might include:

- What is our cost per unit?
- How long are cycle times?
- How quickly does our inventory turn over?
- What is the percentage of defects per thousand units?

Effectiveness, on the other hand, focuses on "doing the right thing." It is strategic in nature. Questions relating to effectiveness include:

- Who is our customer?
- What value do we currently provide to our customer?
- What needs are emerging in our market(s)?

During our interviews with successful leaders, we were frequently reminded that you need to make a concerted effort to ensure that your organization is effective before you focus on efficiency, so let's take a closer look at these three questions.

Who Is Our Customer?
Although the question "Who is our customer?" may seem fairly basic, for many companies it can be very difficult to answer. Consider an automobile manufacturer. You may have "internal" customers if you are a service group within the company. Maybe your customers are the dealers who sell the cars. Or maybe the customer is the person who actually buys the car. There are many stakeholders, and each one has a different set of needs. So it is important that you, as the leader, make sure everyone understands that there are different types of customers, even though you may operate in a single business. It just depends on which slice of the business your specific business unit serves.

What Value Do We Provide to Our Customer?

What are the specific needs your company fulfills for customers? Although the difference between focusing on customers and focusing on value may seem subtle, the latter is a very different lens to look through. Focusing only on *who* the customer is may actually deter growth, because it will deter efforts to identify new needs for customers—quite possibly needs that customers may not even know exist. Do you think Steve Jobs focused exclusively on customers when introducing the iTouch, iPod, and iPad? No! Customers could not demand products and technologies that did not yet exist. Focusing on value is much more strategic; it can open the door to a plethora of opportunities.

What Needs Are Emerging in Our Markets?

How can you get out ahead of the curve to anticipate customers' needs, before customers even know these needs exist? Value innovations like the smartphone and iPad *created* needs in order to achieve growth. Proactive leaders ask this question as a means of looking to the future. Michael Dell, CEO of Dell Inc., explained his mind-set in this way: "We know that virtually everybody is going to buy their computer over the Internet in five to ten years. We want to dominate that market and have a leadership position in sales of computers through new distribution channels."[1] Dell hasn't been sitting back focusing all of his efforts on current customer needs. He is using efficiency (the company's ability to have new distribution channels in place) as a tool to improve his effectiveness.

WHY EFFECTIVENESS TRUMPS EFFICIENCY

Without an understanding of the importance of effectiveness, a focus on efficiency can misguide a company.

An organization can be very efficient at some activity, but if the activity doesn't generate value, as defined by the market, then the efficiency not only poorly orchestrates resources in an activity that doesn't matter, but it may even destroy value. It's a zero-sum situation—allocating resources to efficiency that doesn't contribute to value-added activities takes resources away from those activities.

Some leaders become so inwardly focused on processes, they end up spinning their wheels. For example, in 1988, the R.J. Reynolds Tobacco Company embarked on a process to make smoking cigarettes more efficient. CEO Jerry Long introduced a new kind of cigarette, the "Premier," which used a complicated system to heat and vaporize the tobacco. This new type of cigarette presumably burned cleaner, yielding a measureable decrease in toxins to the smoker, as well as to those who would be breathing in the secondhand smoke. Investment in the Premier cigarette exceeded $1 billion. Although it appeared to have the same attributes as a regular cigarette, smokers were highly unsatisfied.[2] The problems with the cigarette—ranging from the difficulty of lighting them in the wind to the fact that smokers had to inhale harder—left a bad taste in consumers' mouths (literally and figuratively). Moreover, smokers did not even *want* a healthier alternative if it meant decreasing their satisfaction. R.J. Reynolds dropped the product less than a year after it was introduced into the market. The company had just developed the most efficient cigarette in the world. Unfortunately for Jerry Long, the cigarette was efficient at doing the wrong thing.

When a leader focuses on effectiveness first, can the organization still survive or even thrive in spite of operational inefficiencies? The answer, surprisingly, is yes. Remember that effectiveness focuses on value. Customers want their needs to be satisfied. When their needs are satisfied, they are happy, even if the company is not efficient. They don't care how you do it, as long as you do it. Think about it this way: When you put a key in the ignition of your car, you expect the engine to start when you turn the key. You don't really care that when you turn the key, power flows out of the ignition circuit, causing the points to open and close, sending power through the coil, creating a large surge of voltage that jumps the gap in the spark plugs, igniting the gas/air mixture that is pressurized in the piston chamber. You just want the engine to run.

Tony Hsieh, CEO of Zappos, knows firsthand that effectiveness is king, that providing value to your customers is paramount, no matter what it takes. Zappos isn't just an online shoe store. According to Hsieh, Zappos is in the business of "delivering happiness." However, in 2002, Zappos faced a significant challenge when its logistics model failed. Hsieh had decided to outsource logistics management to a third-party logistics firm called eLogistics in Kentucky. Within a week after inventory was moved to eLogistics, one of Zappos' employees went to visit and reported back that "everything at eLogistics is a mess. It is a bigger problem than we all thought . . ."[3] (It did not help that in the same week a semi-truck loaded with Zappos shoes overturned.) For an online retailer, this could have been a disaster. Hsieh quickly fixed the efficiency problem. His solution was to bring logistics back in-house.

But what about "delivering happiness"? Here is the difference between a typical leader and a leader who understands the importance of effectiveness. Zappos immediately contacted all of its customers to let them know what was going on. When Hsieh's operational efficiencies failed, his first priority was making sure his customers were kept in the loop. He was being effective in the face of being inefficient. Stated differently, even though he wasn't able to deliver the actual product on time, Hsieh was building relationships with his customers—relationships built on honesty and transparency. Most leaders would have seen these inefficiencies only as a huge blunder, but Hsieh used this situation as an opportunity. There's the difference between a typical leader and a great leader.

How could an online retailer survive when its logistics operations were so flawed? Even though Zappos was missing its ship dates during this time, not only did the company survive, but it continued on its aggressive growth trajectory. Hsieh was able to succeed because he was so effective. He understood what customers defined as value, and he designed a world-class customer service program. So even when efficiencies failed, the company was still able to succeed.

HOW LEADERS GET TRAPPED IN AN EFFICIENCY MIND-SET

Hsieh's story and many others provide concrete proof that effectiveness trumps efficiency—a tenet that is fundamental to good leadership. Yet our research has clearly shown that many leaders don't *want* to understand why it's more important to be "doing the right thing" rather than "doing things right." You read that correctly—they really *do not want to understand*. Thinking about effectiveness before efficiency is difficult. Efficiencies are easier to address. You simply focus on ways to do things—things you are already doing—a little bit better. It is relatively safe; it's measurable; it's satisfying. In contrast, effectiveness has to do with big-picture issues. Are we even doing the right thing in the first place? This can be a stressful question to answer. It may mean questioning your company's actual existence! And many leaders don't want to deal with this possibility. They want to put their heads down, keep moving (not necessarily forward), and just continue on with what they are already doing. To these leaders, thinking about effectiveness is nothing short of a threat.

Every organization is constantly evolving, undergoing new and unanticipated challenges. Often a leader gets stuck in an efficiency mind-set because she is caught up in the details. And when the details become overwhelming, then crisis management quickly becomes the *modus operandi* and putting out the largest fire is the focus. According to our interviews, this detail-chasing, reactive mentality is a primary cause of getting stuck in efficiency. When a leader is increasingly putting out today's fires—or even trying to catch up with putting out yesterday's fires—she becomes overwhelmed with emergencies, leaving no time to step back and see the big-picture. Efficiencies become paramount, cost-cutting evolves into the primary focus, and effectiveness is put on the back burner. Once a leader gets stuck in an efficiency mind-set, things can get out of hand.

What happens to a leader who gets so entrenched with putting out fires that he goes overboard in trying to achieve efficiencies? For one thing, he might find himself included on the *American Express Open Forum* "10 Dumbest Business Mistakes" list, like Japanese airline Nippon Airways. In 2009, Nippon announced it would ask all passengers to use the restroom before boarding flights. During a four-week experiment, the company had agents at the gates asking passengers to relieve themselves before getting on the plane.[4] Why, you may ask? All in the name of efficiency. Nippon's new bathroom rule was an attempt to reduce fuel consumption, resulting in decreased carbon emissions, as well as decreased cost. Any traveler could have warned them that their customers would likely be embarrassed and offended by the request.

SHOOTING STARS

Nippon Airways' misguided (and short-lived) rule is good for a roll of the eyes and a chuckle; it's less amusing when the result of emphasizing efficiencies and ignoring effectiveness leads to the demise of the whole company. Two preeminent examples of companies that fall into the quick-burnout "overefficiency" category are Pets.com and Webvan.

The Demise of Pets.com

Pets.com built an extensive infrastructure and a national brand overnight, becoming one of the hottest new IPOs on the NASDAQ. But focusing on efficiencies rather than effectiveness killed the company in only 268 days.

Pets.com was a San Francisco–based internet retailer that Greg McLemore launched in August 1998. The company sold pet accessories and supplies and provided information about caring for pets. It was a virtual company, having no brick-and-mortar stores. Pets.com aspired to be the leader in online pet supplies.

In early 1999 Pets.com was purchased by a major venture capitalist firm, Hummer Winblad, and Julie Wainwright was named CEO. At the time Pets.com was launched, there were several other firms competing for the same market space, including Petstore.com, PetPlanet, and Petsmart.com. Pets.com emerged as the industry leader, as it was the first of the pack to be operationally efficient. Wainwright envisioned leveraging these operational efficiencies to make the company the one-stop shop for customers' pet-supply needs.[5]

Wainwright invested considerable resources in designing an efficient website. The website was easy to use and attracted a lot of customers. Pets.com also spent considerable resources in its warehousing network in order to realize economies of scale and capitalize on efficiencies. All of the investments that Pets.com was making in its infrastructure were similar to those of other players in the market. However, Pets.com was able to differentiate itself from other dot-coms when it invested in developing its brand.

Pets.com also spent a lot of money when it contracted with TBWA\Chiat\Day, the advertising firm that had just created the talking Chihuahua for Taco Bell. They came up with a creative new character for Pets.com—a dog sock puppet with a microphone. It was a very plain sock puppet with button eyes and spaghetti-like arms, and it was an overnight success.[6] The sock-puppet dog created a following similar to that of a pop star. Within a very short time, the puppet appeared on nationally broadcast television shows like *Good Morning America, Nightline,* and *Live with Regis and Kathie Lee.* There was even a giant balloon character of the sock puppet in the 1999 Macy's Thanksgiving Day Parade, and it was interviewed in *People* magazine. The biggest victory for the sock puppet came from a Super Bowl ad in 2000 that cost Pets.com over $1.2 million. In it, the sock puppet told the world why it should shop at Pets.com: "Because pets can't drive." The commercial had the highest recall rate of any ad in the Super Bowl.[7]

Could it get any better than this? Here was a company that had access to considerable resources; a high-profile CEO; a well-developed, highly efficient website; and a best-in-practice warehouse network with the potential to create significant efficiencies. And now it had a nationally recognized brand. Clearly this was a company poised for greatness—right?

Unfortunately for Pets.com, they had invested considerable resources to create a highly efficient organization, but Wainwright and the backers of Pets.com never stopped to determine whether e-tailing pet supplies and accessories online was an effective business idea. It wasn't. First of all, Pets.com had entered an extremely low-margin industry. Many pet stores typically made money on services, such as grooming and training, rather than on dog food. Most alarming was that the company hadn't done market research to see whether customers actually wanted to buy pet supplies over the internet. As it turns out, many customers preferred to buy their pet supplies at grocery stores while they were shopping for themselves. Bottom line, Pets.com didn't provide any value to customers; there was nothing to motivate them to do anything different from what they were already doing. Sure, the sock puppet was cute, and even entertaining, but the company offered no unique value.

So even with all of its efficiencies, the company began to rapidly fade. Management announced that the company was in desperate need of revenues. The company's extraordinary success in branding didn't matter when it was finally discovered that the market for buying pet supplies online didn't exist. In 2000, the funds from venture capitalists dried up, and according to CNET's "Top 10 Dot-Com Flops," Pets.com came in at number two.[8]

Webvan's Big Bust

Another company that fell victim to focusing on efficiencies before effectiveness was Webvan, identified as one of the most recognized dot-com failures in history. Its story is surprisingly similar to that of Pets.com.

Founded in 1996 by Louis Borders, the multimillionaire who owned the Borders bookstore chain, Webvan set out to become the biggest online grocer in the United States. The idea was simple: figure out a way to deliver grocery items quickly and inexpensively to people's homes. Borders was determined to change the grocery store industry forever. "Intuitively, I knew I'd have a great financial model if I could eliminate store costs," Borders stated.[9]

Borders thought that the secret to creating such an enterprise was a committed focus on efficiencies. He focused on efficiencies at many levels, including putting together orders, keeping perishable goods fresh, and delivering orders to customers within a thirty-minute time frame. Webvan set out to provide same-day service to customers in twenty-six cities after the first year. Unfortunately, because Borders focused on efficiencies first, Webvan never came close to that goal. And although many start-ups failed during the dot-com bust due to insufficient access to cash, this was not the case with Webvan (nor was it the case with Pets.com), as Webvan spent billions of dollars on developing efficient operations.

Webvan started taking orders in the San Francisco Bay Area in June of 1999 and boasted that it was able to offer products at a price 5 percent less than traditional brick-and-mortar stores.

Borders became chairman of the board, and he hired George Shaheen, former CEO and Managing Partner of Accenture Consulting (formerly Andersen Consulting), to become CEO of Webvan.

Borders and Shaheen were committed to the concept that bigger was better. Everything they did supported the idea that to succeed, they needed to gain economies of scale by maximizing efficiencies. As such, Webvan planned to gain its efficiencies by building giant distribution centers that were three times the size of its competitors'.

As Borders' focus on maximizing efficiencies grew bigger and bigger, so did his investments in creating a world-class, albeit very complicated logistics system where much of the work was automated. Webvan also created a sophisticated supply-chain management network to allow for efficiencies and economies of scale. Webvan's first state-of-the-art distribution center was launched in Oakland, California, with a 330,000-square-foot facility, made up of 18,000 stock-keeping units with varying temperatures for different types of perishable goods. It had a network of conveyor belts, scanners, and 125,000 square feet of picking and staging space. The high-tech order-management process would automatically place items in plastic bins using a bar-code system and send the bins to work stations where pickers would complete the orders along 4.5 miles of conveyor belts.[10] Before even stocking or staffing the warehouse, Webvan invested $35 million in the building. Shaheen entered into a $1 billion contract with Bechtel, a global engineering and construction firm, to build twenty more facilities like the one in Oakland.

Emulating the business logistics model used by Fred Smith, founder of Federal Express, Webvan invested in a complex hub-and-spoke system for its warehouses in each specific geographic region. The elaborate system started with the warehouses and continued with transfer stations where grocery products would be picked up and delivered by Webvan's own fleet of delivery trucks.

Each region served a sixty-mile radius. Webvan also invested in a user-friendly website that allowed customers to order 24/7.

Once Webvan had built its distribution model in the Bay Area, Borders built similar networks in Chicago and Atlanta. They were based on the same model as Oakland's, with online orders processed at a main warehouse and then distributed through satellite facilities. Ultimately, Webvan operated in eight cities after it spent over $1 billion acquiring HomeGrocer.

So here was Louis Borders, now chairman of Webvan, with the most efficient grocery-based logistics management facility in the world. Moreover, he had assembled a group of leaders that he and Shaheen cherry-picked from some of the leading companies in the world, along with a board composed of high-profile leaders like Christos M. Costakos, CEO of E*Trade, and Tim Koogle, Yahoo! CEO. What could possibly go wrong?

In addition to spending a lot of investors' money before making any revenue at all, the "dream team" defended their business models even when investors and industry experts questioned the basic premise of their idea. Specifically, even with the potential for improved efficiencies and decreased costs, industry experts suggested that an online grocery-store model would fail if it tried to compete with brick-and-mortar stores. Analysts cited entry barriers such as start-up capital, low customer acceptance rates, and tight margins. Borders, Shaheen, and the rest of the team simply discounted the questions, explaining they had collected their own data. When Borders was questioned about whether Webvan could become a billion-dollar business, he replied, "Naw, it's going to be $10 billion. Or zero."[11] He was absolutely correct.

Borders and his team fell victim to creating a highly efficient (and admittedly world-class) organization, but they were ineffective. They were really good at doing the wrong thing. As it turns out, although their data showed that many customers were dissatisfied with brick-and-mortar grocery store shopping, they didn't accurately assess whether convenience was a major value driver for customers. Webvan's leadership team assumed customers would be driven by the efficiencies and convenience of ordering grocery items online. Unfortunately for Webvan, customers did not embrace the concept very well. Webvan never understood its markets well enough to assess potential customers' actual level of interest in buying groceries online. Moreover, many customers said it took them longer to figure out and navigate the website to fill their virtual carts than it did to just go to the actual grocery store.

Webvan lost over $347 million in the year 2000.[12] Shaheen was fired, and Borders severed all of his ties with Webvan. In July of 2001, Webvan went into bankruptcy, firing over two thousand employees and wasting over $1 billion of investors' money. Webvan was never profitable, not even for one quarter. Webvan became one of the most costly victims in the long list of dot-com failures.

So what important lessons do we learn from R.J. Reynolds, Zappos, Pets.com, and Webvan? Once you know you are *doing the right thing, then* it's time to start figuring out ways to *do things right.* It's much better to be an effective organization, fulfilling the needs of your customers even as you need to ramp up efficiencies, rather than an organization that is very efficient at doing the wrong thing well.

AVOIDING THE EFFICIENCIES TRAP

There are two key approaches a leader can use to avoid the common mistake of putting efficiency before effectiveness. The first is a matter of balance—specifically, balance between having a strategic lens and an operational lens. Or to use a well-known metaphor, balancing between seeing the forest and seeing the trees. A good leader needs to do both. The second approach is making sure that you truly understand how the customer defines value, as opposed to how the management team feels about customer value. This can be done only by effectively collecting the "right" data.

Seeing the Forest and the Trees

Great leaders have certain qualities; fortunately, many of them can be learned. For one thing, great leaders are able to be aggressive strategic thinkers, stepping back and continually exploring the "big-picture" at the same time as they are able to think operationally and get things done. To be a great leader, it is not sufficient to simply be able to see the big-picture. Once a leader understands the big-picture and creates a value-focused organization, she must also initiate and maintain action. She must also "do things right."

Understanding the benefits of a value-focused organization can, in and of itself, be a fix for ineffective allocation of resources. In Chapter Two we covered a similar idea: the importance of defining your company based on the needs you fulfill rather than the products or services you offer. It's equally important to correct any imbalance between effectiveness and efficiency. In Chapter Two we also talked about how to use a value-focused approach to decide when it was best to pursue a new business opportunity. In this chapter, we use a similar approach, but rather than addressing the question, "Should I pursue a new business?" we look at the business you're already in. To achieve the optimal balance between effectiveness and efficiency, a good leader needs to identify underlying customer needs, rather than the product or service that the company offers. It is a whole different way of looking at the organization.

A classic example of a product-based versus needs-based perspective is found in the U.S. railroad industry around the turn of the twentieth century. At that time railroads were a dominant form of transportation in the United States. Not surprisingly, some of the richest people in the world were the owners of the railroads. If you asked railroad owners to look at themselves strategically and define their business, they would have answered that they were in the railroad business—a product-based focus. In contrast, if they had done something so fundamental as looking at their companies in terms of the need they were fulfilling—transportation— they would have seen themselves through a whole different lens. Instead of seeing an industry such as on-highway trucking as a substitute for trains and a threat to business, they would have seen it as a natural extension of their business. Did they have the money to invest in other modes of transportation? Absolutely. So seeing themselves as transportation companies could have completely changed the future of their organizations.

To habitually balance effectiveness and efficiencies, leaders must be both opportunists and realists. For a leader to look at needs rather than products, she must be somewhat entrepreneurial. She must have the ability to step back to see the forest. At the same time, she must be able to focus on the trees—she must consider an opportunity to deliver value for what it *could be* rather than what she would *wish it to be*. It's okay to dream—and effective leaders can dream up great entrepreneurial growth opportunities. But these same leaders must also determine whether these opportunities are feasible and have the possibility of increasing profitability and, ultimately, shareholder value. If Pets.com and Webvan had used this approach, they would have saved resources at many levels. By playing the realist role, leaders can manage the risks associated with the opportunities they are willing to pursue, and *high* risks become *calculated* risks. In this role, leaders also take action. It is not good enough to simply anticipate needs before customers know the needs exist. Great leaders also need the courage to move on that knowledge. By focusing on the trees when appropriate, an effective leader will figure out ways to make things happen.

How do managers wear both hats? How can they focus on the forest *and* focus on the trees? How can they find time to strategize the future when fires erupt all the time? Our research showed us that great leaders have a distinctive process by which to view their organizations and their markets, and it involves their ability to learn in different ways. Specifically, they are skilled in two modes of learning:

1. *Coarse-grained learning.* This holistic view of learning focuses on the big-picture. It is not very detail oriented, but it is critical to conceptualizing value. It is similar to the way a child would approach a new discovery—eyes wide open, taking in everything with no preconceived biases. This big-picture learning allows leaders to understand effectiveness issues. As discussed in Chapter Two, Sir Richard Branson, CEO of the Virgin Group, is a master at coarse-grained learning, at seeing big-picture opportunities.

2. *Fine-grained learning.* This type of learning focuses on detail. It has a bias toward action; leaders use it to try to figure out ways to ramp up operations to meet new opportunities and manage growth. Pragmatic, fine-grained learning allows leaders to understand effectiveness issues. Again, recall that Branson has approximately 125 notebooks full of ideas. Although many of these ideas are about new growth opportunities, many others are about doing things better.

Each of us has a propensity to favor one way of learning. We all have our own comfort zones. And it is not surprising that people tend to matriculate to careers that match these comfort zones. For example, if someone is more comfortable using coarse-grained learning, she may end up as an artist or in sales. Conversely, if someone is more comfortable with fine-grained learning, he may end up as an accountant or an engineer. Even though everyone has their own comfort zone, effective leaders need to bridge the gap between coarse- and fine-grained learning and do both. Effective leaders need to stretch outside of their comfort zones in order to see their organizations through both lenses. Being able to do this will minimize the possibility that effectiveness and efficiency get out of balance.

The good news is that you can achieve a balance between coarse- and fine-grained thinking relatively easily. The first step is awareness—to identify your natural tendencies. Do you prefer to focus on the big-picture, where there may be no definitive right-or-wrong answer, or do you prefer to analyze details? Knowing your natural tendencies will expose your blind spot. Once you figure this out, it then becomes a conscious effort to try to see through the other lens. However, awareness alone may not be enough. It can be extremely difficult for a coarse-grained thinker to have the patience to study details. As a matter of fact, many coarse-grained thinkers have no interest in or ability to know the details. In contrast, many fine-grained thinkers don't have the desire to think beyond the details. Ambiguity can be a scary thing for them. Coarse-grained thinkers and fine-grained thinkers process information very differently. It may be difficult to see through the other lens. You may have to find a counterpart—someone whose natural tendency is opposite of yours—to fill in the blanks that you can't see.

Accessing the "Right" Data

It is a terrible thing for a leader to spend considerable time and money collecting data and to confidently make decisions based on it, only to learn that the data was wrong. He would have been better off not collecting any information at all.

So what are the common reasons for bad data, and how can a leader avoid making this costly mistake? There are two approaches to ensuring you have the right data: going to the right source, and asking the right questions. Although these approaches seem like common sense, they're not used all that often.

The Right Source

Why is it that so often, when leaders want to try to identify value drivers for their customers, they do anything but ask the customers what they think? According to data from our interviews, the most common reason why leaders don't ask customers directly is because they are concerned that customers might feel as though the company is imposing. Who likes filling out surveys, anyway? So, too often, they instead ask other leaders in the organization. Or maybe they ask suppliers or creditors. But if you want to know what customers are thinking, you must ask them. Customers are a tremendous source of information. Unfortunately, Wainwright and her top-management team at Pets.com did not use this resource.

3M Corporation has masterfully met customer needs for decades, and it credits its success in part to staying close to customers. Customers can not only share their perceptions regarding how they define value, but also serve as a barometer to let the company know how it is delivering—how it's doing in the "fulfilling needs" category.

Great leaders also know that to get the pulse of their markets, they must draw on feedback from existing customers *and* potential customers. Capgemini Consulting performed a "Leader versus Laggard" survey in 2010, and found that leading companies are much more effective at using customer survey information than are laggard companies. Here's the deal, and it's a truth we return to again and again in this book: *how* you do something is often more important than *what* you actually do. Asking customers to participate in a survey does not have to be perceived as an imposition; if done correctly, it can actually form the foundation for a long-term relationship. Instead of "imposing" on customers by asking them to fill out surveys, reframe the scenario to "partner" with customers. Let them know you care about what they think. Because the better you understand what they think, they better you can serve their needs.

The Right Questions

Companies often embark on data collection efforts only to find out (or worse, not find out) that the data they collected is inappropriate. The trouble is, when companies design surveys, they are most interested in satisfaction: employee satisfaction, customer satisfaction, and the list goes on. But truly effective leaders *don't care about satisfaction.* Yes, you read that right. They don't care about satisfaction—or rather, not satisfaction alone.

Let's say you conduct a survey and find out that customers are disgruntled with your customer service programs. What would most leaders do? They would start investing resources in making customer service better. They would focus on efficiencies (hiring processes, wait times for answering the phone, and so on). An effective leader, in contrast, wants to know how satisfaction ratings compare to *importance* ratings. If a customer is dissatisfied about something, but it's *not important to them,* do you want to spend money trying to change things? Probably not. It is the combination of satisfaction ratings *and* importance ratings that matter, but leaders often don't think about the second part.

Webvan surveyed potential customers and found out that they were frustrated by having to go to the grocery store every week. What leaders at Webvan failed to do was ask customers how important this frustration was. And as we have learned, clearly the frustration of going to the store on a weekly basis was not enough to motivate customers to shop for groceries online. If Webvan had measured importance along with satisfaction, they would have had a very different take on their data. Instead, they collected bad data, and confidently used it to defend their business model, even as they were stepping out over the cliff.

If a leader is trying to understand the basic needs and value drivers of his market, the survey should be designed to measure how respondents rate typical purchasing drivers (such as price, quality, serviceability, reputation, and delivery) in terms of satisfaction *and* importance. The red flag appears when customers identify dissatisfaction combined with high importance.

■ ■ ■

Many of the concepts in this chapter boil down to an issue of balance. As a leader, you need to balance between effectiveness and efficiencies. You need to balance between coarse-grained information (the forest) and fine-grained information (the trees). Finally, you need to balance between satisfaction and importance in the data you use.

KEY TAKEAWAYS

Lessons Learned from Mistakes
- When efficiencies come before effectiveness, a leader can very efficiently guide her company into doing the wrong thing.
- Consider efficiencies (doing things right) only after you can ensure that you are doing the right thing (being effective).
- It is easy to fall into the trap of putting efficiencies first when a leader gets bogged down in day-to-day issues. This becomes a self-perpetuating spiral, with the leader forced into reactive thinking at the expense of proactive thinking.

Successful Navigation
- Make sure that you are doing the right thing before you concern yourself with doing things right.
- Know that effectiveness is defined by needs and values, not products.
- Leaders who stretch their comfort zone can learn to be both coarse-grained thinkers and fine-grained thinkers. Another approach is to recognize which is your strength and find a counterpart with the opposite strength to complement you.
- Getting the right data to define effectiveness requires asking the right people (your customers and potential customers) the right questions, including satisfaction and importance.

To find out more about whether you tend to be a coarse-grained thinker or a fine-grained thinker, visit www.TheWisdomOfFailure.com.

PART TWO

Drama Management

FIVE

The Playground in the Workplace

Leaders Who Rule by Bullying

Firist, an imperative: don't skip this chapter. If you think of old-school management as just that—*old*, outdated, a remnant of the days when workers were less empowered, bosses less versed in soft communication skills, and the workforce based more in the factory than in the cubicle—think again. Bosses who are old school—by which we mean those who are either overt bullies or more subtle about it—are everywhere. And if you think the tension between old- and new-school management is obsolete, over and done, you need look no further than *NFL Sunday* to see the battle continues.

The game: Seattle Seahawks versus New York Giants. As the players fought a tough battle on the field, two other dramas played out on the sidelines. On one side, Pete Carroll, head coach of the Seattle Seahawks, paced, jumped up and down excitedly, and patted players on the back as they returned to the sideline from play. Though his words were difficult for the masses to make out, his body language made clear they were of the "Attaboy!" variety. Carroll, who became famous for reviving USC's football program, also penned a book about management that espoused his philosophy: *To inspire achievement, help people remove all obstacles to that achievement so they can tap into their best selves.* On the sideline of the game, Carroll was putting his philosophy into practice, boosting his players' energy and morale.

On the other side, Tom Coughlin, head coach of the New York Giants, paced and yelled at players when they came off the field. A player botched a play, and Coach Coughlin was in his face, letting the player and the nationwide audience know that he really screwed up.

Coughlin's behavior was all the more interesting because several years prior, his job had been in trouble, in part because of locker room complaints about his aggressive style and his rough handling of the media. He was asked by the team's ownership to tone it down. Coughlin's contract was renewed for just the 2007 season, and he got the message. He famously diverged from his old-school management style. He became a nicer, more communicative coach who went bowling with his players, was less overtly critical, and even set up a committee of veteran players to help him communicate with everyone else.[1] The result was a Super Bowl underdog victory to cap off that season, a book about his conversion—and a five-year contract extension.

Midway into that contract, judging by his demeanor against the Seahawks, it looked like Coughlin's conversion to a new style of management had been only temporary. The battle of sidelines played out for the world to see—Seahawks versus Giants, Carroll versus Coughlin, new-school versus old-school management. The winner of the Seahawks/Giants game is incidental (it was the Seahawks, but just barely), because an effective strategy for one game cannot accurately reflect a team's long-term staying power, any more than strong sales numbers one quarter can accurately reflect an effective long-term manager. The point, rather, is that the NFL is full of Tom Coughlins, and so are the NBA, the WNBA, the NHL, and their counterparts in the worlds of arts and science. The business world—no matter your business—is populated with them, too.

Still, you may feel tempted to move on to reading about the next business mistake, confident in the knowledge that *you* are not an old-school manager, and neither is anyone who works for you. If you read this chapter with an open mind, you just might change your opinion, seeing that—through no malicious intent of your own—you are either engaging in or tolerating bullying behavior. Even if you come through this chapter crystal clean yourself, it is still critical to understand bullying, because it leaves a streak of filmy residue behind it, affecting the way teams operate and relate to their boss long after the bully has left the building. You might find yourself responsible for just such a team.

In a recent CareerBuilder survey of 5,700 workers, 27 percent of them said they had been bullied in the workplace.[2] That number may be even higher, according to another survey, commissioned by the Workplace Bullying Institute (WBI), which found that 35 percent of respondents had experienced bullying.[3] Few managers are likely to admit (even to themselves) that they are bullies, but given the statistics of the *bullied,* the *bullies* exist in significant numbers. Some well-meaning leaders may be bullies without knowing it. And some leaders—though not bullies themselves—may be tolerating old-school managers in their organization, for reasons grounded in everything from the calculated to the clueless.

In this chapter we unpack a leadership mistake that many offenders are unaware they are making. We delve into the two types of old-school bully management: the overt and the covert. And just as important, we discuss the fine line between what is bullying and what is simply assertive management. We look at the consequences of the old-school approach, and we consider why, if we know bullying is bad and few people *want* to be thought of as bullies, we do it—or tolerate it—in such large numbers anyway. Finally, we offer guidance for avoiding old-school management, repairing a team that has been victim to it, and, if necessary, changing your approach for longer than it takes to win a Super Bowl.

THE OLD-SCHOOL MANAGER

According to WBI, a full 81 percent of bullies are the boss, 14 percent of bullies bully a colleague, and 5 percent bully a higher-up. More statistics to make us feel bad about ourselves: 97 percent of coworkers are aware of bullying when it happens but don't help.[4] It's the office park version of the beating in the schoolyard, in which everyone circles around a fight but no one steps in to end it. If you are the bully, there's little your audience will do to make you stop. One attorney recently told us that she is aware a colleague of hers is being tormented by the partner for whom they both work. She sees the abuse daily, but few others do, because their particular group works on a different floor than the rest of the office. The only person who could possibly put an end to it is the managing partner, but she is unsure he would be receptive to a complaint. Worried about her own job security, and making her mandated hours for the year, the witness is likely to stay quiet—and stay put.

Sometimes bullying happens in plain view of an entire office, but other times it is less blatant, or, as in the case just described, physically removed enough that it's not very visible. That leads us to the two types of bullying—the overt variety, where there's little doubt what's happening, and the possibly more dangerous covert type, from which the damage is every bit as lasting, but less apparent.

The Overt Bully

When Washington State Senator Pam Roach was banned from the Senate Republican Caucus, it was not the first time the politician had been accused of workplace bullying. Roach was elected to the Washington State Senate in 1990 and has made news ever since with her harsh remarks and behavior. According to a *Seattle Times* article, Roach was cited for violating the senate's bullying policy—which forbids "demeaning and/or derogatory" behavior or comments if they interfere with work or create an "intimidating, hostile, or offensive work environment"—five times between 1998 and 2010.[5]

After an internal investigation in the Washington State Senate in 2010, Senator Roach's colleagues sent her a letter explaining that "it would be best to physically separate you from the caucus staff and from other Republican senators while we are working on the floor." The letter concluded by suggesting she partake in various counseling offers from the Senate to deal with her anger management.

The incident prompting the investigation involved the state Republicans' attorney, Michael Hoover. During a caucus meeting, Hoover had raised questions about a senator's desire to post material and photos from a rally on her official website, based on the ethical questionability of using public funds for political purposes. Though others present disagreed with Hoover's assessment, Roach, according to Hoover, went "from zero to ten on the angry scale."[6] She berated him and told him he should be fired. These attacks resulted in Hoover feeling intimidated and others feeling uncomfortable on the caucus floor.

Though it would appear to most reasonable people that Roach's behavior merited disciplinary action, Roach claimed her banishment stemmed from a personal vendetta, asserting that Senate Minority Leader Mike Hewitt did not like her. These attempts to justify her behavior on the caucus floor deflected attention from the real news of the disciplinary action. Victims of Roach's bullying—which a staff member referred to as "being Roached"[7]—had not been able to make a lasting change through their individual efforts, but by banding together, the senate Republican caucus finally succeeded. Unfortunately, not all bullies get called out in such a public way, and so we never hear about them.

Another classic example we heard plenty about is that of Al Dunlap. The former head of Sunbeam was known as "Rambo in

Pinstripes"; he wrote a book titled *Mean Business*, leaving little question as to the management style he preferred. Dunlap earned his reputation by going into struggling companies and turning them around, slashing staff and intimidating workers into success. He was also a tornado-like force. Some Sunbeam managers believed there was only a hair's breadth between his verbal rages and physical violence, and his first act at the helm of the company was to berate the executives at a long meeting. "It was like a dog barking at you for hours," according to one of those executives. "He just yelled, ranted, and raved. He was condescending, belligerent, and disrespectful."[8]

Roach and Dunlap both used intimidation, a common bully tactic used to threaten employees to the point where they no longer speak up or offer opinions. Intimidation can be either physical or emotional—only a razor's edge difference exists between the two. People have immediate physical responses when being severely verbally threatened, to the point where the only thing worse is being hit by a fist. Verbal abuse can escalate into emotional violence. People's lips quiver. They become weak. They retreat, pass out, or get sick.

In one of our interviews, an officer of the company said, "You know the culture has changed when I feel like I need to suit up in a bulletproof vest just to go to work." Another C-level said, "I felt like we all should issue handguns at staff meetings. At least we'd all have a fighting chance." These interviewees' language matches the severity and blatant manner of the bullying. There is nothing subtle about it.

The behavior of leaders like the ones featured here is undeniably horrible, and although they may weigh more heavily on the drama scale than others, our interviews found no shortage of bosses like them. We heard about bosses who had earned the nicknames "Hair-trigger Harry," "Yelly Nell," and "Bumbling Bob," and even a trio of bullying managers whose name sounds more like an upstart cover band: "Drama Dan and the Dastardly Duo."

As Drama Dan and company showed us, overt bullying *does* still happen.

The Covert Bully

The covert bully is every bit as dangerous as the overt one—perhaps more so, because his behavior is less easily called out and more socially acceptable. While many leaders would be mortified to have their staff see them yelling at someone, those same leaders might think it's perfectly appropriate to send a string of emails asking a staff member his whereabouts if he takes a short absence from his desk.

Covert bullying includes projecting blame, increasing workload, guilt-tripping, excessively monitoring an employee's time, using sarcasm, and socially isolating employees. The covert bully can more easily justify his tactics. It is much more difficult to dodge an accusation of shouting or threatening than an accusation of assigning an unreasonable amount of work, or setting an employee up for failure by mandating an impossible deadline. Meryl Streep's character Miranda Priestly, in the film *The Devil Wears Prada*, is a perfect—albeit extreme—example of the covert bully. As the editor-in-chief of *Runway* magazine, she is an ice queen. She never raises more than an eyebrow and her speech is quiet and controlled, yet she makes impossible requests of her staff, such as procuring a yet-to-be-released Harry Potter book in a matter of hours, or finding her a flight during a storm so powerful that it's shut down air traffic. "Get this for me or you are useless/unemployable" is the blatant message, but expressed softly, and termination can be justified as no more than "the employee was unable to complete assignments." Miranda Priestly is not of the real world, but the film was adapted from a book by Lauren Weisberger—who, in the real world, was once an assistant to *Vogue* editor and famous ice queen Anna Wintour.

In one well-publicized case of covert bullying, Jennifer Shih, once a financial analyst for Warner Bros. Entertainment, claimed to be a victim of this type of harassment. She sued her former employer, claiming that her boss gave her more work than others, gave her a hard time about taking time off for maternity leave, and upon her return made her document her time spent pumping breast milk.[9] Assuming the allegations are true, Shih—and victims like her—has suffered deeply. Often an overt bully's behavior is so over-the-top that everyone bands together to complain—or at the very least, to commiserate about it. But victims of covert bullying may not have obvious avenues of support, because others can't discern what's happening. The victims may even question whether they're being bullied at all, because it's so difficult for them to point a finger at situations that might be read two ways in isolation, but when accumulated over a period of time have one clear meaning.

Bullying or Assertive Leadership?

When is a leader a bully, and when is he simply an aggressive leader? A leader might give an unfavorable performance review, but that does not make him a bully. A leader might set a deadline that a staff member perceives as unreasonable, but in reality it is not a clear call. One litmus test, in this case, might be whether the staff member feels he can discuss the deadline with the leader, even if he doesn't end up getting his way in the end. But note that this doesn't mean a leader has to run a business as a democracy. Every decision does not have to be open to debate; in fact, some successful leaders are direct and commanding to the extent that their subordinates don't question them very often—yet they are assertive leaders, not bullies.

Both Oprah Winfrey and Ford CEO Alan Mulally are well known for firmly holding people accountable, yet they fall more on the assertive side of the line than on the bullying side. When Mulally took over at Ford, for example, he began holding a weekly meeting with his direct reports. To cover everything they needed to discuss, they used a chart that was color coded based on whether that area was on track. If it wasn't on track, it was to be coded red, orange, or yellow, depending on the severity of the problem. If all was on track, that area would be colored green and they'd move right on.

At first, all of the metrics were green, yet Mulally knew everything couldn't possibly be on track, given they'd lost a lot of money the year before. He asked, "Is there anything that's not going well here?" and emphasized that it was okay to color your area of responsibility a yellow or red. The next week, someone colored his area bright red because there was a production delay. According to Mulally, the room became silent with everyone's anticipation. "So what was Alan going to do?" Mulally recalled. "Was a hook going to come out? Was Mark [the executive who had colored his area red] going to disappear? So I started to clap. I said, 'This is tremendous visibility, Mark. What can we do to help you?' "[10] Solutions and ideas were bandied about, and the red area had improved by the next meeting.

Mulally epitomizes the assertive leader who does not cross the line to bullying. He set the tone as one of support, not punishment, and the color-coded system was great for that. But as he also admits, "You can imagine the accountability [in the color-coded system]."[11] If something went wrong in someone's area, the person could not hide it. It had to be addressed in front of everyone. In color. That's assertive, tough leadership, but if Mulally had been a bully, no one would ever have had the courage to color their area red. And they never would have gotten the problem-solving support of their colleagues.

Another framework for determining someone's bully culpability is that of *context*. In what environment is the behavior taking place? If you're a leader whose company is in crisis, you may have to be very assertive to break the pattern of employee behavior. It may be necessary, even admirable, to shake employees out of their comfort zone. That leader might tell staff that the pressure of the competitor is unreal, and that if a certain milestone isn't reached, the company is dead. If this information is true, then that leader is not guilty of bullying. Rather, she is being open, honest, and communicative with her team. She is rallying the troops against a common adversary. If, however, the company is not in crisis, the information crosses over from being accurate and useful to being a scare tactic.

With covert bullying, in particular, it is important to examine the *frequency* of the bullying behavior. According to the Workplace Bullying Institute survey results, bullying is a prolonged pattern, lasting an average of 16.5 months.[12] A single passive-aggressive email from a leader asking where you are might not, in and of itself, be an example of bullying, but days on end of similar emails, combined with guilt trips, combined with any other number of aggressive behaviors, can constitute an undeniable, provable pattern. For instance, a professor might get bad schedules from a department chair who doesn't like her. Or a software developer might continually be assigned the most tedious project by a boss who seems to have it in for him. One bad schedule, one bad assignment does not constitute a bully pattern. But over a period of months and years, it definitely sends a message.

Just as it's hard for the victims to name what's happening, it's hard for the perpetrators to recognize that when they make certain assignments, they are penalizing people they don't like. They justify their decision without examining its root cause. *It's not like I'm threatening anyone,* they may reason. Here's what they're *not* asking themselves: Am I making this person's life uncomfortable on a regular basis? If I'm really honest with myself, is there part of me that enjoys doing so? Why is that?

Another way to differentiate between an assertive leader and a bullying leader is reason itself. Would a reasonable person think that behavior is okay? Would most people consider a certain action acceptable? If it were written up in the newspaper for the world to see, would it create outrage, or would people simply move on to the next article? And finally, you can look at the behavior of employees and how it changes over time. An interesting example of this is unions. Many unions exist today because of a bullying manager of yesteryear. The reasons unions were formulated—even though union members must give up rights in order to join—was that management got so bad that employees felt they had no other choice. If you have assertive management, you probably won't have unions forming; if you have bullying management, they will.

THE CONSEQUENCES OF OLD-SCHOOL MANAGEMENT

In cases like Al Dunlap's, the consequences of old-school management are plain to see. When the consultant Dunlap hired to suggest personnel cuts at Sunbeam came back with more modest numbers than Dunlap expected, he suggested the consultant was "getting weak-kneed in his old age." Dunlap clearly reveled in slashing entire departments, and he did so—including outsourcing Sunbeam's entire computer staff. The problem with this zeal emerged quickly: computers were down for months, and customers like Wal-Mart had to be invoiced manually.

Even more dramatically, Dunlap's intimidation tactics led to the crossing of ethical lines, in the form of faulty accounting practices. He set impractical goals and encouraged people to believe that their livelihood rested on making those numbers. Workers resorted to questionable practices they never would have agreed to otherwise, and those who wouldn't, quit. The resignation of key personnel was just one signal to Wall Street that Sunbeam had a major problem. By the time Dunlap was fired, Sunbeam had a shortfall of $200 million in a single quarter.[13]

Two hundred million is a painfully quantifiable number, and Sunbeam's losses became legendary. But losses like theirs play out in smaller scales all over. At a Silicon Valley company that calculated the cost of a notorious bully, figuring his extra costs week by week compared to a more civilized employee, they determined this employee's behavior had cost $160,000. Though in some cases a concrete number can be assigned, many of the costs of old-school management are more difficult to measure. They come in the form of lost productivity—a tricky number to measure—but according to the Level Playing Field Institute, if a Fortune 500 company suffers just 2 percent in lost productivity, that can amount to $8 million a year. And productivity *is* lost, with bullied employees spending anywhere from 10 to 52 percent of their day fending off harassment,[14] and everyone else wasting time watching the drama around them unfold, at a cost of as much as a 40-percent decline in their productivity.[15]

When an individual is bullied, he often suffers from physical or psychological symptoms. The Workplace Bullying Institute says that 41 percent of bullying victims become depressed, 76 percent suffer from severe anxiety, 84 percent experience sleep disruption, and 40 percent of those who leave their jobs do so because of health issues.[16] The organization then feels the effects from this individual in very concrete ways: through increased absenteeism, turnover, stress, and decreased morale and motivation. These effects can ultimately influence the productivity of the workplace, customer service, and the overall corporate image.

The consequences of a bully's behavior last long after he has left. A leader might come into an organization and find that his staff is terrified of him before he's said a word. The leader wants open participation, a creative exchange of ideas, but no one wants to come forward. That leader must go backward, remaking the team, instead of spending his time moving the company forward.

WHY GOOD PEOPLE BECOME OLD-SCHOOL LEADERS

Some people with extreme personalities, like those who would revel in a nickname like "Rambo in Pinstripes," might enjoy the "bully" moniker, but it's safe to assume most people don't *want* to be considered mean. What's more, clearly bullying behavior has financial consequences. So why would a fundamentally good person who understands the standards of decency resort to this behavior? Understanding the answer to this question goes a long way toward preventing bullying—and stopping it if it's already happening.

Often a person's greatest strength is also her greatest weakness. Managing these strengths and weaknesses is about managing context. The same colleagues who banned Pam Roach from the caucus room acknowledged that she is a passionate advocate for her constituents. Passion is a great asset for any politician, but only if pointed in the right direction.

The same strength/weakness dichotomy might apply to leaders of companies, as behavior that is acceptable in beating the competition carries over to internal relations. When Procter & Gamble—the behemoth manufacturer of consumer goods—made it known they were going to move into the bleach market, the leadership at Clorox—the household cleaning giant—did not sit idly by. Rather, the leadership used intimidation to keep P&G out of their business. When Procter & Gamble decided to test market its new bleach product, Vibrant, in Portland, Maine, Clorox aggressively delivered a free gallon of *their* bleach to the doorstep of every household in the area. The result: nobody in Portland would need bleach for many months to come. Clorox successfully intimidated Proctor & Gamble. According to A. G. Lafley, CEO of P&G, "They basically sent us a message that said, 'Don't ever think about entering the bleach category.'"[17] And according to Lafley, these bullying tactics were quite effective.

In this case, the behaviors of Clorox's leadership team were admirable. But what if they had internalized the conflict and used the same intimidation tactic internally? What if they had felt the aggressive stance that worked well with P&G would also work well when it came to improving productivity? If they had said to

employees, "Don't even think about getting out of here at a reasonable hour unless you churn out this quotient of product," their
style would have earned them not respect, but rather the "Chainsaw" reputation of an Al Dunlap, and could have led to agitation,
low morale, and possibly even unethical behavior.

Generating results is a large part of any leader's job. Leaders
may unintentionally pass along that pressure to underlings, or
they may feel it is the most effective and efficient way to motivate
staff. Effective leaders will inspire emotion, but how they do
it—and what emotion they inspire—is what makes the difference
between a leader who is merely effective in the short term and a
leader who is inspiring in the long term. Some leaders may not
feel they have time to inspire good performance, so they will force
it instead. Going back to our football story, it takes precious time
to adopt Carroll's style, whereby you uncover what's keeping
players from performing their best. It's much easier to shout
"Perform your best, dammit!" Those scare tactics *will* work, in
many scenarios. But not over the long term.

There is another category of old-school leader whose path to
this behavior is led more by personality than by circumstance, and
though we will delve further into this issue in Part Three, the type
merits a brief explanation here. A socially inept manager may
never smile; may talk in short, clipped, phrases; or may make
inappropriate comments without realizing they are inappropriate. The socially inept leader probably has no business being in a
position where she manages people, and may have gotten there
because she has superior technical skills, or some other specific
skill. To reward her performance, she is promoted to a job for
which she is not suited. In the television program *The Office,*
for years the humor lay in the fact that manager Michael Scott
was so socially immature that he didn't understand the inappro-
priateness of actions such as forcing employees to come out as
homosexual, or making other sexist, racist, or offensive claims.
Although Michael Scott is an exaggeration, part of the reason we

find him funny is because we relate; his type *does* exist in the workplace. However, a manager's cluelessness is not an excuse. Perception is reality, and if a leader's staff perceives her as inappropriate or a bully, she *is*.

Over two thousand years ago, the Chinese philosopher Lao Tzu said that the best leader is the one who helps people so that eventually they don't need him. Next comes the leader who is loved and admired. Next, one who is feared. And worst of all is the one who lets people push him around—who, in effect, is no leader at all.[18]

There is much wisdom we can pull from Lao Tzu's ranking, but the most poignant to us stems from his description of the worst type of leader—the one who is pushed around—and whose best recourse is to move one step up on the ladder to become fearsome. Weak leaders may fear being pushed around to such an extent that they overcompensate—they feel the need to prove that they are here, that they are powerful and strong. They will push people around simply because they need to show they can.

Whether we look at ancient texts or corporations of today, we see that self-esteem matters in leadership; old-school management is both ancient and contemporary. When a leader has poor self-esteem, bullying is often close behind. What's more, bullying breeds bullying, to the extent that some company cultures become rife with self-loathing at every level.

WHY GOOD PEOPLE TOLERATE OLD-SCHOOL MANAGERS

We've pondered why otherwise good people resort to bully tactics; now let's consider why the good people above them accept this behavior. The drama of this dynamic played out all over the headlines in the spring of 2011, when David Sokol, heir apparent to Warren Buffett at Berkshire Hathaway, suddenly resigned amidst rumors of misusing insider information for his own gain. In the wake of his departure, staff came forward to reveal Sokol's brass-knuckled ways, such as his monthly updating of a notebook that ranked his aides in the order in which he would fire them, or suggesting that a company get rid of employees in poor health or employees going through a divorce.

Sokol's trajectory from hardscrabble youth to heir apparent to disgraced bully is interesting, a story of a hard worker who was enticed by material wealth (he collected expensive homes) and blinded by ego. But far more interesting is the question of why Buffett—who has a reputation for benevolence and for valuing skilled managers and trying to keep them, and who is almost impossibly *grounded* (he owns just one home, which he bought for $31,500 in 1958)—was so close to handing over the keys to the store to one whose values seemed so very different from his. The answer to this question has implications for those leaders everywhere who may think that an old-school management culture has nothing to do with them personally but are nonetheless culpable in its drama.

The most obvious explanation for why good leaders tolerate bullying managers is the bottom line. The Silicon Valley company we mentioned earlier, which calculated the cost of a bully at $160,000, notably did not fire the bully, a top-ranking salesperson for the company. Rather, they deducted 60 percent of what they figured he cost them from his bonus.[19] To them, it was a numbers game. They considered this person's behavior part of the cost of doing business—a means of rationalizing behavior that is never acceptable and that has costs that are not easily quantifiable, but hefty nonetheless. For his part, Sokol made money for Buffett, who may not have even *looked* at the numbers behind the numbers: numbers involving absenteeism, turnover, health care costs.[20] It's possible that Buffett willfully looked the other way because Sokol was generating results. It could also be that Buffett had a blind spot for Sokol, who came from modest roots and was self-made, like Buffett himself. Or there's the fact that Buffett prides himself on being a hands-off manager; perhaps he truly did not know the impact of Sokol's behavior on Berkshire employees.

This last reason brings us to another: a leader may tolerate bullying behavior because there is no system in place for the leader to learn about it and deal with it. In the case of Pam Roach, there was a clearly stated policy against harassment, and her colleagues could point to it in their reasoning for banning her from the caucus floor. But many organizations have no such policy, and the results can be disastrous, as they were in the case of Kevin Morrissey.

The signs abounded that Kevin Morrissey was in trouble, including numerous phone calls to the University of Virginia's human resource department, ombudsman, faculty and employee assistance center, and even the university president. The fifty-two-year-old managing editor at the *Virginia Quarterly Review* (VQR) was reaching out for help, and when he could not find it, he ultimately took his life on July 30 at an old coal tower near campus.

Morrissey's sister Maria and his colleagues reported that Kevin suffered from depression, a condition in which bullying by his boss, Ted Genoways, played no small role. Genoways denied the allegations and claimed there were no reports against him, that he and Kevin were longtime friends, but Kevin Morrissey's colleagues tell a different story. Coworkers began to notice a difference in Morrissey in his last few months and claimed his relationship with Genoways worsened, without any solution. Genoways would yell at Morrissey behind closed doors and act dismissive of him in public—clear signs of bullying behavior.

One coworker of Kevin's said that Morrissey had "repeated meetings with people in human resources, the office of the university ombudsman, and the president." The same coworker said that four staff members, including Morrissey, went to the president's staff and told them "that we were finding work conditions under Ted completely untenable. [The president's staff] sort of said, 'Oh, working with creative people is sometimes difficult.' "[21]

The WBI suggests that VQR was negligent, enabling the bully. According to the university's internal audit report, "UVA personnel responded to employee concerns in accordance with institutional policies and procedures, given the information they were provided. However, there was a lack of clarity with regard to certain roles, as well as a perceived lack of independent institutional authority to engage and resolve issues for employees while operating with a general good faith desire to respect employee confidences." Without a proper system in place to report these allegations, the University simply did nothing.[22]

The UVA example is a dramatic one, but the point it leads to is applicable even if the lack of an effective system doesn't result in such a tragic outcome. The attorney we mentioned at the start of the chapter, for instance, fears going to her managing partner about the bullying situation because she doesn't know how he will respond. The only other human resource representative at her firm is the bully himself. It's a problem without a clear path to a solution.

Although the story at UVA is tragic, and extreme, its culture of "CYA" is all too common. Institutions become so concerned with process, they lose track of moving forward—it's the number one problem with bureaucracies, be they government, corporate, or academic. These bureaucracies are supreme nesting grounds for covert bullies. The bullies know that repercussions are unlikely, given all the red tape, so they are empowered to continue their harmful behavior.

ENDING OLD-SCHOOL MANAGEMENT AND REPAIRING THE DAMAGE

The Giants' Tom Coughlin, compelled to change his behavior for fear he'd lose his job, did make some dramatic strides toward becoming a more new-school manager. But they seem to have fizzled once that fear was gone; again, fear is not a useful motivational tool for lasting change. So what is? If you recognize that you have old-school management characteristics, and that's the only way you've ever managed, how do you change? If you've inherited a team that has developed behavior patterns to accommodate an old-school approach, how do you fix the problem and keep from becoming the type of manager they're used to? And if you want to eliminate bullying in your organization, what's the best approach?

Recognize

Are you the bully? No? Are you sure? Leaders should never stop being self-aware, and sometimes they need some help in that pursuit. Ask yourself if you are differentiating between the way you treat employees, and the way you treat competitors, or if you use equally aggressive tactics with both. How do you approach inspiring workers? If you use fear as a way to provoke action, you have crossed an important line. Ask colleagues to provide anonymous feedback about your performance. Ask: "Am I approachable?" "Do you feel you can disagree with me?" "What can I do to be more accessible?" Accept their answers with a spirit of openness, and then ask them for feedback again after some time has passed.

How do your managers approach inspiring others? Have you promoted people to a manager level when they have an aggressive personality? If you suspect a bully is working under you, look at the numbers behind the numbers. Do you have an inordinate amount of absences in any department? Is productivity affected under that department's leader? What does the turnover rate look like? If you recognize a problem and identify offenders, you have several options. The first and most obvious is to replace them. But if you want to work with them before letting them go, you have some options.

Repurpose

Perhaps the bully is a bad fit for that particular job, but you'd hate to lose him because of other skills he brings to the organization. In the case of someone who has advanced through the organization because of exceptional technical skills or sales skills, you don't want to lose him—you just don't want him to be in charge of a team of people for which a different skill set is paramount. If he has a particularly aggressive personality that crosses over to the bullying side, focus those skills toward your competitors, where his traits can be of value to the company.

Reform

Many aggressive leaders *can* change their ways. Probation, anger management training—any number of programs are available for those who want to repair their old-school ways. Soft-skills training programs are the order of the day, and sending your bully off to school to learn better habits is a great initial way to approach the problem. One word of warning, however: a two-day seminar, or even a year-long class, cannot be counted on to stomp out bullying tendencies. Any effective reform must involve a maintenance element. We knew a vice president at Caterpillar who was known far and wide as the biggest bully among seventy thousand employees. One day he saw the light, rejected his bullying ways, and even gave talks to students about the wrongs he'd done and how he's righted them. All was great, until circumstances became more stressful and intense—then he reverted right back to being a tyrant.

Define

Sexual harassment training has become de rigueur in the corporate world, and the problem is finally becoming controlled in the workplace. As workplace health writer and advocate Ellen Cobb notes, "Think about sexual harassment. It's not done. And yet until not that long ago it was something that was done flagrantly—and constantly—with a wink and a nod."[23] She argues that part of the reason it happens less is because of public perception. Sexual harassment is easy to define, easy to spot, and easy to verbalize—and it's easy to draft a policy prohibiting it. Workplace bullying is four times more prevalent, yet because it's less easily and commonly defined, it's a struggle to get anything done about it.

As the leader of an organization, you can bring awareness to bullying. You might form a committee to draft an antibullying policy, which would define it clearly and lay out, step by step, what should happen if bullying occurs. Communicate the policy to all employees, and express your commitment to ending the behavior at all levels of the organization.

The next level of policy redefinition may prove more difficult. To cultivate a bully-free environment, you must also examine some of the systems and policies that your workplace may have followed for years. Are there incentives in place that encourage workers to compete against one another in an unhealthy manner? Are there systems that undermine relationships? Are unrealistic goals set, such that managers may feel overly pressured and more likely to resort to bullying behavior to meet those goals? Though these systems can be difficult to break down and rebuild, the result in improved morale and productivity will make it a worthwhile pursuit.

IF THE MILITARY CAN DO IT, SO CAN YOU

If it seems like bullying is so ingrained in your organization's culture that change is out of reach, consider the change in the military over the past few decades. Although the hard-core drill sergeant of *An Officer and a Gentleman* may never become entirely extinct, now there is more emphasis on the psychological health of soldiers, as well as awareness about how an old-school culture can lead to events like those at Abu Ghraib, wherein soldiers took advantage of a responsibility to guard and interrogate in order to indulge in gratuitous bullying—and created international outrage.

Before his death in 2007, we had discussions with General Wayne Downing about the changes he'd seen in the military and the ones he'd been a part of. General Downing was a four-star army officer who commanded Special Operations forces and became a senior counterterrorism advisor to President George W. Bush. General Downing's thirty-four years in uniform afforded him a front-row seat at—and a voice in—the military's culture changes. He was a frequent and well-known critic of bureaucratic rigidity, and he challenged the old-school premise that when a soldier is given an order he must follow without question. General Downing instead advocated a policy that the military does now embrace, one whereby a soldier has the authority to question an order if it falls outside his role.

In addition to this "allow questioning" philosophy, Downing also was a strong proponent of debriefings—wherein the players in an incident come together to discuss what went wrong and how to learn from it—and the importance of systematizing those debriefings. Debriefings are now an integral part of military policy, and one of their most important purposes is to put bullies on notice. Debriefings send a message of accountability, no matter your rank. No one would have accused General Downing of being a softy, and indeed the military isn't exactly in danger of becoming a kumbaya culture, but reason and efficacy dictate that bully tactics do not help the military achieve its goals—any more than they help your organization achieve its goals.

KEY TAKEAWAYS

Lessons Learned from Mistakes

- Bullies are costly: their behavior leads to employee absenteeism, turnover, and low morale, and in extreme cases can serve to encourage illegal or unethical practices.

- Covert bullying, although more subtle than overt bullying, is even more damaging to a victim because of its chronic nature and lack of support for the victim.
- It may be tempting to justify a bully's presence because he or she generates results. But although intimidation tactics may inspire results for a time, these tactics are not a sustainable way to motivate staff.
- If a bully reigns, staff will fear speaking up about errors, thus missing out on opportunities to receive help and get a project back on track.
- Bullies thrive in bureaucracies where a focus on process leads to a lack of accountability.

Successful Navigation
- Examine your actions over a period of time, and solicit feedback to determine whether you engage in bullying behavior.
- Have a zero-tolerance philosophy about bullying in your organization, make that philosophy well known, and implement it.
- Encourage accountability—both of yourself and of those you lead. Give people who have been bullied a system within which to report it.
- Examine current practices to see whether they promote bullying behavior or employee intimidation. If they do, find ways to change them to eliminate the intimidation while still getting the results your organization needs.

SIX

When Utopia Becomes Dystopia

Problems with Dysfunctional Harmony

At the opposite end of the spectrum from the bully lurks another troublesome leader—one who can be just as damaging. Whereas the bully may thrive on making people feel uncomfortable when he enters a room, the *pleaser* thrives on just the opposite. She wants everyone to like and approve of her, to feel comfortable around her, to believe she is on their side. And just as everyone gets along with the pleaser, the pleaser boss also wants all of them to get along with *one another*. She wants people on the outside to perceive her company as a realm of peace and harmony—happy worker bees in a seemingly utopian hive.

That's the "harmony" part. But the "dysfunctional" modifier comes in because a worker who appears happy is not necessarily happy, and these workplaces are often saturated with drama. Agreeing with one's coworkers and one's boss all the time does not lead to a conflict-free environment—it creates a passive-aggressive one. The pleaser may be creating a workplace similar to the oft-parodied family dinner where no one airs any grievances as they politely ask for more mashed potatoes, but discontent permeates the air nonetheless. As we discuss in this chapter, dysfunctional harmony erodes trust, stifles creative thinking, damages morale, and hurts the bottom line. We profile leaders vulnerable to various forms of harmful positivity, and also one or two who have overcome their instinct to please without going all the way to the other end of the spectrum and turning into bullies, or who have managed to break the patterns of a "comfort culture" in which no one is truly comfortable. We show how to diagnose the pleaser problem in yourself and your company, how to avoid it, and how to fix an environment where everyone seems to gets along, yet no one is happy.

WHY WE WANT UTOPIA— AND WHY WE SHOULDN'T

Though there are some people like the more extreme bullies we profiled in Chapter Five who relish being feared, far more bosses want to be loved. It's human nature. Even by the time we start high school, we're primed for the popularity contest—if we're not struggling to fly beneath the radar, then we're vying for the top spot of homecoming king or queen.

We also spend a great deal of time at our workplace—for many people, most of our waking hours. Just as we want our workspace to be comfortable as a result—our chair positioned just so, our plant and photos bringing a sense of home—so, too, we want our relationships at work to be friendly. We probably have long-time friends we never see because we don't have time, and yet we see our coworkers each and every workday. Why not make those coworkers into friends? Isn't it even more pleasant to go to work if we get to work with our buddies?

Harmony may also be deeply ingrained in the pleaser's personality. Business aside, she may avoid conflict in *all* areas of her life. She may be the type of person who would never send back a steak for being overcooked, or confront a friend with whom she's angry. In her professional life, this trait may even have served her well, as her superiors all benefited from her eagerness to please and promoted her as a result.

Finally, many leaders may consider likeability and harmony a calculated business strategy. When workers are happy, leaders reason, they do great work. A happy team is a productive team, they think. A CEO can motivate the best performance from her workers if she is beloved, and if those workers also love one another, all the better.

All of these reasons for wanting a utopian workplace are legitimate. Perhaps that's why dysfunctional harmony is so common. For while it *is* beneficial for workers to be happy and to like the boss, you have to make sure that's the reality and not a façade. Just beneath the surface of all the smiles and slaps on the back a very disgruntled workforce may exist, and the company's productivity may even suffer from all the politics of pleasing.

Constructive Conflict Is Missing

In 2005, bestselling author and historian Doris Kearns Goodwin published a book titled *Team of Rivals: The Political Genius of Abraham Lincoln,* chronicling the way Lincoln's greatest competitors for the presidency became his most valued advisors. The process of debate and disagreement, Goodwin revealed, enriched Lincoln's decision-making process. Her work raises a question for our political leaders—and any leader, for that matter: Can a team of people who all think the same way do as well as a team with disparate voices? Doesn't lively and honest discussion lead to more sophisticated, well-thought-out decisions?

The error of the pleaser boss is that he does not value debate, because to him, debate signals discord. He is inclined to hire people who are pleasers, just like he is. His team, once assembled, is more likely to resemble a line of bobbleheads than anything else. His eagerness for consensus sends a message to the team that they should not object to any proposal too strongly, even if their objections are valid and could make the product or decision stronger.

An employee at a toy company had just such a problem with her boss; she described meetings with him as fruitless. "It never goes well, because he won't let me say no," she explained. "He doesn't let me be negative. I can't tell him the problems— he doesn't want to hear the problems. He's too rose-colored glasses." She's worked for him for seven years, and for most of that time she has silenced her opinions.

The pleaser boss fears conflict to an unhealthy degree. Some degree of conflict aversion is understandable. Conflict can be destructive, leading to tears and stress and ugly scenes with people storming out of rooms. Indisputably, destructive conflict should be avoided—but in their avoidance, leaders must be careful not to swing too far in the opposite direction. "If it is well managed, conflict can have positive outcomes," according to Brenda McManigle of the Center for Creative Leadership. "Conflict can lead to better decision making, expose key issues, stimulate critical thinking, and fuel creativity and innovation."[1]

Anil Menon of Emory University also recognizes the underlying value of conflict. Psychologists, he has noticed, often mention positive, constructive outcomes of well-managed conflicts in therapeutic settings. Why shouldn't this be true in a business setting as well? With that hypothesis, he analyzed the answers of top marketing executives to questions about new product introduction in their companies. The survey asked questions specifically about conflict. In companies where conflict was constructive, "managers guided discussions that included vigorous challenging of ideas, beliefs, and assumptions" and in the end, "mistakes were avoided, weaknesses were spotted early, differences were settled amicably, and the new products they introduced did significantly better in the marketplace."[2]

In other words, Lincoln was on to something.

Bosses Make Bad Friends

Imagine that a leader needs to promote one of two people. One may be a better candidate than the other, but the pleaser-leader will be inclined to promote whichever one of them would be angry or vocal if denied the spot. Because the leader cares too much about being liked, her judgment is impaired. When a leader cares too much about being liked, her ability to give negative feedback is impacted. Assume she has to give a less-than-excellent performance review to an employee. The purpose of the review is to help the employee improve, but that means the employee must acknowledge certain behaviors and commit to changing them. No matter how carefully couched, the feedback will not please the employee. If the leader hates conflict, she is apt to give a performance review that is stronger than it should be. She is likely to brush the criticism under the rug while she focuses on what the employee wants to hear. The leader may even convince herself that if she can just build the employee's confidence, then the employee's performance will improve. Not so. The leader has lost an opportunity, and so has the employee. That employee will not grow as much in her job. The leader will not help make a decent performer into a great performer.

The consequences of performance reviews that are less than honest can be even more far-reaching, to the extent that they harm a company's culture. A top-performing senior associate at a mid-sized Portland law firm found herself increasingly frustrated by the support staff's lack of effort. The support staff—from paralegals to secretaries to document typesetters—would consistently complain when the associate requested something, and they would consistently do the bare minimum. The staff's apathy and lack of client focus was deeply entrenched in their culture and affected the associate's ability to do her job well. The frustrated associate took her complaints to the firm's COO, homing in on the support staff's gravest offenders. The COO listened patiently to her complaints, then presented her with copies of the offenders' performance reviews: they indicated performances that were consistently above average. The associate was infuriated, but when she calmed down, she wasn't that surprised. Performance reviews were not emphasized at their firm. It was true that once a year a form would be circulated to the attorneys who worked with a certain staff member the most, asking them to rate that staff member's performance. But the questions were vague, the rating system was loose, and—most problematic of all—the firm's managing partner, Ken, was well known for tuning out negative feedback. He viewed his firm like a family, and negative comments about anyone in his family were customarily buried. Attorneys had stopped bothering with honest performance reviews, because they knew they were aboard a ship that wouldn't be rocked no matter what.

We'll return to Ken in a moment, but first, consider the repercussions of this culture of overly positive performance reviews. The top-performing associate loved many things about the firm, but the daily battles with support staff and the resulting frustration made her receptive to other job offers. And though the lawyers suffered when their requests of staff weren't received or performed well, ultimately the lawyers' requests were made on the clients' behalf. The firm may have been able to get away with weak staff during good times, but during bad economic times, every inch of effort mattered.

Ken's focus on making staff feel they were part of a big happy family carried over to the way he dealt with the firm's lawyers, and the results were also negative. By making attorneys' employment so personal, he created the impression they could never leave without betraying the "family." If someone did leave—and many did—to pursue a clerkship opportunity, or a different area of law, or even a different type of firm, Ken spoke disparagingly about the person. He implied that that attorney had never been up to snuff and that the firm was better and stronger without him or her. The consequences of this behavior were twofold: On the one hand, those who were still employed with the firm feared that leaving meant they would burn a bridge, so their loyalty felt less like a choice and more like an obligation. And on the other hand, Ken's criticism inevitably got back to the attorneys who left. Those attorneys, though possibly in a position to send referrals to their old firm, were left with hard feelings about their former "family."

Ken's ill-advised badmouthing brings up yet another danger of a boss who's too cozy with employees: gossip. Gossip is rampant in every workplace, and the more casual time the leader spends with employees, the harder the leader will find it to avoid engaging in gossip—or at least listening to it. According to a Turkish proverb, "Who gossips to you will gossip of you." At best, gossip undermines professionalism. At worst, it erodes trust.

Trust Erodes

A leader who avoids conflict creates a cluster of passive-aggressive pathologies, with consequences that spread far beyond the employee they happen to be talking to at the moment. Just as the leader who craves harmony is unlikely to give a completely honest performance review, he is also unlikely to reveal a distressing business forecast to his staff. His desire to tell people what they want to hear is so ingrained, he will do so even if it means not telling the truth.

At a mid-sized California company that produced games for adults as well as for children, the financial outlook was bleak. Though the adult group and the children's group historically maintained separate editorial, design, and production departments, the president felt it necessary to combine the production departments into one. Editorial and design naturally feared their departments would follow suit, but the president—who prided himself on being a good, likeable guy—assured them there was no intention of doing so, going so far as to explain that it wouldn't make any sense for their business. Soon after that, members of the executive team leaked to staff the information that merging the departments was indeed being considered. Rumors circulated, and for months no one felt certain about where the company was headed. A year after the production departments merged, the head of human resources informed the adult art and editorial departments that they would indeed be combined with juvenile's, but claimed that the idea had come up only three weeks before. That afternoon, when the president formally announced the change at the company meeting, he told everyone that merging the departments had been the plan from the get-go, assuming that this information would reassure them (and obviously forgetting that he'd said the opposite the previous year).

The good news was that, despite the blended departments, no jobs were lost. The bad news was that because of the way the situation was handled, many of the staff ceased to trust their leadership. How could they know whether they were being told the truth or just what their president thought they wanted to hear? Far from feeling assured when their president said, "Don't worry—everyone still has a job," they felt insecure. How could they be sure what was really going on behind closed doors, when no straight answer ever emerged?

The reason for the president's attitude is easy to comprehend. He had built the company from the ground up, and it was like a child to him. He took its successes and failures very personally, and he cared immensely for the company's employees. The company was his utopia, and if it had flaws, he didn't want to acknowledge them. He also wanted his employees to be as invested in the company as he himself was, and he probably feared that being truthful with them about the decisions he was facing would give them pause. He may have justified his decision to lie by reasoning that he didn't know for sure what he was going to do, and he didn't want people to worry about something that might not come to pass. The problem is, the truth has a way of coming out, one way or the other. The only control he really had was over whether (and how) he delivered the truth, or whether it wafted down in rumors. Because he gave in to his desire to tell people what they wanted to hear instead of the truth, he lost the trust and loyalty of his staff. Some resigned; others detached emotionally. An employee who is emotionally detached may stay and do adequate work, but she has no incentive to give her all. She has no investment other than collecting her paycheck and going home. And without a deeper connection to the company, there's little to prevent her from looking around for a new job.

Initiative Suffers

Just as toxic as the president who told people what he thought they wanted to hear, there is the leader who appears to be listening and taking staff opinions into account when he really has no intention of doing so. This is an equally passive-aggressive behavior, with equally damaging consequences—and it's a behavior that has been around for decades, if not centuries. In a timeless article on leadership written in 1961, W.C.H. Prentice called out this false democratic behavior, writing that when parents tell their children they can participate in decisions and the children discover they actually do not, "They develop a strong sense of injustice and rebellion."[3] Though there are definite differences in the boss-employee relationship, Prentice tapped into a universal truth of leadership. Sometimes, you just have to say, "I'm sorry, I can't have this decision made by committee; this is one I have to make on my own." Certainly that's a justifiable call. What's not justifiable is the ruse that the decision is up for a vote when really it is not. Staff will see through it—if not the first time, then by the second or third time. And when they do, the consequences are far more damaging than if the leader had just been direct with them in the first place. According to another article, "[P]assive aggressive organizations are dotted with frustrated world-beaters who cannot understand why their most promising projects can't gain traction. After a couple of years, such individuals either quit or become demoralized into ineffectuality by the thanklessness and futility of effort."[4]

If the pleaser-leader happens to have a hard time truly delegating, the consequences of a false democracy reach farcical levels. In 2005, a trio from Booz Allen Hamilton studied a snack food company that had been so successful in the United States that it expanded to Latin America. The company's founder was known for being incredibly hands-on, and although he appointed a vice president to oversee sales in Latin America, he himself flew to Brazil almost weekly. He made decisions contrary to the local operation's suggestions, but he continued the charade that the local operations had a powerful voice—even calling their authority out in formal procedure. Everyone playacted as a result; staff in Latin America understood they had no power, that the founder was going to do what he wanted, but they played along anyway.[5] This is dysfunctional harmony at its most apparent—a situation seemingly ripe for satire—yet it happens all over the business world. In a recent Booz Allen Hamilton survey of fifty thousand individuals, passive-aggressive behavior was identified as the most common factor leading to "unhealthy" organizations.[6]

The Bottom Line Sinks

Though thus far the consequences of dysfunctional harmony we've pointed out have been very general—loss of trust, loss of employee investment, loss of referred business and creative energy—hard numbers show that passive-aggressive organizations where dysfunctional harmony reigns are perceived as much less successful than companies that are resilient, or companies that do not qualify as being passive-aggressive. In the Booz Allen Hamilton survey, 81 percent of respondents at resilient organizations felt that information flowed freely across organizational boundaries, compared to just 20 percent of respondents at passive-aggressive organizations. And 51 percent of respondents at resilient organizations felt their company was more profitable than average, compared to just 28 percent of those at passive-aggressive organizations.

Still, many leaders will insist that being liked does not necessarily equate to a passive-aggressive organization or dysfunctional harmony. This is true enough, but the real issue is not whether or not a leader is liked; the issue is whether she feels she *needs* to be. If the leader cares too much about employees' needs and perceptions, she loses sight of the big picture. One of the most discussed examples of this mistake is Malden Mills.

Aaron Feuerstein was the majority shareholder, president, and CEO of manufacturer Malden Mills at the end of 1995, when three of its eight Lawrence, Massachusetts, factory buildings burned to the ground. Malden Mills had been around a long time—since 1906—and as it employed three thousand workers in Lawrence, its importance to the community was huge. To make matters worse, the fire happened just a couple of weeks before Christmas.

Feuerstein had important decisions to make. He could have used the insurance money to start a factory elsewhere, choosing a locale with lower labor costs. He could have simply taken the insurance money and closed the business. Or he could have expressed sympathy to the workers for the unfortunate circumstances out of his control, laid them all off without pay, and spent the necessary time to rebuild the factory in Lawrence.

Feuerstein did none of these things. He felt he had a responsibility to take care of his workers and his community. Two days after the fire, he told his employees he would pay their full wages for 30 days. He ultimately extended that to 90 days for the paychecks, and 180 days for benefits. The generous proposition to pay workers when they couldn't work cost Malden Mills $25 million.

Undoubtedly, Feuerstein's decision was a kind one, one that made him incredibly popular and universally liked. But was it a wise business decision? In an interview with *CBS News/60 Minutes*, Feuerstein said yes, it was good business, "but that isn't why I did it. I did it because it was the right thing to do." Often, the fact that it's the right thing to do also makes it the right business decision, and "good" acts are rewarded by loyalty, excellent productivity, and great PR. That certainly appeared to be the case with

Malden at first. After Malden rebuilt the factories and hired back all the workers, the workers repaid the company. Business grew 40 percent; customer and employee retention reached 95 percent; off-quality products dropped from 6 to 7 percent before the fire to just 2 percent; and production increased from 130,000 to 200,000 yards per week.[7] But the extra effort and loyalty weren't enough. Malden Mills had spent too much while making too little; they could not dig themselves out of $140 million of debt, much of it stemming from the rebuild.[8] The company was forced to declare bankruptcy multiple times. Feuerstein lost his job in 2004. Ultimately, Malden Mills became Polartec, which employs only a thousand people in Lawrence.

Feuerstein is the ultimate principled manager. Even if his main motivation wasn't to be liked, but rather to do the right thing, it certainly resulted in employees liking him quite a lot that Christmas. And everyone else liked him, too—in addition to the flattering *60 Minutes* profile, he was celebrated by the media and was invited to speak at colleges and universities all around the country.[9]

An interesting exercise is to contrast Feuerstein's reputation with Jack Welch's, as the Cato Institute's Radley Balko did. "During his tenure," Balko wrote, "Welch was considered by many to be the epitome of the ruthless, cold-hearted, profit-minded corporate executive. He laid off thousands of workers in his efforts to streamline and change the focus of the company." And yet, he argues, "For every job he slashed, he eventually created dozens of new ones. For all the praise heaped on Feuerstein and scorn heaped on Welch, it is Welch, not Feuerstein, whose 'cold-hearted' capitalist management style did the most good for the most people."[10] Ironically, GE was the chief stakeholder of a group of corporate lenders who saved Malden Mills from going under completely. Those one thousand employees who remain in Lawrence may well owe their jobs to "cold-hearted" Jack Welch.

The Malden Mills story raises all manner of philosophical discussions about the ends justifying the means, the role of business in society, and whether a company that *ought* to do "the right thing" by bailing out displaced employees in fact has the means to do so. It's this last point that brings us back to dysfunctional harmony. A leader must always keep her eye on the big picture, and if she does not have the means to follow through with a principled stand, she can't. It's bad business, and it's not going to be good for employees no matter how principled it seems.

Sometimes you will have to give employees bad news—either about their performance or about the company as a whole. You *can* give employees the bad news in a kind way, and you can do it without being passive-aggressive and without omitting critical information. They may not all leave the room liking you, and sometimes that's okay.

AVOIDING DYSFUNCTIONAL HARMONY WITHOUT BEING A BULLY

You *can* avoid the family dinner where everyone's smiling but no one's happy. And you can do so without being the jerk who starts picking on everyone in order to start a fight. The answer begins with a simple acknowledgment: Business is inherently full of conflict. You have competitors. Staff will come and go. People will make mistakes as they go through the process of learning the business. Disharmony exists in business, so accept it. Don't try to gloss over it with niceties, or spend an inordinate amount of effort and energy making work an artificially nice place. It won't work, for all of the reasons we have convincingly (we hope) explained, and if you're not convinced, we have more statistics to prove it. Consider that despite your best intentions, the big happy family scenario won't *ever* work for about a third of your employees. It turns out that 28 percent of people are pessimists, who will distrust you fundamentally.[11] So even if 72 percent of your employees are ready to wear matching pajamas in the name of solidarity, you'll still have a significant number on the outside, whispering behind your back.

Now that we've convinced you, here's how to detect and fix the mistake of dysfunctional harmony.

Identify Dysfunctional Harmony in Yourself or Your Workplace
Have you recognized yourself in this chapter? Maybe you see a little of yourself in leaders like Ken or the president of the California games company. If so, dysfunctional harmony may be something you need to work on in yourself and in your company. You may have to take a long look at whether you are overly eager to please, and if so, why. Here are some questions to ask yourself:

○ Do people challenge your opinions? Allstate Insurance's George Ruebenson said he considered himself "lucky" if his leaders felt comfortable enough to get in his face once in a while, keeping him reeled in. Although not everyone would characterize debate quite this way, it's worth asking yourself: When was the last time a position I took was openly challenged? At your next meeting, pay attention to the dynamics. Express a controversial opinion, and see what happens. Does anyone blink an eye? If not, it may be that open expression is stifled. Your staff may be asking for mashed potatoes when what they really want to say is, "What the hell is he thinking?" They're not silent out of fear, like the subordinates we describe in Chapter Five. But they're not saying what they mean, which is just as damaging.

○ How often do you meet behind closed doors? Is it always necessary? Are you as transparent as you can be? If closed doors, sealed documents, and hushed conversations are a part of your everyday work life (and you don't work on national security issues or do undercover detective work), then your workplace may suffer from unhealthy speculation about what's going on behind those doors.

○   Do you dread giving performance reviews? When you leave them, do you feel like you left something unsaid? If so, you should examine your relationship with conflict. You might be sweeping dirt under the rug that you'd be much better off cleaning up.

○   Choose several big decisions facing your company and analyze them. Are you making progress toward solving them, or are you nibbling around the issues—that is, dealing with more easily solvable problems at the perimeter while the messy heart of it sits untouched? If you're nibbling when you should be biting, you may have a problem with postponing or avoiding conflict.

○   Look at your teams. Does everyone generally have the same point of view? Do you ever mix up teams to invite different viewpoints? If your groups are homogeneous, your desire for consensus may be overtaking healthy debate.

Motivate Your Employees the Hard Way—with Transparency and Honest Communication

One of the keys to effective leadership lies in the nuance of motivation. Sure, you can motivate through the carrot and the stick, but the real work happens when you neither threaten nor cajole.

If old-school, bullying management represents the problems of the stick, dysfunctionally harmonious management represents the problems of the carrot. A leader can't rule by fear, and a leader must offer more than just fun, entertainment, and likeability. Those things may help achieve certain goals in the short term, but success won't be lasting. It's far more difficult to inspire great work by understanding what inspires each employee and then speaking to that specifically. W.C.H. Prentice writes, "[E]ach player must not only fully understand his part and its relation to the group effort; he must also *want* to carry it out."[12] We would argue that the two are related. If a player is the recipient of effective communication, if he understands his part, he is more inclined to carry it out. Hence communication is crucial to motivating employees and avoiding dysfunctional harmony. For all of the many complex factors that create the dysfunctional harmony malady, the main cure boils down to four simple words: say what you mean.

Be honest while being tactful. Take the time to explain decisions, especially those that negatively affect your group. Doing so will help them to move forward. In the example of the California game company with the merged departments, the president could have just said, "We don't know whether we'll be merging the departments. As we see how this year plays out, it may come to make sense, depending on our sales numbers. Still, I will do everything I can to protect jobs, and I'll keep you posted throughout the year." Some employees would have been alarmed at this news, and they might not have appreciated its messenger. But when the president ultimately did merge the departments, he wouldn't have lost anyone's trust, because everyone knew all along it was a possibility. Further, since the president tied the merge decision to sales, everyone would have understood that they played a role in whether the departments merged. They would have felt motivated to move forward.

Commit to a culture of transparency. Use company newsletters, handbooks, bulletin boards, and lunchroom chats to inform workers what's going on. Of course, there will still be information you are obligated to be discreet about, for legal reasons or because there's no reason for Jill in accounting to know that Bill in IT is due for a difficult performance review. But if you're withholding information because you're afraid your employees can't handle it, or you're concerned that they themselves won't be discreet with it, fight that urge and share. You will build trust in the process, and you will ward off a workplace of smiles on the surface and dark whispers beneath.

Aim to Be Respected, Not Necessarily Liked

In academia, the best compliment you can get from a student is that you were really tough, but really fair. In fact, if your students like you too much, you're probably doing something wrong. One professor we know of fell into this very trap. She was a performer, and like many performers, she craved approval. She set out to entertain the students with each lecture, and the students loved her class. The entertainment factor took precedence over academic rigor. Assignments were easy, and everyone did well in the class. The professor even brought in pizza on the day students filled out their evaluations, a clear way of signaling, "Like me, like me, like me!"

It worked, yet it didn't. This professor didn't give her students enough credit, for they panned her in their evaluations, and she was let go. Sure, they *liked* her. But they already had plenty of friends; they wanted a professor.

This is not to say that a manager shouldn't try to make work fun, or that a professor shouldn't make class enjoyable. Another professor we know is famous for bringing homemade cookies into her economics class each semester. But before anyone takes a bite, they do a rigorous exercise on the economic theory of supply and demand. How much is this cookie worth? How much would you pay? What if X? What if Y? It's a far cry from pizza on evaluation day, and the economics professor is also known for being a tough grader who keeps students on the ball. Her students may not want to go watch a football game with her after class, but they want her to teach them.

Any parent will tell you the dynamic is similar with kids. Some parents will never say no, for a variety of motivations: they want peace and harmony, they want their kid to be happy, they want their kid to love them. Most people also realize that as much as we'd like to say yes all the time, we can't. Although our kids may hate us for it for a while, they will eventually come to understand why we set certain limits. And they'll be better behaved for having those limits.

Bring in Disparate Voices, and Encourage Debate Wisely

In the documentary *A View from the Top*, Sir Edmund Hillary described the ideal team as one of cautious tension. He believed that as you climb up a mountain, if everyone is in total harmony, it's less likely that you will summit the mountain, and you will be in much greater danger.[13] Climbing the mountain is inherently dangerous, in the same way that running a business has inherent conflict. You do have to have a basic trust of your colleagues, otherwise you'd spend all of your time going back over their work, which no leadership book would advocate. That said, a slight level of discord keeps you from becoming complacent. In that respect, cautious tension is not unlike defensive driving. We spend a lot of time creating a comfortable ride, yet the best drivers never get too comfortable. They follow the rules to get to their destination, but they're also on the lookout for those sharing the road with them, half expecting them to run a red light or take an illegal left turn.

Fight the artificiality of the comfortable ride, as every successful CEO we interviewed did. The first step toward doing so is building heterogeneous work teams. An accountant will see a problem differently from an engineer. Functionally, they have different views and perspectives, and possibly very different personalities, as well. Channel your inner Abraham Lincoln and create a team of rivals.

The second step is to set the tone for constructive debate. First and foremost, a leader must be in touch with the rhythms of her work environment. If everyone is crashing on getting a new product delivered, stress levels are likely to be high, and it is not the right time to have a discussion about improving team dynamics. Second, know that as the leader, everyone's eyes and ears will be on you for signals. Show that you are genuinely open and eager for some healthy debate. Set participants' minds at ease—tell them to say what they mean, and assure them that their idea won't leave the conference room if they don't want it to. Though this may sound like it's in direct conflict with the transparency mandate, it's not. Transparency doesn't mean you tell everybody everything—it means that you trust employees enough to tell them what they should know, secure that they will keep proprietary knowledge discreet.

Part of setting the tone means facilitating compromise, using clear yet respectful language (avoiding hot-button expressions), repeating ideas and points of view once they've been stated, and setting common goals.

Make the Chain of Command Clear—and True

In Menon's study of conflict, he found that conflict was more constructive and communication stronger when managers' roles were clear. It makes sense. In the case of the snack food company in Latin America, though there was a hierarchy, no one adhered to it. If they had, then the Latin America team would have been empowered to make their decisions without input from the founder, avoiding the charade of pretending to have input when really everyone understood they did not.

A clear chain of command also prevents whispered suppositions and bitterness. At a greeting card company, a manager we'll call Shelly would identify team "leaders," but those leaders had no actual authority over anyone. Their roles were vague; the leaders felt entitled to assert more control than they actually had; and everyone else resented them. (The leaders also happened to be the same people perceived as "favorites," compounding the problem.) If Shelly had simply officially promoted the leaders to managers, or otherwise made clear in writing what authority they had and did not have, much of the dissatisfaction of the team as a whole could have been avoided.

Adhering to a clear chain of command helps the boss be clear about when he needs to back away, but also when he needs to step up. To this end, it's important to understand the psychology of being a subordinate. It is not easy to be a subordinate; it means you must take orders from others, sometimes in opposition to what you would do, had you the authority. To accept this position, the subordinate needs to have a firm understanding of a larger order, of a bigger picture. That has been a truism for over a half century, as Prentice's 1961 article attests. He says that one of the "saddest" things among leaders is the manager that tries too hard to be liked. The results—workers lose respect for their leader.[14] We're not arguing that the leader needs to be feared and kept at a far remove—that would swing too much toward the old-school leadership we discussed in Chapter Five. But there is a balance the boss needs to strike between being a fair advocate for his staff and being their best friend.

Again, the character of Michael Scott on *The Office* provides an extreme example to help us illustrate our point. Whereas typically Michael's behaviors highlight what not to do, in at least one case, Michael inadvertently teaches us a business lesson by doing the right thing. When Stanley, the notoriously sour-faced salesman, is openly insubordinate to Michael at a company meeting, Michael does everything he can think of to avoid a confrontation with him. Michael wants to preserve dysfunctional harmony and his belief that his staff—every last one—adores him. When Michael and Stanley do finally have a meeting, Michael suggests that Stanley doesn't respect him because he doesn't know him well enough. When that possibility is refuted by Stanley, Michael is forced to draw an important line: "All right," he tells Stanley. "You don't respect me. I accept that. But listen to me: you can't talk to me that way in this office. You just can't. I am your boss. I can't allow it."[15]

For the first time, Michael has been tough on Stanley, and for the first time, Stanley shows respect for his boss, responding to Michael's line-setting with "Fair enough." Michael has been forced to remove his "best friend" mentality and behave like a leader.

If You're Accepting Feedback, Show It

If you have a brainstorming meeting, or if someone makes a suggestion that everyone gets on board with, make it clear whether the suggestion will be taken or not. If not, explain the reasoning. Give people the opportunity to seek clarity on your reasoning. If you *do* take the suggestion, articulate where and how you've done so. Give credit where credit is due. Say you had a brainstorming session about ways to improve your billing process. If someone suggests a viable idea that you decide to take, when you roll out the new policy, indicate where the suggestion came from. Remind everyone about it at the next brainstorming meeting, to reinforce the fact that they do have a voice.

On the other hand, do not seek feedback if you know you won't be able to take it. If your company is moving to a new headquarters and you know that the board will dictate its location, don't ask employees to weigh in. You will only hurt your credibility when you ask for input in the future.

Look at the Big Picture

Always, always ask yourself whether a decision is in the best interest of the company. Are you being overly influenced by a favored employee or a strong-willed staff member whose ire you dread? Are you so focused on wanting employees' approval that you will roll out a health care plan that your company can't afford in the long term? Walk the line between *ought to* and *can*. Do the right thing, but only if it's truly viable for the company. Employees will understand, because making hard decisions is part of your job and what they expect of you. If they don't agree, that's okay, too—you are not going to reach consensus all of the time, and by virtue of your title and the competitive landscape that is business, some people will not be happy.

The good news is that sometimes doing the right thing is also a sensible investment in the future. One of the CEOs in our study, Paul Macek, considers a decision that made him a lot of enemies in the short term one of the greatest long-term accomplishments of his career. Macek is now the CEO of Proctor Hospital; in 2001 he was put in charge of two hospitals in the BJC Healthcare network. The hospitals, located in the St. Louis suburbs, suffered from $16 million in operating losses *per year*. After the BJC board brought Macek in as a change agent, he got to work, investigating the problems at the Christian NE and Christian NW campuses. Although Christian NE had high operating costs, it was turning enough of a profit to support Christian NW, and many in the community felt it should go on doing so. Christian NW was crucial to their community. Not only did it provide jobs, but its ER and other services were highly valued, if not highly profitable. Politicians, clergy, employees, and community members were outspoken in their desire to maintain the status quo and avoid rocking the boat.

Macek noted their concerns. But he also noted that Christian NW's 200-bed hospital was consistently at 25-percent capacity. The hospital had too much competition from other hospitals, plain and simple. In addition, the hospital had no clear physician recruitment in place, its operating costs were way too high, and it was unable to support clinical programs. None of this information was fun for those emotionally invested in the hospital to hear, and Macek did not relish being the messenger. "It was emotionally charged," Macek said. "The mayor, politicians, clergy, were all adamant about keeping the hospital open, even if it meant operating at a loss." Ultimately, however, Macek's analysis left him little choice but to close Christian NW. "What the market needed and what we wanted to support didn't match up," he said.

Layoffs ensued. But so did a public promise that although Christian NW was shutting down, BJC was opening a new facility at the former site with an emergency room and outpatient care. Macek said no one believed his promise. He made the announcement at a public meeting that was very painful for everyone. "There were a lot of very angry, disappointed people. I will never forget the employees—many who had spent their entire career at Christian NW—sitting in that auditorium, and the emotion and the name-calling that resulted from the news."

Macek did make good on his promise, and the new ER facility rose up from the ground as they demolished the old. The new, award-winning facility is profitable, offers excellent patient care, does not operate at a loss, and is still an important part of the community. A snapshot of the two buildings—one on its way out, the other starting fresh in the background—still holds a prominent placement in Macek's office. It serves as a reminder about the importance of making tough choices, and that sometimes, to rebuild, you first have to tear down.

Leaders who want to transform an environment rife with dysfunctional harmony should take comfort and inspiration from Macek's experience. Lasting change may not be easy, but it is possible.

Mia, a vice president at a company in San Francisco, offers the further heartening information that a repair job for a dysfunctional workplace does not always have to be initiated by top management. Her company offered a textbook case of dysfunctional harmony. On the surface, everyone got along. Nobody challenged anyone else in department meetings. Actually, there was one meeting in which a junior associate questioned something the CEO said. After the meeting, everyone paired off to talk behind closed doors about what they didn't want to say in the open. The CEO took Mia aside and said of the hapless junior associate, "That's not the way we do things here—we all get along."

Mia became so fed up with the environment—one that she believed was perpetuated by the CEO—that she called a meeting of vice presidents in order to make her case. (She was fully aware of the irony that they were meeting behind the CEO's back!) She came prepared with data. "We have a problem," she said. "In the last five years, we've lost eight really good people. Though publicly they always offered a legitimate, easily palatable story about why they were leaving, in private they were explicit that it was a leadership issue." Mia asked everyone to take a survey from Patrick Lencioni's bestselling book, *The Five Dysfunctions of a Team,* to see how they fared. They did not fare well, unsurprisingly, and together the group of vice presidents decided to change their culture. They highlighted the five most critical flaws they saw in their culture, and they planned for five retreats—one to tackle each flaw. They included their CEO in the retreats, as well as mid- and lower-level employees. "Everyone had to be a part of the process," Mia said, "in order to make it work."

Mia's story—the care she took to build her case and to involve everyone in the process of changing their culture— offers up a great deal of possibility. On the individual level or on the group level, there's no need to ever say, "That's just the way it is." People can change, cultures can shift, and our ways of relating to one another always have room—and possibility—for improvement.

KEY TAKEAWAYS

Lessons Learned from Mistakes

- When you want consensus too badly, you miss out on valuable debate.
- Leaders who seek to be too friendly lose impartiality and credibility.
- Hiding bad news is useless and erodes trust.
- Soliciting feedback and then failing to incorporate it stifles initiative and creative thought.
- Decisions that are too employee-based can hurt the big-picture health of the company.

Successful Navigation

- Honestly and persistently assess whether you are prone to a pleaser mentality.
- Commit to a transparent work environment in which open communication is valued.
- Aim to be respected, not liked.
- Encourage debate by selecting a variety of participants with varying perspectives and priorities and by setting the tone.
- Make your chain of command clear to everyone, and stick to it.
- Accept—and incorporate—feedback when you can, and don't pretend to when you cannot.

- Always test your impartiality. Are you basing your team-leadership decision on the big picture? Is it something the company can do and not just something you feel you ought to do to bank good will?

To find out more about whether your company has a passive-aggressive culture, visit www.TheWisdomOfFailure.com.

SEVEN

The Battle Within

Distracted Purpose

L et's go back to that dinner table where everyone's sitting, eating a meal together. In a culture of dysfunctional harmony, everyone smiles through the tension as they ask for the mashed potatoes. In a culture of distracted purpose, they may not be talking at all. And if they are, they're likely to be shouting or interrupting each other. They may even be throwing the food as much as they're eating it, or insulting the cook or the host. There's no guise of harmony—just complete lack of teamwork at best, and open hostility at worst.

We've all seen those companies, even if we haven't had the displeasure of working for one. Linda, an executive at a multinational company headquartered in Dallas, is unfortunate enough to work for such a company. When she walks into a meeting of directors and their higher-ups, it's like walking into a food fight. She is prepared for battle, prepared to attack and defend. The underlying dynamic, she says, is that "everyone wants to feel important, and everyone wants to feel like they have something to say that is the most important, monumental thing ever. Even if the speaker doesn't understand the business, they want to look like they are participating." For those who actually do know the business, it's a frustrating meeting. "We end up going off course from what should be a straightforward business deal into politics and people just talking to talk."

Even worse than being a waste of time, in these meetings the environment soon becomes heated. With everyone jockeying for favor, they perceive that the best way to earn that favor is to deride others. "There's a lot of condescension," Linda says. "People get really derogatory, asking, 'Well, didn't you think of this? Why didn't you think of that?' It becomes a competition to see who can ask the most obscure question to make you look bad."

And what are the leaders doing during the melee? Like spectators at a boxing match, they sit back, watching the show. Once the argument seems to be at its height, Linda says, they step in and make the final call. "I don't know if the point of this is to let people talk it all the way through from several different angles," Linda explains, "but it goes too far. It comes off as a lack of clear leadership, and it's just not effective."

The big-picture consequences of this environment are not hard to imagine. No one is motivated to do their job, Linda explains, because they know they'll be put in the hot seat. Productivity and forward progression are severely stunted. Linda has been with the company for only a few years, and she can't point a finger at the moment the environment became toxic—it was already that way when she arrived. But she is increasingly frustrated by her leaders' decision to encourage the boxing match.

The central goal of leadership is to create something greater than the sum of the parts. You want teamwork, you want synergy. You want those people around the table to bring their resources to bear, to combine their power and coordinate their strategies. As everyone knows, a superhero team—from the Avengers to the Incredibles—can kick a lot more ass than a lone hero, no matter how super that hero may be. Yet when the team is afflicted with distracted purpose, either the parts aren't fitting together, or they're fighting each other when they do.

In this chapter we show you how leaders struggle with this all-too-common mistake. Some leaders think competition is healthy and keeps everyone on their best game, while ignoring the very real tensions that competition creates. Other leaders practice blatant favoritism, which erodes trust and causes distracting politics. Still others have no sense of how to balance the strengths and weaknesses on their teams; they put people in the wrong jobs and let them linger there, to the detriment of organizational efficiency and focus. Finally, some leaders enthusiastically initiate synergy efforts without taking an analytical look at whether the endeavor makes sense in the first place. We go over the many faces of distracted purpose, and offer suggestions about how to prevent it or mitigate its consequences. From encouraging "co-opetition" (cooperative competition) to practicing safe synergy, we explain how to replace food fighters with a team that makes sense, works together, and keeps the organization's mission at the forefront.

DISTRACTION SOUP: THE FORMS OF DISTRACTED PURPOSE

The problems that lead companies like Linda's down the food fight path come in an array of forms. On their own or in combination, these issues mean that a company's leadership has taken its eyes off the proverbial ball. The leader may believe internal competition is the spark necessary to ignite stellar performance among employees, when such competition actually makes everyone focus on the wrong things and lose sight of their common goals. Another problem, favoritism, causes people to focus their energies on perceived unfairness rather than the job at hand. Or perhaps the leader has difficulty bringing everyone's strengths to the fore, letting weak performers remain in roles they should leave. And as much as a leader might crave synergy, sometimes her efforts to achieve it are her company's undoing.

Costly Competition

Our need to compete runs deep, whether a boss pushes us in that direction or not. Motivational speaker and trainer Avery Henderson uses a game to demonstrate this. When he conducts team-building training, he separates attendees into two groups and introduces the game. The main goal, he instructs, is to get as many points as possible. The groups separate to strategize, and when they return, Henderson explains, "in 99 percent of the cases, the game will be played competitively between the two groups. While trying to score points, they use valuable resources to block the other group from scoring." They *don't* use those resources or that time to score as many points as possible, which is the game's sole goal. Henderson often gets blamed for setting the attendees up to compete by dividing them. "I point out that I called them groups, not teams," he explains. "The competitive paradigm is so ingrained in our thought processes that the division of the group is enough to skew what is being said."[1]

It makes sense. From the time we first play Monopoly as kids to the way our parents get the family out the door on time by making it a race, we are socialized to try to get a leg up. In business, especially, we keep a very close eye on our competition, and striving to keep up with or beat that competition usually makes us a stronger business. Competition keeps us motivated, and it keeps us honest with our customers, as we know there will be repercussions from our rivals if we are not honest. The "compete!" button we all have, although so important to use in external dealings, can turn into a self-destruct button if used internally. That's because if we compete with our fellow team members, we are more apt to engage in behaviors that are counter to our company's goals. We hoard information because we think it gives us an individual edge, when really the dissemination of that information would help the company as a whole. We spend time and energy putting down our colleagues instead of helping them achieve, when their achieving is what would actually help the company the most. Inappropriate competition leads to grudges, gossip, heads of departments fighting over budgets, and worse.

Perhaps the most recognizable example of unhealthy competition comes from car dealerships—holdouts in a larger business climate that has begun to shun the commission structure and the corrosive competition that comes with it. At a car dealership it's not uncommon to have rewards in place for the "best sales of the weekend." As salesmen compete, they burn one another's leads and manipulate customers in a way that serves their own needs, not the needs of the company. And the result? Most of us hate dealing with car salesmen—it's one of the least-trusted jobs on the professional scale. The role has become synonymous with insincerity and deceit, and fodder for jokes and insults. The entire car sales industry is rife with competition, and thus change is slower in coming than in other industries, but the greater retail world provides an example of where the market is trending when it comes to internal competition. Shoppers don't like to be hassled and pressured by salespeople the moment they walk in the door, and they will be far more likely to shop somewhere that does not have a commission structure baiting its employees. Many retailers who maintain commissions lose valuable customers—and their dollars.

A clear example of the costs of competition happened at an advertising agency, the creative staff of which were divided into two groups, based on the nature of the account the group handled. One group—let's call them Group A—found themselves slammed, so they asked Group B whether one of their designers whose work was slow could help. The leader of Group B immediately said no. When someone from Group A asked why, the leader of Group B said, "We're going to get busier, and we'll need all of our designers." That may be the case, but why not lend a designer who was slow *while he was slow,* with the understanding that when work picked up for Group B, he'd need to return to his usual duties? The reason was competition. Instead of focusing on the health of the company as a whole, Group B's leader focused on her group's performance, perhaps not wanting to draw the attention of leadership to the fact that her group was slow—perhaps fearing that if she did, she would lose that designer to Group A permanently. Instead, Group A paid money to hire a freelancer, while the designer from Group B played solitaire for a few days. By refusing to share resources, the agency was literally doubling their costs for a certain task: they paid the freelancer, and they paid the designer from Group B who had nothing to do but play solitaire.

The "cost of solitaire" can be measured easily enough, but plenty of negative results of competition cannot be. When competition is rampant, we don't trust the people we sit down with each day. Just as we may be keeping information from them, we suspect they are keeping it from us. In this loaded environment, who can really do her best work?

Favoritism and Perceived Unfairness

Shelly, a manager at a greeting card company, often became friends with her employees. She loved hosting dinners for staff, going out for long lunches, and fostering a feeling of community and family. She believed that the more bonded the team, the more seamless their communication and ability to work together.

In the course of becoming so close with her employees, however, some of Shelly's connections became deeper than others. Some employees played on her desire for closeness to get closer to her than their colleagues were. They spent more and more time in her office with the door closed. They babysat her daughter and mentioned the fact to anyone who would listen. Everyone else noticed and smelled favoritism. When the favored employees were given the best projects or otherwise called out for commendation, even though they actually deserved the accolades, their colleagues were suspicious. Though Shelly claimed to accept everyone, an "in crowd" dynamic emerged. The repercussions continued. If an employee had a legitimate complaint about a colleague, he would not go to Shelly about it if the colleague was a member of the in crowd. He feared that Shelly's relationship with the favored colleague would affect her judgment. Even worse, when teams met without Shelly present, they didn't trust one another. The ones outside of the in crowd viewed their favored peers as informants. Potentially productive debates were stifled, due to the fear Shelly would hear about it secondhand and through someone else's eyes. Morale was negatively affected, and the seamlessness of team communication—the very thing Shelly was trying to foster—suffered greatly.

As is often said in business, perception is reality. It may very well have been the case that though Shelly spent more time with some staff than others, she considered it a business necessity and really didn't favor any one employee over another. It doesn't matter. And it's much easier than you may think to be perceived as unfair. Carol Bartz, who was chief executive of Autodesk for fourteen years, remembered bearing witness to favoritism in her days as a sales representative. Her team leader gave a plum territory to someone whom coworkers considered an underperformer. Bartz transferred away from that team leader as soon as she could, and the experience stayed with her. Yet when she was Autodesk CEO, a staffer complained to her, saying, "Everybody thinks that so-and-so is your favorite."[2] Even with an awareness about favoritism and the best intentions, leaders can get caught in a trap whereby others think they're playing favorites.

Where employees perceive unfairness, the company suffers—because either people don't trust one another, as we saw with Shelly's team, or staff members who feel they are being treated unfairly are distracted or, even worse, react angrily. Organizations that are seen as unfair by employees have higher rates of negative behaviors like stealing and bad-mouthing.[3]

Favoritism often looks the way we described it with Shelly's team, but there are other forms to guard against, as well.

Nepotism is against many company's policies, but where it is permitted, it can be caustic, as employees assume the boss will give his family member advantages based not on merit, but on their relationship. In family businesses, where nepotism is not an "ism" but an anticipated and embraced practice, the value of the company goes down, on average, when the business is passed to a son or daughter instead of hiring a professional CEO.[4]

Cronyism, another form of favoritism, involves hiring someone because she is a friend, not because of her qualifications. Practically speaking, hiring friends or close acquaintances happens all the time, and it can be a great way to bring talent into your company. But it falls under the unflattering moniker of cronyism when the new hire is not up to the job, and when other in-house employees could have filled the role with aplomb. Patronage is a sneakier, more subtle form of nepotism or cronyism. The leader might not hire family and friends herself, but she promotes certain people knowing that, when they are in a position to hire, they will choose applicants who are close to the leader. The unfairness component quadruples.

Finally, possibly the most toxic form of favoritism results when a boss and a subordinate engage in a romantic relationship. Revelations of relationships of this nature have brought down leaders from Boeing's Harry Stonecipher to the World Bank's Paul Wolfowitz. It would be easy to minimize this particular form of favoritism as a rarity, or an extreme example, but for the fact that we spend much of our waking lives at the office. We do not live in an era in which we spend our days calling on other families socially, attending balls and formal dinners regularly. In the present era, we meet romantic prospects as we're both waiting for the copier to warm up. Romance often begins where we spend the better part of our days, and even if a leader isn't party to one herself, she needs to ensure that office romances are not affecting fair practices throughout the company or creating a perception of unfairness.

Inability to Manage Strengths and Weaknesses

Walt Disney, who built an empire and forever changed the entertainment world, did not list his creative, visionary skills as his greatest accomplishment, but rather said, "Of all the things I have done, the most vital was coordinating the talents of those who work for me and pointing them at certain goals."[5]

It seems like a given: put Gwendolen, a big-picture person with excellent interpersonal skills, in an account services role, and have Roger, who is detail-oriented but not a people person, act as Gwendolen's assistant. As individuals, neither one of them could achieve as much as the two together. To clients, they are a dream team. One of the most basic parts of a leader's job is making sure the right people are in the right spot, so that their strengths help one another and their weaknesses are mitigated.

If it's such a given, why is it so hard to do? It may be that the leader has trouble with dysfunctional harmony (see Chapter Six) and freezes when faced with a situation in which he needs to confront someone's weakness. It may be that he is focusing so much on big-picture strategy that he's not paying close enough attention to the implementation of that strategy. Another leader may simply have blinders on regarding personnel matters. This is where what is actually a problem of managing strengths and weaknesses looks like favoritism, as it's far too easy to seek out your top performer again and again, when you should be casting a wider net.

Priceline.com's Jeff Hoffman used a sports analogy to describe the challenges of managing strengths and weaknesses. The Chicago Cubs had an all-star center fielder, Marlon Byrd. Byrd is a fantastic athlete, so beloved by Cubs fans that they would often chant "The Byrd is the word" when he was up at bat. Byrd was probably the Cubs' greatest asset. Yet if the coach determined that he needed to use his best asset as much as possible—a reasonable supposition in the business world—he might put Byrd on the mound to throw pitches. No coach in his right mind would make such a move. Just because Byrd is an excellent athlete and an asset to the team doesn't mean anyone would make the leap to assuming he has the skill set to be the team's pitcher. Yet similar leaps are made all the time in business. If you have a star performer whom clients love and who seems capable of a wide array of tasks, it's tempting to broaden her role and go to her whenever there's something that needs doing. The result is that she may feel overwhelmed and not be able to put forward her best work. She may actually not be good at everything you've asked her to do. Others may feel resentful that you are giving her so much responsibility. And if she burns out and leaves, you have not just one slot to fill, but many. As a leader, you must think like a baseball coach and leverage strengths instead of playing favorites. Don't put a strong performer on the pitcher's mound just because she's strong.

A related area where leaders commonly get derailed is their inability to define a job well. How can you ensure that someone's strengths are right for the job if you don't have a solid handle on what the job is in the first place? Especially in instances when an opening may fall in a completely new area for a company, many leaders will hire someone and cross their fingers that somehow, magically, that person will do it right. It doesn't work. The leader doing the hiring does not necessarily have to be able to do the job herself, but she must understand exactly what the job is. She must respect the time it takes to learn the strengths required of the person who fills the job as well as the weaknesses to guard against. She can do this either by looking around at other companies with similar jobs or by envisioning the desired outcomes for that position and working backward to determine what it will take to get there.

An Obsession with Synergy

All leaders *should* want the strong, collaborative superhero team in place, because it's good sense and good business. Yet some leaders are so excited about the transformative power of synergy, they think it is *the* answer to all their problems, and the legacy for which they will be remembered. It becomes synergy for the sake of synergy, rather than synergy for the sake of effectiveness, as discussed in Chapter Three. But just as someone determined to get in shape can sabotage his good intentions—and even hurt himself—by virtue of his excess enthusiasm, so can leaders work against their goals by pushing synergy too hard. And unfortunately, it's difficult to chalk failed pursuits of synergy up to learning experiences when the consequences are felt so deeply. There's the opportunity cost, for one, because managers are distracted from their core business and other, more promising ventures. Failed synergy programs can also leave a trail of broken customer relationships, unhappy employees, and weakened brands.

According to Michael Goold and Andrew Campbell, business writers and directors of the Ashridge Strategic Management Centre, four central problems are associated with failed synergy efforts. The first is a judgment problem. If leaders want synergy too badly, that desire clouds their judgment about whether or not it even makes strategic sense for certain groups to combine, or certain product lines to be coordinated. When their eagerness gets in the way of sound business judgment, the synergy project fails and dissuades other, better-advised attempts at synergy. *Project A didn't work,* management might say, *so why try Project B?* But what if Project B is actually a much better idea than Project A? We see questionable judgment of this ilk constantly; in the case of acquisitions in particular, we've seen too many instances when enthusiasm wanes and then burns out disastrously. The root problem is usually that an acquisition has an emotional component that can get in the way of good judgment. If a company decides it wants to acquire another company, its leadership will do or think whatever they must to justify that decision. The stakes simply *feel* too high not to make the decision come out the way the leadership wants it to.

Leaders who desire synergy to a fault also don't listen to their managers who tell them that a synergy effort doesn't make sense. That leader has a "parenting bias"—the second problem—wherein he assumes that unit managers are naturally resistant to cooperation. That leader becomes like the parent saying to her kids, "Get along and do this together, and don't come out of your room until you can be nice to one another!" But what if that leader had a different assumption—one that held that if units don't want to work together, it's simply because they know it doesn't make sense? After all, unit managers know their unique slice of the business better than anyone. Why not trust them to have good reasons for questioning a synergy effort?

Third, even if a synergy effort makes sound business sense, and even if every party is on board, an overeager leader can leave out a critical question: Do we have someone who can execute this effort? Do we have the skills to pull it off? "The members of the management team may lack the operating knowledge, personal relationships, or facilitative skills required to achieve meaningful collaboration,"[6] say Goold and Campbell. Or they may simply be impatient or lack the charisma necessary to pull it off.

Finally, Goold and Campbell point out the "pizza problem"— the unexpected (if clear in hindsight) ways in which a synergy effort can destroy the very elements it's trying to strengthen. A consulting company decided to bring together its strategy and IT consultants to work on a new service for a client. When the combined team was working late one night, the strategy consultants suggested ordering pizza and charging it to the client. The IT consultants were surprised—they weren't typically allowed to do this, so why were the strategy consultants? The disparity led to a conversation about other disparities, including the fact that the strategy consultants were paid much more and enjoyed better fringe benefits. In this case, things began to fall apart over dinner. Many of the firm's best IT consultants ended up resigning. Leaders will rush to promote cooperative efforts and synergy, but rarely will they put the brakes on a potentially lucrative initiative because they fear it might negatively affect the culture.[7]

Synergy can be a little like morphine. If times are tough, you may think a synergy endeavor will take the pain away—and often it does. But morphine also masks pain you would do well to observe. Pain alerts you to something important you may need to change. An apt example of a company that fell into the synergy-morphine trap is Pioneer Seed Corporation. Jerry Chicione, former chair and CEO of Pioneer Seed, was part of our study; he shared that the company was originally "a home-grown, established company with loyal employees—many of them farmers—who fully expected to work for Pioneer Seed all their lives." It was a relatively simple business model. Through its research department, Pioneer developed new and better hybrid seed corn products, which it then sold to its customers. Pioneer led its industry, commanding, at one time, nearly 45 percent of the North American seed corn market. Pioneer's field agronomists were experts at determining which new hybrids would yield more for their customers; yields (the amount of bushels harvested per acre) kept going up.

Then came biotech. What had once been the primary purpose of this commodity-based seed group—improving the quality and yield of seeds—could now be done in a laboratory. Biotech produced results that would have taken generations of crops to achieve. Pioneer Seed Corporation cried out in pain, so what did they do? Applied a little morphine. They built a division of young seed geneticists. The result was that employees of the family farm seed culture were now in direct competition with the new white-coated Ph.D.s who built seed crops out of DNA, in the same company. *We'll still do it the old way*, Pioneer Seed was saying, *but we'll also do it the new way*. The forced synergy was a disaster. The two groups looked different, felt different, and spent an inordinate amount of time at odds with one another. The leadership at Pioneer Seed threw up their hands. They felt that if the divisions weren't going to get along, they could fight it out and see who came out on top. That's right—in the absence of collaboration, Pioneer Seed overcorrected and encouraged outright competition between the two groups. They failed again. Pioneer ultimately spent so much money that it needed to lay off 25 percent of its workforce. The 150-year-old seed company almost imploded, and ultimately it was purchased by DuPont. Leaders at Pioneer knew they had to change, but they were so determined to protect their history that they were incapable of making the hard move forward, opting instead to split the difference and dull the pain with a misguided effort at synergy between old and new technologies.

In many ways, Pioneer's leaders made the same mistakes as the leaders profiled in Chapter Six, leaders who did not want to make difficult—if necessary—decisions. And synergy, their way of accommodating their flawed thinking, led to distracted purpose.

RESCUING YOUR TEAM FROM DISTRACTED PURPOSE

As we've seen, a wide array of problems and dynamics feed into distracted purpose. And it can seem overwhelming to imagine fixing a team that is not working well together. Our first piece of advice on the repair issue is—relax. Know that even the closest families have strife, even the most evolved couples have long-standing issues they struggle to resolve, and even the most well-intentioned business will have elements of distracted purpose.

Second, tackle the problems one at a time. Determine which are your most pressing problems, which are present but can wait, and which don't come into play for you at all. Third, don't let that wait be *too* long. It's tempting to pour energy into the biggest problems and never touch those less-pressing problems at all. They may not need to be fixed today, but they do need to be fixed, or else they will result in the next fire to put out. In this section we suggest, one by one, some fixes for the most common symptoms of distracted purpose.

Discourage Competition by Encouraging Co-opetition

The easiest way to discourage competition in the workplace is to simply not encourage it. Don't put people in the position where they have nothing to gain but much to lose if they don't come out on top of a sales finish. Don't set up situations in which departments are competing against one another for budgets and coveted resources. Rather than have them be incentivized by how their group does in relation to another group, base their compensation on the company's goal. For example, at Bradley University, where Larry works, leaders decided to invest a considerable amount of money in one particular college. This decision drew the ire of workers at other colleges, who felt those resources should be shared with them. Instead of letting the groups fester in competition, leaders spent a great deal of time educating naysayers about how the allocation of resources was going to help them, too—explaining the concrete improvements everyone would see by virtue of the increasing visibility of the college that was receiving the funds.

It's a given that no one likes to lose, so don't set up a situation in which there will be winners and losers, because all you're doing is ensuring that *someone* is going to be unhappy. Encourage an environment that supports the much-coveted "win-win"—the mutual benefit possible in all human interactions.

Realistically, as much as you discourage competition, know that it *will* be present. As long as there are plum assignments and promotions, there will be people who get them and people who don't, and a competitive energy around the issue. This may be an opportunity for you to embrace co-opetition—the idea that competitors can each benefit when they work together. Co-opetition has been a favorite concept in the business community for fifteen years, from the time a book by that name was published to great acclaim. Co-opetition most commonly comes into play in an external context, when businesses are in fierce competition with one another yet share certain resources because it makes sense for both to do so. Internally, you can use co-opetition by making sure that the things people are competing over are, ironically, values of teamwork and harmony. As Avery Henderson puts it, make the measuring stick for career promotions "how well a person fosters teamwork, serves internal and external customers, problem solves, and helps to meet the organization's goals . . ."[8] Internal co-opetition continually drives the competitive urge back to the goal of bettering the team.

Play Fair

Are you closer to certain staff members than to others? Would others perceive that you are? Probably the answer to both questions is yes. According to a new study, a vast majority of business leaders say favoritism plays a factor in promotions. Eighty-four percent of the 303 senior business executives surveyed said favoritism takes place at their organizations; 23 percent acknowledged practicing it themselves (which probably means far more of them actually *do* practice it); and 9 percent said favoritism was a factor in their last promotion. Jonathan Gardner, the report's author, felt the true number was likely much higher still, because "No one at this level of executive was going to admit it blatantly."[9] If we are truly honest with ourselves, the statistics make sense. It's human nature to gravitate toward certain people more than others— especially if those people either are like us or make it clear that they *like* us. Just as a lecturer will tend to make eye contact with the listener who is smiling and nodding rather than listeners who cast their eyes downward, so too we seek out certain people day to day because they make us feel good about ourselves. Acknowledging all of that, you can still avoid favoritism by following some guidelines. First, conduct an anonymous poll of your staff to learn whether they perceive favoritism; use this to assess how big a problem you have. To correct your favoritism problem:

○ Pay attention to how much time you spend with each staff member and whether it's merited or not. If necessary, keep a list, either in your head or on paper, so that you can chart those five-minute hallway conversations that turn into hour-long chats in your office.

○ Have clear policies explaining how promotions, hiring, and project-lead decisions are made. Make sure those policies are enforced and that others have a chance to review them. Do the policies themselves favor one group or person over another? Similarly, have policies regarding office romances. To whom are people required to disclose their relationship, and when? What parameters are set around their working relationship?

○ Educate your staff about the policies. It's no use having them if people aren't aware of them!

○ Communicate openly and often about your reasoning. Business author, speaker, and consultant Robert Whipple suggests that if you decide to give someone a key job, explain your reasons for doing so at a staff meeting. Explain, for instance, that this person has done the job well before, but that if someone else would like to do it next time, they should let their wishes be known so that they can be trained to take it on. In other words, be clear that the field is open.[10] By doing so, you are expressing flexibility, demonstrating openness as to your thought process, and showing willingness to develop other staff.

○ Be careful not to overcorrect. If you have a top performer with whom you also happen to personally connect, you may feel tempted to underplay her strengths for fear of seeming to favor her. That's unfair to that top performer who, let's not forget, is a great asset to the company. If you have a go-to person, by all means, use his strengths—but let him and others know why you are doing so, and that they have an opportunity to be a go-to person as well.

○   Shake things up. Imagine the artistic director of a ballet who always gives the same popular ballerina the best solos. Now imagine he surprises everyone in the company by giving the solo to a talented dancer from the corps de ballet. Though for the next show he returns to his usual stable of consistent performers, he also makes it a habit to make unexpected casting choices semi-regularly. It's much harder for the dance company—and the audience—to accuse him of playing favorites.

Leverage Cliques

Even if you achieve high marks on the fairness front, know that favoritisms and groupings will happen even without your participation. Some people just click more than others; as a result, they will leave others out. The key to keeping this dynamic from creating competition and a sense of unfairness is in leveraging it. According to Wharton management professor researcher Jennifer S. Mueller, when cliques are managed correctly, they have enormous potential for benefiting the entire organization because they "can perform better, transfer complex information to one another with higher resolution, and so forth."[11]

Support Workers' Strengths and Help Their Weaknesses

Make sure everyone is in the right seat at the table. You wouldn't seat a left-handed guest in the middle of a crowded dinner table, when chances are those around him will be right-handed, and he and his neighbor will bump elbows all evening. Pay attention to people's needs, and to their skills, even if those skills do not come into play for them daily. An executive assistant may also be an incredible computer whiz, and there may be a way for him to help launch a new technical endeavor that challenges him while playing to his strengths. At the same time, don't be so blinded by someone's skill that you toss that person every task that comes along. Consistently ask yourself: Am I putting a center fielder on the pitcher's mound? If the answer is yes, stop.

Conversely, if someone is struggling in her role, don't pass over those weaknesses—either for lack of time or because it won't be a fun conversation. Allow room for error, of course, but if the underperformer is consistently underperforming, change her role. Find her a fit that plays more to her strengths, and explain that it's in her best interest as well as the best interest of the company to have her there.

Once an employee is in the right spot, help her develop herself—for instance, by setting her up with a mentor, or by creating a system in which she fully owns her job. For example, Jack Stack—whom we met in Chapter Two—believes in full transparency of the balance sheet, to such an extent that all employees know how to read profit-and-loss statements, and from there they understand what their value is and how they benefit the company. He then teaches them how to measure their own success, using balance sheets to help them chart for themselves where they're finding success and where they need to improve.

We met a memorable guy at Parsons, a machine shop in Illinois with roughly nine hundred employees, who illustrates the potential of self-development. This individual was the water recycling manager, and we remarked that it sounded like a dirty job. "No way," he said. "This is one of the most important jobs at the facility." He went on to describe the consequences if the plant failed to get the water to its cleanliness standards. He was genuinely excited about his job, and he spent considerable time actively perfecting it. He had the right skill set for his job to begin with, of course, and then he had the tools to perfect both the job and his skills, and he was energized by his sense of the importance of his role to the whole organization. He was the manager of his own success.

Practice Safe Synergy

The best antidotes for the leader who is overly eager to synergize—and thus more prone to make errors in the process—are awareness and discipline. Slow down. Think clearly. Outline your goals in concrete terms, rather than using vague terms like "sharing best practices" and "cross-fertilizing ideas." Goold and Campbell use the example of a food manufacturer's CEO who wanted to "leverage its international brands"—a fuzzy goal in and of itself.[12] When one of the people charged with implementing this vision—a category manager—tried to persuade a subsidiary to use a marketing campaign that had been successful in other countries, the local manager resisted. "That campaign wouldn't work in Argentina," he said. "What I would like is advice on new-product-development processes." When the category manager explained that she was trying to create an international brand, which meant they needed to standardize their marketing, the local manager had a completely different take on what leveraging their brands meant. "[I]f we want to leverage our brands," he countered, "we need to focus on product development." The category manager met with similar resistance with other local managers, all of whom had their own ideas about how to leverage the international brand. It's not that people disputed the sense in leveraging the brand—it's that everyone had a different take on what that meant in the first place.

What the category manager ultimately did—and what leaders striving for successful synergy should do—was to break down exactly what "leveraging international brands" meant. "By disaggregating a broad goal into more precisely defined objectives," explain Goold and Campbell, "managers will be better able to evaluate costs and benefits and, when appropriate, create concrete implementation plans."[13]

Finally, though we've warned about the dangers of overriding managers who say synergy doesn't make sense, there *is* a time to do so. Start from the assumption that if cooperation between groups makes sense, managers will go for it, but also pay attention to why a manager or group is against it. There is room for a little healthy doubt with every set of assumptions, and sometimes those reluctant managers are wrong.

Goold and Campbell give an example of a German subsidiary of a multinational company that was protective of one of its products. Put simply, they didn't want to share. The German managers feared their French and Italian colleagues wouldn't position it as a premium product and would undermine price levels throughout Europe, hurting the fabulous profits the Germans were seeing in their market. "The standoff was resolved only when corporate executives walked the German managers through the cost-benefit calculations step by step and guaranteed that prices would be kept above a certain minimum in all countries."[14] Another situation in which it would be appropriate to step in arises when the managers *are* letting competition and their own need to have an edge affect their willingness to work together. Assume that this is the exception, not the rule, but don't overlook it when it happens. You could miss out on important synergy opportunities.

■ ■ ■

Purpose is a strong, wonderful word, one that connotes clarity, strength, and discipline of thought. No leader can operate well without that clarity. Yet the process of holding on to that purpose, keeping it free of distractions, is complex. It involves a delicate balancing act. Synergy and competition, for instance, can be great assets to a company. Sometimes synergy does create efficiency and opportunity; sometimes competition does result in stronger, more engaged employees. It's when these ideas are taken too far—when they are pursued for their own sake without proper attention to the circumstances and realistic outcomes—that trouble erupts, and purpose is lost. A great leader will strike this balance correctly, while keeping purpose paramount.

KEY TAKEAWAYS

Lessons Learned from Mistakes

- Competition is rampant in our culture, yet in a work environment it can backfire easily, creating an environment of distrust and thwarting synergy efforts.
- Favoritism—whether real or perceived—causes distraction, with workers focused on unfairness and office politics instead of on the company's goals.
- The wrong person in the job causes the team as a whole to suffer—you would not put a center fielder in the pitcher's mound, and you should not have a talented salesperson filling a human resources job just because she is talented.
- Synergy goes awry when a leader wants it so badly that he is not aware of his own biases.

Successful Navigation

- Encourage co-opetition, whereby employees work together for mutual benefit and compete in a way in which everyone has something to gain and the competition serves the purpose of the business.
- Understand that you probably do favor certain employees. Be aware of both your real biases and your perceived favoritism, and fight against the inclination by opening up tasks and mixing up assignments, all with a spirit of openness about your thought processes.
- Leverage all your workers' skills and also account for their weaknesses. The company will benefit from each worker's being in the right role, and the workers will feel they are able to bring their talents to the fore.
- Put the brakes on synergy efforts, going forward only after you have discerned the basis of any resistance and have genuine buy-in, someone with the skills to bring the project to fruition, and a clear, disaggregated list of objectives.

PART THREE

Personality Issues

EIGHT

Standing in the Way

Hoarding Power and Responsibility

Figuratively, her eyes are burning a hole in the back of his head. Literally, he can feel the warmth of her breath on the nape of his neck. It's an all-too-familiar scenario. She is standing over her subordinate's shoulder, again, watching every move he makes. She can't trust him with any semblance of responsibility. She can't trust anyone. She is so consumed with controlling everything that not only does she ineffectively allocate her own time, but she also gets in the way of her employees. She hoards everything—information, authority, power, control, credit—to such an extreme that her employees become dependent on her for everything. Not only are they stripped of the ability to effectively do their own jobs, but they will never have the chance to develop new skills or take on additional responsibilities.

Although terms like "control freak" and "micromanager" are often associated with these types of behaviors, the problem goes much deeper. As we will discuss in this chapter, hoarding is the inability to let go of the big things—power and authority—in addition to being consumed with many of the little things, like meaningless details. In Chapter Nine we will talk about disengaged leaders. What we talk about in this chapter is the exact opposite. Whereas disengaged leaders suffer from their inability to actively manage, with hoarders, the pendulum has swung too far in the other direction. They need to be in charge of everything, so they overmanage.

Our research has shown that hoarding is a common problem among ineffective leaders. According to responses from our survey, almost 45 percent of managers admitted they were guilty of hoarding. Not only did we find this in our large study of executives, but anecdotally it was a common theme in our interviews with some of industries' most successful leaders. Priceline.com's Jeff Hoffman told us he had seen many overcontrolling managers throughout his career. Similarly, other studies have found that the number of leaders who overcontrol has reached alarming proportions. According to Harry Chambers—author of *My Way or the Highway: The Micromanagement Survival Guide*—71 percent of workers report themselves victims of a controlling work environment. In another recent study, by Hurley and Ryman, a survey of 300 managers illustrated that approximately 30 percent of them were too controlling.[1] And yet another study by Bernthal and Wellins, surveying 1,500 leaders, identified overcontrolling as one of the most common causes of leadership failure.[2] It's a big deal.

When hoarders move up the chain to upper-level leadership positions without resolving their issues, they end up "managing" (and overmanaging, at that) instead of leading. Motivational speaker and author Estienne de Beer puts it this way: "The dilemma in today's corporate world is that many teams are totally overmanaged and completely under-led."[3]

The result is almost always failure. Consider the hoarding nature of Jill Barad, former CEO of Mattel. Barad worked her way up the corporate ladder, on the way taking the Barbie line from $235 million to $1.5 billion. Employees described her as obsessed. She had a reputation for her "overweening attention to detail, monitoring doll designs down to minor detail on the faces." Yet she was proud of her controlling nature, stating that "what I do in my job, first and foremost, is protect Barbie."[4]

In her role as a product manager, Barad's style often sped up the process. But once she became CEO, her hoarding nature became toxic. Insiders said she was seen as meddlesome. "It is a blatant problem. Why is the chairman looking at every design concept?" a former executive lamented.[5] Barad was described as obsessed over the slightest details of "her" toys while working at Mattel. Insiders said she had severe problems delegating authority to subordinates.[6] These tactics earned her a reputation of viciousness.[7]

Barad's reputation wasn't the only casualty—Mattel itself suffered from Barad's inability to delegate any responsibilities to her employees. Her management style created unnecessary work for her vice presidents, as they would scurry to anticipate every possible reaction she might have. James A. Eskridge, Barad's direct report, coined the term "Jill Factor," referring to her management style. He explained Barad's ability to instigate "learned powerlessness,"[8] a common trait of hoarding leaders, wherein they condition perfectly capable staff members to behave as helpless children.

Barad's hoarding tendencies ultimately led to her demise. In 1997 she'd become the first female CEO of a Fortune 500 company. By the beginning of 2000 she was forced to resign.[9]

It was Andrew Carnegie who said, "No man will make a great leader who wants to do it all himself, or to get all the credit for doing it." It never ends well, yet it's incredibly common. In this chapter we talk about what hoarding is in leadership terms, why Barad and so many other leaders make the mistake of hoarding, what its consequences are, and how to avoid it.

THE WHAT AND WHY OF HOARDING

Control freaks and micromanagers demonstrate a flawed leadership style, but these behaviors alone do not a hoarder make. Control freaks and many micromanagers are at one end of the continuum, sweating the small stuff, whereas hoarders sweat the small stuff *and* can't let go of the big stuff. In other words, you can be a micromanager or control freak without being a hoarder, but if you're a hoarder, chances are excellent that you are also a micromanager and control freak.

Micromanagement, according to the *Merriam-Webster Dictionary,* is "manage[ment] especially with excessive control or attention on details." Often these details are minor, and horror stories about micromanagement abound. A micromanager's obsession with the small stuff can become extreme, leading to his entanglement in the most minute details. The result is inefficiency and disgruntled workers.

The control freak is a close cousin to the micromanager. Many leaders feel that to be effective, they must be in "control" of their employees. Intimately connected with day-to-day activities, they perceive themselves as always putting out fires, of never having time to step back to take a strategic look. And although this may be true, these constraints are largely self-imposed. They insist that day-to-day decisions come through them. Expenditures under $10 must be approved, subordinates' emails vetted—in extreme cases, these leaders may even monitor employees' use of the company bathroom. The control freak wants to know what every employee is doing, all of the time.

Put these traits of obsessive control together, add some ego, and raise the stakes, and you've got the hoarder—the leader who oversees every little thing and takes credit for everything, big or small. The leader who runs an organization as its gatekeeper, security guard, and master puppeteer.

The nightmare stories spawned by hoarding behavior are endless. Phill Benson, a former employee at a large IT consulting organization in Central Florida, told us a few about a previous boss. His supervisor needed everything documented on a continuous basis. Nothing was considered acceptable unless there was a report detailing everything, most of it meaningless data that not only wasted the time of his supervisor to read but also wasted Benson's time to have to produce. Benson recollects, "Whenever I had to turn in receipts from business trips, not only would I have to produce the itemized receipts, but I would have to write out report after report, detailing where I ate, why I ate there, who I was eating with and what we were talking about, even for receipts less than $5.00."

The worst horror story we heard came from Kevin Weingarten, a former employee of a large Boston-based consulting firm. "Every time I prepared a report for a client, before the report went out, my supervisor would 'take a crack at it.' There were so many changes to my documents that, literally, the comments in track changes [Microsoft Word] were longer than the report itself," he said. "There was not a single sentence that remained intact." Eventually, Weingarten's old boss was fired for poor management, and Weingarten flourished in the new environment. "When my new leader came in, it was like a weight had been lifted off of my shoulders," recalls Weingarten. "All of a sudden I was productive, my reports were seen as being high quality, and clients were happy." Instead of sticking himself in the middle of every client relationship and getting hung up on controlling the smallest of details, Weingarten's new leader let his subordinates do their jobs.

We can see these behaviors in everyday life, too, not just in the professional world. Consider the parent who does all of her child's homework. Although the intent is not to control, the parent can't let go. She knows that she is better at third-grade math than her child is, and she wants her child to get good grades for homework. So she does the work for her child, and the child gets good grades. As this child gets older and starts to apply for jobs, guess who writes the cover letters?

The urge to hoard often stems from arrogance. A hoarding manager may believe "No one has the skills necessary to do a good job. I am more talented, so I need to do all of the work for them if we are ever going to succeed as a company." Hoarding managers usually have an inflated perception of themselves and think very little of others. Because ultimate responsibility was given to the leader, he justifies the overuse of control to ensure that the job will be done correctly.

George Ruebenson, retired president at Allstate, believes a main reason managers hoard decision-making power is to justify their own existence. He has seen managers take the position that it is necessary to hoard "so that you are not replaceable." He went on to say that often hoarding can make an ineffective manager "feel a false sense of importance." The more she controls, she thinks, the more difficult it will be to replace her. But Ruebenson also warned of the feeling that hoarding engenders in your employees: "Why don't you think we can handle this on our own?"

If a hoarder is concerned about justifying her own existence, she may not want her subordinates to get more recognition than she herself does; she may control the situation to make sure that she receives credit for successes yet manages to avoid blame for failures. (We will talk about this specific attribute in more detail in the next chapter.)

Ironically, many leaders engage in hoarding to *avoid* mistakes. Remember when we talked about perfectionism in the first chapter? Perfectionism is not only a leading reason why leaders don't learn from their mistakes; it is also a major driver of hoarding. When the drive for perfectionism becomes too powerful, the desire to succeed is overshadowed by the fear of making mistakes. Managers don't want to be seen as incompetent or ineffective. It happens all the time in football: a team builds up a sizeable lead for the first three quarters of the game by doing the right things, only to lose the game in the fourth quarter because the team stopped doing what made them effective and started playing to *not lose*, rather than playing to win. The same thing is true with hoarders who suffer from perfectionism. They feel an innate need to control all decisions, transforming their purpose to "playing to not lose" rather than "playing to win." It is the hoarding, and everything that flows from it, that ultimately leads to their demise.

CONSEQUENCES OF HOARDING

When a leader hoards power and control, the impact can be significant, not only on the leader and his subordinates, but also on his organization as a whole. Employees want to be treated with respect and integrity; they want to be trusted, and they want the opportunity to grow. Consequently, when working for a hoarding leader, high-performing employees who can leave the dysfunctional environment will usually set out to find better working conditions. The employees who don't have the opportunity to find another job—usually those with average and weaker performance—end up staying. The fact that these employees are weaker performers, combined with having a boss who demeans and controls them, creates a demoralizing environment in which they eventually lose hope. Ironically, the fact that high performers leave and weaker performers stay only reinforces the hoarder's need to control power and decision making. It is a negative cycle, in which hoarding creates a weaker workforce and a weaker workforce justifies the hoarder's behaviors.

The costs to the organization are dramatic. Nearly one-third of employees that have worked for a micromanaging supervisor end up leaving the company.[10] Not only are turnover costs often significant, but long-term quality of the workforce is jeopardized, resulting in lower productivity. Moreover, when a leader hoards, he is so busy trying to control everything that he does not have the time to step back and actually lead his people. The company suffers as a result.

Workers know when they are not trusted. They lose confidence and self-esteem, and they do not have the opportunity to learn and develop. The organization may eventually see victims of hoarders as incompetent, when the truth is they could thrive in a healthy environment. Eventually the employees become disengaged and unmotivated. In the end, disengaged employees give their time to the organization but not their effort or enthusiasm. They lose all desire to take on responsibility, risk, and creativity. The workforce becomes a group of aimlessly wandering drifters, devoid of passion or hope. Employees no longer make suggestions or share ideas. They are unwilling to make sacrifices (for example, working harder), but instead aim for the lowest acceptable level of productivity to keep their jobs. And, to varying degrees, hoarding managers can treat their employees in such a demeaning way that it significantly affects the employees' emotional and physical health.

Effective leaders learn that they must have faith in their subordinates. In the absence of this faith, they would never delegate anything. Not only will a work environment without trust create inefficiencies, but subordinates will never have the chance to gain the skills necessary to be leaders themselves. Consumer advocate Ralph Nader observed, "I start with the premise that the function of leadership is to produce more leaders, not more followers."[11] Leaders who hoard thwart the opportunity to develop future leaders, and they don't see the development of others as part of their job at all.

Hoarding and the Power of Expectation

Have you ever watched a professional golfer before he hits the ball? He stands behind the ball, looking toward his target. Although it may seem like he is staring off into space, he is actually visualizing the shot he wants to hit—he is creating an expectation to succeed. Does this guarantee that he will hit the perfect shot? No. But a substantial amount of research shows that it will improve his chances of success.

There is tremendous power in expectation. The "Pygmalion effect" demonstrates how expectation is closely linked to behavior.

It has been identified in assessing the degree to which teachers' expectations influence students' performance in the classroom.[12] In a study conducted by Rosenthal and Jacobson in a public elementary school, it was found that when faculty expected students to perform poorly, students did perform poorly. But when faculty valued their students and expected them to succeed, students' performance improved. The research was able to demonstrate that we actually do live up to others' expectations, whether they are positive or negative. The same thing is true with leadership in business. When you expect others to act in a certain way, they are more likely to exhibit the expected behavior. For example, as a leader, if you expect others to succeed, your expectations will increase the likelihood that they will succeed. Conversely, if you expect your employees to fail, the likelihood of failure will increase. When a leader hoards and then expects his subordinates to be dependent on him, it increases the likelihood that they will need him in order to complete a task. When a leader sets his employees up to fail if they try to make decisions on their own, they may start believing that they need him to hoard power in order to succeed. He appears to be the hero, saving his employees from imminent doom, when his behaviors are actually responsible for the failure.

Sometimes a hoarder will try to empower his people, only to use the opportunity to justify that his role as a leader is to control. For example, a hoarder may delegate a task to his employee: preparation of a proposal for a customer. If the hoarder expects the employee to fail at this, the most likely outcome is that he *will* fail. When the employee tries to prepare the proposal on his own, subconsciously he knows that no matter how hard he works on the proposal, it will not be good enough for his boss. So inevitably he turns to his boss for help along the way. The boss now feels justified to hoard. His employees need him. Is that such a bad thing? More often than not, as we are seeing, the answer is *yes*.

Hoarders' Long Tails

Worse yet, not only does hoarding perpetuate hoarding, but a leader who cannot give up control is also setting a bad example for younger leaders. His subordinates are more likely to follow in his footsteps and do the same thing when they get a chance to lead. As Jim Owens told us in Chapter Two, "leadership has a long tail." Because leadership is learned, employees may have a higher propensity to think, "Well, my boss used to do everything for us so that we wouldn't fail, so I must do the same thing so my subordinates don't fail." And the pattern repeats itself.

In their research, referenced earlier in this chapter, Hurley and Ryman interviewed managers and their subordinates about their experiences when working in a highly controlled environment. One subordinate offered this explanation of an offending manager: "I don't think he saw himself this way, but his style of leadership devalued the people around him. We never really felt like he trusted us." The subordinate continued, "As a result, there was little or no creativity and no one felt empowered or fulfilled."

Clearly, lack of trust and overcontrol were big problems for this leader. But note the first sentence of the quote: "I don't think he saw himself this way . . ." Often hoarders don't realize they are hoarding. They actually believe they are good leaders, doing the right and necessary things. It is hard for them to see themselves accurately—and even harder to accept their own shortcomings.

ARE YOU A HOARDER?

About one in three managers is overly controlling. When you are in your next meeting, look at the leader on your left. Now look at the one on your right. Now do the math. Odds are, one of you is a hoarder. Is it you? Before you answer, here's the catch: most hoarders sincerely believe that they are doing the necessary and right things in order to succeed, not only for themselves, but also for their employees. So you can't necessarily trust your gut answer to the hoarder question. Here are some signs and symptoms that may indicate that *you* are hoarding.

Low Tolerance for Ambiguity

How comfortable are you with uncertainty and ambiguity? Some leaders are fine with uncertainty, and some even enjoy uncertainty because it "makes things interesting." However, most hoarding leaders are not, by nature, comfortable with uncertainty. They do whatever they can to minimize uncertainty in an attempt to manage risk. Hoarders are creatures of habit. They strive for predictability.

Interestingly, what is going on inside the head of a hoarder is counterintuitive to how he appears on the outside. On the inside, hoarders are often anxious and fearful of uncertainty. On the outside, they try to minimize this anxiety by controlling as much as they possibly can. The only way they can feel safe is by minimizing ambiguity.

Focused on the Trees and on Putting Out Fires

This heading may sound like a job description for a park ranger, but this dual focus is actually a subtle indicator of hoarding. Do you find yourself immersed in details, overly concerned with the minutiae, and less concerned with the big picture? Hoarders are more comfortable studying the trees, or even the pattern of the bark on a particular tree, than stepping back and seeing the entire forest. Looking at the forest can be scary to a hoarder. Why? Going back to what we learned in Chapter Four, analyzing the forest—the big picture—means uncertainty and ambiguity. Focusing on a particular tree feels much safer and more manageable. So in business, a hoarder will tend to focus his attention on day-to-day decisions rather than big-picture strategic decisions.

Do you feel too busy putting out fires to step back and think strategically? Then you have to ask yourself, are you always putting out fires because of the nature of your job, or are you focusing on the fires to avoid having to think big? This is a difficult question to answer, but it is well worth your time to think about it.

Confusing Authority with Ability

It is often necessary for a leader to provide detailed instructions for subordinates, especially on critically important projects for which employees don't have much experience. This is good, healthy leadership. To diagnose hoarding, look instead at smaller, repetitive issues. Instead of giving general instructions for these issues, hoarders continue giving detailed instructions. Does this sound familiar?

As we have discussed in earlier chapters, often the "why" is more telling than the "what." The reason a hoarder does these things is more important than the behaviors themselves. There are some circumstances in which it is acceptable to control decision making. If your employees are working at jobs for which they lack the knowledge, skills, or ability to do a good job, then by all means consider taking more control. Or if you have a disgruntled worker, he may need to be watched carefully. Exercising control in these circumstances does not make you a hoarder.

In contrast, the reason hoarders control decision making is that they cannot trust anyone to do the right thing. Ever. They don't believe in their employees. They may have developed this state of mind for several reasons, including past experience, misperceptions of employees' actual abilities, lack of confidence in their teams, and, in some cases, even paranoia. The result? They believe that the only way to get something done is either by doing it themselves or by tightening the reins on their employees.

It can be even worse. Perhaps you think you are a good leader, and you delegate decision making to your subordinates, but you require them to always consult with you (that is, depend on you) on minor issues, which strips them of any actual authority over the decision-making process. Moreover, you tend to get irritated when employees do not consult you, even when they could make the decisions on their own. Or you assign decisions to your employees, and before any decisions can be made, you step in to "save the day" and make the decision for them.

If you feel that you need to always exercise your authority because you believe you have to in order to get a task completed correctly, you have one of two problems. Either you are really bad at making effective hiring decisions, and you hire only incompetent people, or you are a hoarder.

"My Way or the Highway" Thinking

Does everything need to be done your way? Do you always have to be right? Do you feel you are the only one with enough skill to actually make decisions? If you are a hoarder, you may have difficulty accurately answering these questions; admitting that you are sometimes wrong means you are not always correct. Another tough one, indeed.

It is human nature to feel that your way is the best way. Whether we are giving someone advice on how to drive a car or how to drive a golf ball, we all like to think that our opinions not only matter but are correct. Otherwise, why would we share them?

Author Sydney Finkelstein, one of the foremost experts on CEO failure, argues that an excess of "my way or the highway" attitude is a key contributor to overcontrolling behavior. Symptoms that your confidence has gone too far include self-perceptions like these:

- If I believe in myself, you should too.
- Don't worry about anything, because I already know all of the answers.
- I don't need anyone else.[13]

Former CEO of Rubbermaid Wolfgang Schmitt fell into virtually all of these categories. According to Finkelstein, Schmitt was particularly fond of showing off his ability to quickly work through challenging problems. One of his former managers recalls sarcastically, "Wolf knows everything about everything." Because Schmitt felt that he knew better than everyone else, he made almost all of the company's key decisions unilaterally. The unfortunate result: he took Rubbermaid from being one of *Fortune*'s most admired companies in 1993 to being bought out by Newell just a few years later.

Too Much Focus on Process

How much useless documentation is cluttering your inbox? Hoarders will request reports that report on how reports are being reported! Hoarders want documentation on virtually everything, creating an environment one of our interviewees described as "report-a-palooza." Rather than focusing on performance, hoarders will focus on unproductive detail. Often they get blindsided by something they should have seen—and could have seen, if only they had lifted their heads up for a second.

Focusing only on process and not outcomes often results in delayed or poor decisions, redirects behaviors away from accomplishing goals, and impoverishes the flow of appropriate information among employees and even customers. Hoarders will make these sacrifices, though, in order to maintain "proper" control.

STOP MANAGING AND START LEADING: OVERCOMING THE URGE TO HOARD

At the risk of sounding like we're writing a mindfulness manual, it must be said that leadership is a fluid journey. We never "complete" the journey, and we are always learning. However, it is important to constantly reflect on how the journey is going and on what we can do to enhance the learning process.

In this chapter we have focused on the ill effects of hoarding. We know hoarding is detrimental to the leader, to subordinates, and to the organization. We know the causes of hoarding, as well. In this final section of the chapter, we focus first on how to transition from being a hoarding manager to being an effective leader. Second, we look in depth at the role of empowering employees as a means to help you either stop hoarding or avoid hoarding in the first place.

Lessons for the Hoarding Manager
So you are among the one in three managers who hoards. You have seen why this is bad, and you want to change. The good news is that as far as leadership mistakes go, hoarding is a relatively easy fix. You *can* transition from hoarding manager to effective leader. Here's how.

Work on Building Trust
For a hoarding manager, the best way to build healthier relationships with your employees is usually the most direct. Meet with them face-to-face and let them know you are serious about changing your ways. You may have to make numerous attempts before they trust you. Remember, they may have difficulty trusting you because you have had difficulty trusting them. Finally, you need to acknowledge to them that your leadership approach has had negative consequences, and you need to be willing to admit you were wrong. This will accomplish much more than you may expect in terms of building trust.

Get the Hard Facts
Once you have established a rapport with your employees, ask for their help—a hard task if you're a hoarder, as it's counterintuitive

to what you have done in the past. Ask employees to call you out every time you exhibit hoarding behaviors. Not only will this give you valuable feedback, but it will also enhance your relationship with employees. Rather than stripping them of power and authority, the simple fact that you are asking them to call you out when you hoard gives them a sense of power. Once you have some data, focus on analyzing it in these three key areas:

- When is the hoarding most likely to occur? Is it at the initial rollout of a project, or does hoarding become more apparent near the end of a project, when deadlines increase levels of stress?
- Why are you hoarding? Go back to the causes and signs section of this chapter and find out the root cause or causes behind your hoarding.
- What are the catalysts that lead to hoarding? Are big projects the most likely suspects when you hoard? Or is it the minute details? Do you hoard only in certain circumstances or all the time?

Communicate Like a Coach, Not a Boss

To start changing your behavior, you first must acknowledge and accept that things are going to have to change in several areas—namely, you will need to prioritize higher expectations, increased trust, and improved communications. It can help to view your role as that of an encouraging coach.

First and foremost, expect more from your subordinates. Encourage them to succeed. Remember the Pygmalion effect we discussed earlier in the chapter? It works both ways! If you start setting higher expectations for your employees *and* you trust them, you should see an improvement in their performance. Remember that positive expectations have a positive impact on performance.

Second, make a concerted effort to communicate better. The better you communicate, the less intense the feeling that you have to hoard. Increase the amount of one-on-one feedback with your employees as well as group communications. When providing feedback to employees, remain positive, complimenting them whenever possible while being truthful (you don't want to fall into the trap of dysfunctional harmony described in Chapter Six). If you think of yourself as a coach rather than a boss, the tenor of all these conversations will change.

Another communication tool that can improve your relationships with subordinates is to ask questions—not for the sake of trying to catch errors, but rather to have the opportunity to listen. Good leaders are great listeners. Hoarders are poor listeners. Work on your listening skills. And when employees offer input, even if you may not like it, accept what they are saying. Although these suggestions may seem like common sense (and they are), they are counterintuitive for many hoarders.

Using Empowerment to Avoid Hoarding

Whether you are a legitimate hoarder or simply a leader who doesn't want to ever fall into that trap, empowering your employees is an invaluable tool. It allows you to pay attention to what really counts. Trying to hoard power wastes time and energy; empowering your people saves time. But this is not necessarily so at first—think of empowerment like an investment. Up front, it may actually cost you more time, as well as expose your team to more problems, but in the long run, the dividends can be great. For example, if you spend the majority of your time preparing reports that a subordinate could put together, it may take a considerable amount of time up front to train the subordinate to take over. However, the investment will pay off in the long run, not only in terms of saving you time, but also in terms of developing your people.

Remind yourself that delegating responsibility and empowering your people will increase their morale, their sense of worth, and ultimately their productivity. Not only will it increase their satisfaction, but they will ultimately take on a sense of ownership and pride. They will know you trust them, and trust is an invaluable gift that a leader can give her subordinates and her company.

To benefit from empowerment, you need to consider three basic issues: when, who, and how.

When is the right time to empower your employees? The first assessment you need to make is whether it makes sense, strategically, to delegate the task. When you initially empower someone to take on new responsibility, you need to consider the potential for failure in the short term. If the venture fails in the short term, can you recover?

Similarly, consider timelines. It will usually take your subordinate longer the first few times to complete the task, as he is slowly moving along the learning curve. Is there time to give him the knowledge, skills, and abilities to effectively do the job? Timing is critical. If there are tight timelines for the project and you decide to start delegating, setting up an employee to fail may be worse than doing nothing at all. However, when the task can help an employee to grow by developing new skills, that's an argument in favor of delegating.

The next consideration is *to whom* do you give the new responsibilities? Basic logic would of course dictate that you pick the right people, the ones who already possess the necessary skills and need the least supervision. Additionally, though, those who have a strong sense of independence may be the most appropriate, as well as those with a strong need for achievement. Although this may seem very basic, for a hoarder it may seem foreign. It also makes logical sense to avoid those employees who will just go through the motions—the ones who look for the minimum level of acceptable performance necessary to get by. Finally, be considerate of people's workload. Are your candidates already maxed out, or do they have some flexibility? There is an art to helping them maintain balance between emptying out their current inbox and taking on new projects and responsibilities. Finally, as you now know after reading Chapter Seven, don't play favorites, as that will lead to resentment from the rest of your team.

Then there's the question of *how* you empower you employees. The way you frame empowerment can make or break how effectively it works. At one end of the spectrum, employees can view empowerment and delegation of responsibility as a burden. At the other end of the spectrum, they can view it as an opportunity for growth. Make sure that when you delegate, the person takes on the new responsibility with a sense of pride and satisfaction, rather than having a sense of anger or feeling that you are taking advantage of her. There are a few general rules to follow to ensure a positive experience.

First, stress that this is an opportunity for growth and show your subordinate how it may benefit her career if she performs well on her new task. Second, never delegate any task you wouldn't be willing to do yourself. If your efforts at empowerment are perceived as "dumping," the whole concept of empowerment fails. Third, let the person know exactly why you are choosing her for the job. Take this as an opportunity to build her self-esteem.

Finally, if you have identified yourself as a hoarder, once you have delegated you will need to let go. This will be hard, but fight the urge to look over the shoulder of the person you delegated to. If he needs help, let him come to you. If you fall back into old habits, the whole exercise of empowerment will not only fail for now, but you may make it difficult, if not impossible, to pursue it in the future.

A final element of empowering your people is effectively following up. When your employees succeed in completing a new task, share the success. Give credit where credit is due. Again, for a hoarder this is difficult. In the past you may have held on to all of the credit, but sharing credit and rewards will go a long way to support effective empowerment. It is a paradigm shift: from managing to leading, from directing to partnering.

When thinking about empowerment as a way to overcome hoarding, consider Heifer International. The entire platform of the organization is based on the concept of empowerment. It is one of the largest not-for-profit organizations in the world, at times raising more money than any other international not-for-profit in the U.S. The organization's goal is to work with communities around the world to end hunger and poverty—and to do it through empowerment. Rather than giving food to those in need, they provide live animals—such as cows and goats, chickens and bees—for the recipients to raise and care for. These animals can produce food for many years. Heifer actually empowers communities in need to provide for themselves.

Not surprisingly, Jo Luck, the former CEO of Heifer, is a huge advocate of empowerment. Not only was Heifer based on the foundation of empowerment, but so was Jo Luck's leadership style—whether she was out in the field, empowering a small community to feed itself in the middle of a third-world country, or empowering her own team back in the United States. In our interview with her, she stated that empowerment is one of the most important foundations for effective leadership. Her main point (which echoes the Ralph Nader quote earlier in this chapter): "Our most important role as leaders is to develop future leaders, and the best way to do that is through participation and empowerment."

KEY TAKEAWAYS

Lessons Learned from Mistakes

- Hoarding power and control takes a leader's attention away from important issues and focuses it on less important details.
- Leaders hoard power for many reasons, ranging from perfectionism and other personality issues to a fundamentally flawed perception of his employees.

- When you hoard, you will lose your best employees, and the remaining employees will become disengaged.
- Hoarding displays a lack of trust in your employees' ability, and this becomes a self-fulfilling prophecy (the less you trust them, the less able they become).

Successful Navigation
- Assess your behavior to determine whether you are hoarding. If you are, assess the damage. Go directly to your people to find out how bad it really is.
- Commit publicly to making a change. Then, to realize your good intentions, you must create a safe environment. Let go; start trusting.
- Use effective empowerment to build a sense of trust and respect with your employees. Delegating important tasks has benefits at many levels, and it should be regarded as an investment in future productivity.

NINE

Living Outside the Storm
The Destructive Path of Disengagement

If you take the subway or bus to work, your commute is one filled with sights, smells, and face-to-face interactions with people and their energy, be that energy good or bad. If, on the other hand, you commute to work in your car, your experience of the journey is entirely different. You probably spend that time listening to the radio, talking on your phone (in a hands-free, law-abiding manner, of course), and relating to other drivers only in the sense that you're annoyed with them when they won't let you merge. Disengagement happens to all of us—it's human. Even when we're on the bus, we often want to be able to hide in a book or in the music on our iPods. But disengagement becomes problematic in a leadership situation.

We love to pounce on our political leaders for seeming disengaged. In 1992, President George H. W. Bush famously marveled at supermarket scanners, for instance, and the public cried "We've used scanners for years—who's doing *your* shopping?" When President Obama was campaigning in Iowa, he was harshly criticized for asking the price of arugula at Whole Foods. "Arugula! Whole Foods! Iowa? Disconnected!" *Mother Jones* points out that the price of milk and bread is one of reporters' favorite questions for political candidates, to such a degree that "every presidential candidate should be given a commodities rundown with their morning briefing."[1] Disengagement from the "everyman" has become such a common campaign critique that candidates often exert enormous effort to show that they *are* engaged—drinking beer with voters, bowling, whatever it takes to show that even though, yes, they are very powerful, they are really just like you. Can you imagine these antics from well-known business leaders— Amazon's Jeff Bezos pulling up a chair in your cubicle and saying, "Hey, wanna grab a beer after work? Happy hour at Beakers means $2 beers!"?

Grabbing beers with a Bezos-like boss might seem absurd, but there's something in that image that's worth thinking about. Disengaged leaders are those who never get out of their cars, metaphorically speaking. Whether at the helm of a state government or of a small business, disengaged leaders are those who have become insulated and self-consumed—sometimes over a long period of time—and have removed themselves from the realms of some or all of their key stakeholders. They are aloof—and sometimes completely checked out. Their finger isn't on the pulse of their company or the marketplace anymore; in fact, sometimes they're not even trying to find that pulse. What they see and what actually *is* are often divorced from one another, and the disconnect leads to poor morale among their employees, at best, and illegal activity, at worst. Disengaged leaders may crave being insulated because they believe it is a sign of their status, but they may just be burned out or in the wrong job for their skills, and their position has allowed them to get away with coasting.

This chapter looks at the disengaged leader—with burnouts at one end of the scale and celebrity leaders at the other. We examine the path from engaged manager to "retired without retiring," explore the disconnected world of the celebrity leader, describe how disengaged leadership is detrimental to a company, and offer suggestions for making sure a title on the doorplate doesn't turn into a closed door.

MISFIT AND BURNOUT LEADERS

It's important to note that not all leaders who become detached are guilty of being greedy, status-hungry individuals. There are much more innocent, and arguably much more common paths to disconnection, and those paths involve misfit and burnout.

Jared Heyman is an example of a misfit—that is, someone who found himself in the wrong job, even though he put himself there. Heyman launched Infosurv when he was only twenty years old, and he built it into a $2.1 million company. He worked hard throughout his twenties, and by the time he reached thirty-two, he was ready for the free-wheeling experiences he'd missed out on in his earlier years. He left the company in the hands of a trusted manager and hit the road, sea, and skies—traveling the world on a year-long sabbatical. As it turned out, he wasn't missed terribly by his employees. According to Carl Fusco, whom Heyman had left in command, Heyman's management style involved retreating to his office to work behind a closed door, leaving employees to wonder *what* exactly he was doing in there.[2]

Heyman suffered from burnout, obviously, but he was also in the wrong job. As we've mentioned in other chapters, in many cases the cause of a misfit is a person's stellar performance. He may be good at one thing, so he rises through the ranks until he's appointed for a job for which he may not be suited or may not even want. Or he started the company and along the way took on managerial responsibilities without stopping to consider whether he was suited for them. Heyman was a great creator but not necessarily a great manager. "I don't think I suck as a manager," he told *Inc.* magazine, but Heyman added that he's better in a figurehead role. He likes to do his thing on his own behind closed doors, and he figures others would like that as well. "I give someone a task, and I say, 'Here is the result I want—accomplish it how you see fit.'" Heyman's disengagement was particularly evident when he visited the office after nearly a year of travels and ate pizza with the staff. One senior staff member described Heyman as detached. Though he was eager to share details about his trip, the staff member said, Heyman didn't ask the staff how *they'd* been during his absence. "Look, none of us survive if the staff isn't doing a good job . . ." the staff member said. "You want to take good care of them."[3]

To be clear, Heyman is not a villain. He is smart and accomplished, and as the person who took the risk and worked hard for the company for so long, he was certainly entitled to some time off. But his disengagement—both before the sabbatical and on his return—was not serving the company, nor was he terribly happy at Infosurv.

Companies can outgrow their leaders, too—particularly when the leader suffers from burnout. For an example of a disengaged leader whose company outpaced him, we look at a founder of a retailer in Des Moines; we'll call him Jack Dunn. Dunn started the company right out of college and built it into a highly profitable organization over two decades. He had always been the "idea guy" and was known for his high energy, creativity, and outsized personality. As the company became more and more profitable, Dunn used his increased salary to improve his lifestyle. He traded his beat-up Dodge for a Lexus convertible. He started spending one month a year in California; the month soon became the entire summer. He would still call in, and his sign-off was still needed on most projects. Employees embraced his absences at first, knowing that in his leisure time he was much more apt to give his stamp of approval without its being a long, drawn-out process.

As the years passed, however, Dunn's absences became more problematic. His summers in California were still on the calendar, only he had started taking a month off in the winter, too, to go skiing. He didn't communicate critical information to staff in a timely way—say, if he happened to have scheduled a ski vacation after attending an important trade show—which handicapped his staff's effectiveness and lowered morale. Getting Dunn's sign-off became harder, not because he was exacting, but because he was rarely available. He also wasn't making the important deals necessary to move the business forward.

One year, when Dunn returned to the office after his California summer, he walked around the company's cubicles, excitedly telling everyone about his adventures learning to surf. The cubicle inhabitants, meanwhile, had spent the entire summer working long hours and feeling stressed out over the budget. Dunn was the founder, they knew, and it was his right to do what he wanted, but it was still demoralizing to hear how great his life was when his great life was causing them setbacks and frustration. He seemed insensitive and out of touch, and staff deeply resented his triumphant returns from long absences.

Though Dunn's company had been doing very well when his forays to California began, the economy had since changed, and the business began to struggle. There was a greater need for Dunn's presence and leadership in Des Moines—both to move new products along more efficiently and to calm frayed nerves. If he didn't want to be present, Dunn needed to step aside and appoint a leader in his place. Dunn did neither, maintaining his vacation schedule and his role as the company's copresident. It was no surprise to anyone, except possibly Dunn, that the company was forced to initiate layoffs.

Dunn finally did step away from the business, but it was three or four years after he'd stopped caring. He confessed to one departing employee that he'd grown completely bored by the work. Dunn's income and his status in the company gave him certain rights and privileges, and as he became more detached, he saw less and less of the realities of the marketplace and the complaints of his employees. Dunn is the perfect example of the leader who is "checked out" or "out to lunch," more familiar with the rhythms of the golf course than those of the office.

Executives like Dunn are easy to find, and they are not necessarily of retirement age. When a leader holds herself at a remove from others, when she closes her door as Heyman did or flies off to California as Dunn did, she misses out on important information necessary to running the company. Because Dunn was absent both physically and emotionally, he didn't hear about the obstacles his staff was running into with customers. He did not know his staff was working late nights and weekends, and that even so they remained concerned about their company's viability and their job security. He did not catch on to just how serious the morale problem was, and that turnover could become a serious problem. Leaving his company leaderless, Dunn also left his staff feeling overworked yet uninspired.

Companies like Dunn's are vulnerable to two problems. First, they fall behind in their industry because there is no one providing a vision or motivation to excel (beyond fear of layoffs—never an effective driver beyond the short term). Second, they become hunting grounds for other companies in search of talent. It is hard for productive workers to remain productive in an environment where they are underappreciated. When leaders detach from their people, they are creating a "farm system" or training camp for their competitors.

Though leaders like Heyman and Dunn create a world of problems for their staff, if given the choice, we'd still rather work for one of them than for the other type of disengaged leader: the celebrity.

CELEBRITY LEADERS

In our culture, celebrities are held at a remove from the masses; they are also often held to different standards of behavior. We are so accustomed to this remove that we even say complimentary things about celebrities who are "grounded," as if they should be commended for overcoming their greatness and acting normal. For better or for worse, a thick curtain separates us from them, whether that curtain is in the form of throngs of paparazzi, a private plane, or a VIP rope.

When we talk about celebrity *leadership* as a form of disengaged leadership, we do not necessarily refer to leaders who grace the pages of *Vanity Fair* and the screenplays of Aaron Sorkin. Rather, we are referring to individuals who have allowed that curtain or rope to come between themselves and everyone else— particularly employees, customers, and other stakeholders. You can be a well-known leader, even a famous leader, without exhibiting characteristics of disengagement. But it's awfully difficult.

Many of the behaviors celebrity leaders exhibit are a result of being self-absorbed—a leadership flaw we will detail more extensively in Chapter Ten. But there's an important distinction between a self-absorbed leader and a celebrity leader. The self-absorbed leader's goal, ultimately, is to help the *company*—he just has an overinflated idea of his role in that process. In contrast, the celebrity leader uses the company as a vehicle to help *himself*. His eyes are trained on the world outside of the company, not within it.

Another way to define celebrity leadership is by looking at its direct opposite: servant leadership. Servant leadership is the philosophy that a leader's primary purpose is to serve the interests of the people she leads. With celebrity leadership, a leader's primary purpose is to serve her own interests, sometimes at the *expense* of the people she leads. What those interests are varies from leader to leader. Sometimes the celebrity leader is interested in jetting around the world reinforcing her image; sometimes she's interested in doing very little at all.

On the television sitcom *30 Rock*, executive Jack Donaghy is a caricature of a celebrity leader. He is mortified when his old-school company is taken over by Kabletown, leading to the elimination of the building's gilded, exclusive executive dining room.

It's appalling to him that anyone can dine in what was always a hallowed space for the rich and powerful. Although it's fodder for humor, the dining room phenomenon is actually a very real symbol of a company's culture. In the White House, there's a dining room affectionately called "The White House" that is alternately open to upper-level staffers and their guests or not, depending on the management philosophy of the current administration. And for generations, General Motors had an almost mythical fourteenth floor. The habitat of the high-ranking and powerful, GM's fourteenth floor was graced with mahogany walls, electronically controlled glass doors, its own bathrooms, and its own dining room. Entry was granted only through an elaborate invitation system. Everything in the construction of the fourteenth floor was designed to insulate the company's leadership from everyone else.

GM's fourteenth floor is long gone, but leaders from all sectors still strive to create an aura of inaccessibility. Smithsonian Business Ventures hired one such executive, Gary Beer, to head its business unit. Beer came from the real (entertainment) celebrity world of Sundance Institute, and he brought that celebrity culture with him. He told some of his employees that he'd spent $30,000 in limousine charges over five years. These employees said he told them, "I don't do Yellow cabs."[4]

Beer's lavish spending marked his distance from everyone else at the Smithsonian, as did the fact that he wouldn't even take cabs, let alone public transportation. He also began a relationship with a direct subordinate, who during Beer's tenure became one of the highest-paid employees in the business unit. Beer's desire for the fourteenth floor—and all that privileges there implied—hurt the organization, alienated employees, impaired his judgment, and ultimately led to his ouster in 2007.

As easy as it is to shake our heads at Beer, the fact is, our culture encourages celebrity leaders. We love to read about larger-than-life personalities like Steve Jobs and Michael Eisner, or big, extravagant spenders like Donald Trump. We watch reality shows like *Undercover Boss*, in which a company's CEO joins the masses of hourly workers and engages in activities like making burritos and cleaning up trash. The show—a reality-TV version of Charles Dickens's *A Christmas Carol*—presumes to cut through the barrier caused by celebrity leadership, showing bosses the difficult life of poor Bob Cratchit. In reality, the show serves to shore up that barrier by making the CEO *better* known to the public. For all the boss's on-air comeuppance, there is little doubt that he is trying to make his name and image as public as possible. And we, the viewing public, can't get enough of it.

There are two sides to every story, so it must be acknowledged that there *are* some benefits to celebrity leadership. A celebrity leader can increase the stock price or company valuation. Remember bully Al Dunlap? He was a big name before Sunbeam put him in charge, and as soon as his appointment to the top spot was made public, Sunbeam's shares soared nearly 60 percent, to $18.63. Ironically, for a time his celebrity made the stock too expensive for many investors, even though selling the company was Dunlap's goal.[5] Celebrity leaders can also leverage their name to introduce new products or to attract talented people to their companies. When Hewlett-Packard was accused of becoming stale and irrelevant, its board thought that hiring flashy celebrity leader Carly Fiorina would give the company a rebirth and prove to critics that the company still mattered. The culture underlying Wall Street believes that the bigger the name, the greater the chances for a company's turnaround. Leaders are thus incentivized to *be* the big name, to foster an image of celebrity.

On the down side, the results of celebrity leaders are often dismal. Celebrity leadership tends to create a "yes man" culture, stifling the debates that should be happening to avoid falling into the dysfunctional harmony trap. Al Dunlap drove Sunbeam into the ground. Carly Fiorina was eventually forced to leave HP because she could not pull the company out of the doldrums, but not before she'd presided over thousands of layoffs and hurt the company's longstanding culture. Ironically, HP's board finally determined that they didn't really need a big-name CEO. What they really needed was a hands-on manager, one who spent more time dealing with the day-to-day grind and less time in front of the flash of cameras.

The Consequences of Celebrity Leadership

The celebrity leader is often less concerned with the interests of the company and more with his own interests. He doesn't hear about problems and concerns a leader needs to hear about. He doesn't inspire staff—in fact, he alienates them. Jim Collins, in his groundbreaking and bestselling *Good to Great,* which compared good and great companies, defined great companies as those that achieved an average cumulative stock return of at least three times the market over a fifteen-year period. Collins's research team found that "In over 2/3 of the comparison companies"—that is, companies that *didn't* outperform the market to such a degree— "we noted the presence of a gargantuan personal ego that contributed to the demise or continued mediocrity of the company. These leaders were ambitious for themselves . . . but they failed utterly in the task of creating an enduring great company."[6] For an example of just how bad the consequences can be, we need look no further than Hewlett-Packard under Carly Fiorina.

To be fair, HP was struggling before Fiorina took the CEO slot. The company, started by two engineers in 1937, had long espoused the HP Way, a cultural philosophy that valued societal contribution, teamwork, and exceptionalism. But HP was falling behind, struggling to make the changes necessary for the marketplace while still holding onto their cultural values. According to author Douglas Branson in *The Last Male Bastion,* "The engineering focus, the autonomy within the company, and the lack of marketing buzz ultimately became a source of stagnation. . . . In the late 1990s, insiders said that HP was 'sick and endangered,' 'suffocating.'"[7]

The charismatic Fiorina, an expert marketer, came in from the outside and made her presence known. She seemed to be everywhere at once, traveling around the world, signing up for prestigious speaking engagements, appearing on national television, and gracing magazine covers. *Fortune* named her the most powerful woman in business for five consecutive years. She certainly succeeded in generating buzz about HP, but the buzz led many to wonder whose brand she was building. Lew Platt, her predecessor as CEO, was bemused, saying, "[H]er celebrity style is strange to me. I'm of a different era." And a former executive from Lucent, the grounds from which Fiorina had come, said, "Carly Fiorina is truly focused on the success of Carly Fiorina, and of the organization she is leading. Which comes first, I'm not sure."

One of Fiorina's first acts was to turn eighty-seven separate divisions at HP into just four, a move that was impressive in its grandeur but ill-advised in its haste. (Much of her consolidation has since been undone.) She pushed to acquire the esteemed consulting company PricewaterhouseCoopers Consulting, and when the deal fell apart, she quickly turned her attention to the acquisition of Compaq Computer, a move that was highly contested and one that would require thousands of layoffs. The merger went through, and although HP did well immediately afterward, it performed below analysts' expectations again and again in its five years under "Armani Carly." According to Branson, "Her public persona, her travel, her speeches, and her overweening egoism, at first a novelty, had become a distraction."

Although her most objectively measurable mistakes involved low stock performance and her failure to revive HP, her management mistakes have received equal criticism. She refused to hire a COO to mind the store while she was out traveling. She icily told an interviewer who questioned her on the matter, "I'm running the company the way I think it should be run."[8] It appeared that her ambition did not allow her to see her limitations. And in her buy-in of *celebrity* culture, she failed to value *HP*'s culture. She disregarded the HP way, restructuring so that management became top-down. She closed office doors, and she closed off lines of communication that had always been open—indeed, openness had been a mainstay of HP's culture, one that had long empowered employees. Fiorina went further. In an act of insensitivity that makes Heyman and Dunn look like Santa Claus in comparison, Fiorina bought a personal jet and granted herself and her executives bonuses, even as eighteen thousand employees were dismissed. One employee who worked for HP from 1989 until 2005 wrote of Fiorina, "On the backs of employees, she lived a fairytale life while at HP."[9]

The saddest truth about Fiorina's stint at HP is that it ultimately worked out okay for *her*. She *was* ousted, but only after collecting a celebrity-sized severance package of $21 million. Her national presence set her up well to run for Congress, though she lost that race. The lasting consequences of Fiorina's celebrity leadership were inflicted on the employees of Compaq/HP, which are summed up curtly by Arianna Packard: "I know a little bit about Carly Fiorina, having watched her almost destroy the company my grandfather founded."[10]

Celebrity Leadership and Malfeasance

Once a celebrity leader has become disconnected from the company's needs, the consequences can be far more damaging than hurting morale or even costing jobs. In some cases, the celebrity leader insulates himself to such a degree that he loses touch not only with employees and other stakeholders, but also with wrong and right.

The authors of this book live in Illinois, so we have had a front-row seat for the drama of a man who is both celebrity and celebrity leader: Rod Blagojevich, our former governor and now a national joke. After his scandalous downfall he was most frequently mocked for his horrible hairstyle, Elvis imitations, and foray into reality television, but behind all of the buffoonery was a fascinating story of a leader who became so disengaged—from the people of Illinois and from reality—that when he was arrested he asked if it was a joke; not only did he seem to feel that his reign was impermeable, but he also seemed to genuinely believe he had done nothing unlawful. Though the evidence against him was strong enough to earn him a fourteen-year sentence—one of the stiffest penalties for corruption in a corruption-saddled state—he fought off admission of his guilt until his sentencing, and even so, more than likely he still doesn't comprehend his wrongdoing.

In the time between "Blago's" arrest and his trial, he often attested to feeling hurt and misunderstood when people expressed their dislike for him—even as evidence unfolded that he had told a children's hospital he was withholding money for them until he received a campaign contribution in return. The FBI had tape of him trying to sell the congressional seat of president-elect Barack Obama, yet Blagojevich blithely compared himself to Icarus, the character of Greek myth who flew too close to the sun. He fully believed he would be vindicated, and he did not rule out a political comeback. He was grilled on the charges against him during a panel on political ethics at Northwestern University, after which he said, "I mean, racketeering! Bribery! I can't believe they are directing those things at me!" In reference to the professors who grilled him, he replied, "These people are naïve, and they sit up in their ethical cloud. Some of these people just don't live in the real world."[11]

How is it possible for someone to draw the curtain between reality and myth to such a degree? After all, Blagojevich started out in the milieu of our opening "riding the subway" analogy. He grew up in a white ethnic neighborhood in Chicago. His father worked at a steel plant; his mother took tickets for the Chicago Transit Authority. Blagojevich worked his way through college, and a friend from that time said that Blagojevich "would make it clear that he didn't want to blend in fully with us preppies in the upper middle class, with our khakis and button-down shirts."[12] While practicing law in Chicago, Blagojevich met and married Patti Mell. With the help of his father-in-law, Richard Mell, a strong political player in Chicago, Blagojevich won a seat in the state legislature and then in Congress. Blagojevich decided to run for governor, and with the questionable help of Chris Kelly—a wealthy construction-company owner—raised hundreds of thousands of dollars for the campaign.

"The moment he transitioned from a backbench kind of nobody to congressman to a serious candidate for governor was when he filed with a million dollars," Pete Giangreco, a former Blagojevich media consultant, told the *New Yorker*'s David Mendell. "After that, the thing that made people come to him, to advise him or advocate on policy or whatever—your advice was only as good as how much money you could raise."[13]

As his separation from the reality of his office deepened— during his first term as governor—money became Blagojevich's object—the money itself, not what that money was to be used for. He wanted all the funds he could muster to help him win reelection and propel him to political stardom. When he was elected to a second term, his disengagement from the task of governing became even clearer. Wiretaps revealed that after his reelection Blagojevich complained that he "was kinda getting stuck into this . . . four-year deal." He spent only between two and eight hours a week in the office, and he would sneak away or hide in the bathroom if he was needed to discuss important legislation.

Blagojevich's crash and burn is of monumental proportions; few leaders will resemble him in their behavior or appearance. He is an exaggerated example of a disengaged leader, fully divorced from his staff, his constituents, and the job he was hired to do. But we see in his story the capacity for a leader to lose touch—one that we are all susceptible to on a smaller scale if we don't get out of our cars.

Though nowhere near as delusional as Blago, Penn State's longtime football coach, the late Joe Paterno, offers an even more tragic example of what happens when the blanket of celebrity insulates to the extent that a basic moral compass is lost in its folds. Though Paterno did not set out to become greater than his organization the way Fiorina and Blagojevich did, he nevertheless became a larger-than-life figure, and with that status came grave consequences.

Paterno's career at Penn State began in 1950, and he became revered not only as a coach but also as a sort of university-wide moral and ethical leader. Yet under his leadership a member of his coaching staff—Jerry Sandusky—molested children on the Penn State grounds and right under Paterno's nose. When Sandusky's behavior was flagged to Paterno, he reported the allegations to the athletic director but did nothing more. It's hard to believe that Paterno did not know, at least in a general way, what was going on. But even giving him the benefit of the doubt (which we do), it's unfathomable that, once informed, he approved of Sandusky's actions. Rather, what we think happened is that Paterno had achieved such power and status in his role at Penn State that he felt entitled to wear blinders. In true celebrity leadership style, his ultimate stakeholder was himself and the winning football program that was testament to his achievement. He was far enough *above* the fray that he chose not to see what was going on *in* the fray. In the Bible, Luke 12:48 says, "From everyone who has been given much, much will be demanded; and from the one who has been entrusted with much, much more will be asked." Or, more colloquially, as Uncle Ben tells Peter Parker/Spiderman, "With great power comes great responsibility." With celebrity leadership, these basic ethics are lost and the morality instead becomes, "With great power comes great insulation." In an interview, George Ruebenson, former president of Allstate Property and Casualty, told us sadly that celebrity-leader disconnection is more common than you may think, and that it happens "when you forget you are a steward of the company and its stakeholders."

As horrible as the Penn State situation is, as angry as the public rightfully feels about Paterno's lack of action, we must be very honest with ourselves. It's very easy to watch news reports and pundits and declare how differently we'd behave if in Paterno's place—and yet, would we? If we had had years and years of layers that had built up to hold us aloft—higher than the masses—would we come back down to earth at a moment of reckoning? We can't know for sure. And this is the cautionary nature of celebrity leadership.

AVOIDING THE MISTAKES OF DISENGAGEMENT

Disengagement is a difficult mistake to correct because it requires a baseline of self-awareness that is nearly impossible to teach. For instance, even if you fall into the pro-Fiorina camp, it's undeniable that she was not successful at HP—yet her memoir *Tough Choices* offers no recognition of wrongdoing on her part, but is quick to point fingers at everyone else. Every leader makes errors—no one is infallible. Understanding this and taking a close look at your own weaknesses is the point at which all correction begins.

Ask Yourself the Tough Questions

The most basic question every leader needs to ask himself is whether he wants to be there, and if so, why. David Axelrod—most famous for his role as an advisor to Barack Obama—worked with Blagojevich for a while, but ultimately left. "He couldn't articulate to me why he wanted to be governor, and I thought that was a pretty telling assessment," Axelrod told the *New Yorker*.[14] Though it's fair to say *nobody* wants to be Blago, do you want to do what you're doing? Do you want to be retired? Doing something else?

A report from the Corporate Leadership Council presented questions to assess employee engagement, questions that could very easily be put to the leader. Employees are asked to rate how strongly they agree or disagree with the following statements:

- I believe in what I do every day at work.
- I enjoy working with my team.
- I am proud to work for my organization.
- When needed, I am willing to put in the extra effort to get a job done.
- I am constantly looking for ways to do my job better.
- There are days when I don't put much effort into my job.
- I frequently think about quitting my job and leaving this organization.[15]

Chances are you didn't need to be asked for your responses to know how you feel, but it's very possible you've avoided asking yourself. It can be difficult to make a change, but change you must, if you are not engaged in your work anymore. In the case of Jared Heyman of Infosurv, he decided not to end his globe-trotting and not to come back to the company. It seems clear that Heyman is an idea person, a start-up guy, whose skills best served that role and not the day-to-day running of a company. Heyman, though still traveling, is likely to find his way into another start-up venture one day. The same may be true of Dunn, who began the Des Moines retailer. When and if his new love of surfing dries up (no pun intended), he may find another role as an idea generator—the very task that inspired him to start his company in the first place.

David Campeas is one leader who found his way back from the brink. In 2002, he was a rising vice president at an executive search firm, but he was micromanaged and miserable. He seriously contemplated switching gears dramatically and becoming an elementary school teacher. He didn't feel listened to at work;

he didn't feel valued or in control. He was bored and unhappy. When his company decided to spin off a division, he bought it. His new role engaged his entrepreneurial spirit and restored his energy. Although his work stress is still prevalent, it is inspired stress. And lest you think leaders like Heyman, Dunn, and Campeas are the exception, think again. Campeas became the owner of Princeton Search Group executive search firm (now called PrincetonOne), and he says he sees reflections of his disengaged self in the eyes of high-ranking executives at nearly every company he observes.[16] You may even be one of them.

Open Your Doors

It's pretty obvious that a great solution to a closed-door, insulated culture is to open your doors. Heyman talks about not being the type of manager who walks around and "shoots the shit," and although our competitive workplace prohibits spending hours on end on small talk, sometimes casual discussion is necessary. It's the small conversations that build trust and lead you to the information you need to effectively run your business. How often do you talk to your staff? Do you know who is feeling overwhelmed and who has so much free time that they're bored? How much of your dialogue with staff is about *you*, and how much is about *them*? If you return from a trip, do you spend your first day back telling people about the trip or asking them about their experiences while you were away? Engage, and as you do so, take note: chances are excellent that in the process of engaging staff, you will become engaged in return.

Some leaders may balk at this advice. After all, what follows after you open your doors may require a great deal of time. Like Heyman, you may prefer to sit alone in your office thinking of ideas, not checking in with everyone all of the time. That's perfectly fair, but is it what your job requires? If you'd rather be isolated, are you providing your company with the leadership it needs in your absence, or are you still hoarding control? If you're not personally in touch with the needs of staff, is someone else? And is that someone reporting that information to you?

If you determine that you will be the point of contact, build that open door time into your schedule. Though you probably won't be able to set the exact time parameters, as it will vary, value that role of yours as a task to be completed each day, which means you might have to give up something else. TechRepublic's Scott Robinson suggests that, at least in the tech world, "In the long run, you'll think of this time in much the same way you think about any other day-to-day management duties: easy to anticipate and dispatch. Your open door will cease to be a burden, becoming an indispensable administrative help rather than a drain."[17]

Nourish Thyself

Research shows that people who are coached, praised, and developed have a higher level of engagement. If you are the leader, these factors still apply, but whose job is it to coach, praise, and develop *you*?

If you're engaged with your employees and the content of your job still appeals to you, yet you're still feeling aloof, you have the psychological equivalent of a fracture, and you must work hard to heal it. If there is not already a system in place to nourish you, create one. And a word of warning: compensation isn't the solution here. For example, if you work with a board of directors, let them know that you need their feedback and support. If you are a mid-level manager, insulated from the board, consider turning to your management team. If that's not possible, look outside of your organization for the support you need. Finding others in similar situations can provide the feedback you need.

Remember that your ascension to a leadership position did not eliminate your need for positive feedback. It would be awkward to go to your employees and say, "Hey guys, tell me what you like about me!" Yet there are still ways to receive that information. If there's a program in place for employees to review you, it might be as simple as adding a question that asks what's going well. Or take the example of Rich Products, a company that promotes two-way reinforcement. They have a recognition program called Going the Extra Mile (GEM) designed to shine a light on people who have, well, gone the extra mile. That's not unlike recognition programs at thousands of other companies, but sometimes the rank and file recognize their leaders through GEM. The Chief Operating Officer was recognized for his efforts to train women at the company, and the ninety-one-year-old founder and chairman was recognized for visiting employees while travelling abroad.[18]

If all else fails, try to draw strength from encouraging others. Sometimes that can be even more rewarding and fulfilling than receiving a compliment yourself.

Ask: What Would Darwin (Smith) Do?

In contrast to leaders like Carly Fiorina, we present Darwin Smith. He passed away in 1995 at the age of sixty-nine, and his legacy was a good company—Kimberly-Clark—that became great under his stewardship. Shortly after he took over the company, he made the difficult decision to sell all of the business's traditional paper mills and invest the money in the consumer business, into brands like Huggies and Kleenex. Smith was derided by Wall Street, and analysts suggested he was crazy to think a paper company could compete in the consumer market, but he proved them wrong. In time Kimberly-Clark generated returns to investors that beat the general stock market by over four times. When Smith retired, Huggies was the nation's leading disposable diaper.

Smith had a level of confidence in his abilities—if he hadn't, he wouldn't have had the courage to make such a gutsy switch. But he also had humility. He periodically visited the paper plants, and he was known for having great rapport with line workers—both union and nonunion. He believed in strengthening employees and offered programs wherein they could improve their education and their health. Darwin Smith has little name recognition outside of the paper community. He wasn't interested in joining industry groups or high-profile executive associations. He was shy and reserved. Smith did not want the spotlight, and he would often direct credit back to the company, its people, and customers.[19,20]

Darwin Smith was a servant leader and a model of what Jim Collins terms a Level 5 leader—one who has a blend of personal humility and professional will. These leaders are quick to give others credit for successes, yet they accept responsibility for problems.

It's a given that to be a good leader, you have to have confidence. Just as Darwin Smith had to have confidence to sell the company's mills, Carly Fiorina *had* to have a high opinion of her judgment in order to make difficult decisions—otherwise self-doubt could have paralyzed her. Yet she also needed to counter her confidence with humility, and that's what so many leaders are unable to do. It's the difference between Warren Buffett and David Sokol, whose contrasting lifestyles we described in Chapter Five.[21] Sokol lacked humility, and the slippery slope of his lavish spending ultimately led him to cross that line between wrong and right when it came to insider trading. Another moral compass became lost in celebrity.

It is not simple to become a Level 5 leader. But you can start by understanding your strengths and weaknesses and by hiring great people to make up for those weaknesses. You can "fake it until you make it," which might mean repeatedly going back to the model of leaders like Darwin Smith, using their examples to guide your decisions, and asking "What would Darwin do?" in moments when the moral landscape appears cloudy.

■■■

Even as our celebrity-obsessed culture creates celebrity leadership problems, there are hopeful signs that the tide is turning. Writers and thinkers like Jim Collins, along with organizations like the Great Place to Work Institute, are redefining the successful company and the successful leader. The 2008 economic recession made some celebrity leaders into celebrity villains. Outsized compensation packages like the one Fiorina received are under more scrutiny by a public that has become cynical about the costs of the celebrity CEO versus her value. We write this now in the midst of the Occupy Wall Street protests and the upheaval of a presidential election. Whether our cultural values will change in a lasting way or not has yet to be seen.

KEY TAKEAWAYS

Lessons Learned from Mistakes
- Insulation from the rank and file creates a dangerous divide between the leader and the led, one that leads to disengagement.
- Advancing into the wrong job (a misfit) or staying with a job once you've lost your interest (burnout) both lead to aloof behavior that hurts a company's health.
- Wall Street culture and popular culture often encourage the celebrity leadership phenomenon, even though a celebrity leader usually does not yield positive results.
- When a leader is driven by ego instead of by the interests of her company, she makes poor decisions for the long-term health of that company.
- A lack of engagement can lead to a loss of a moral compass, so that ethical decisions come in second to personal advancement.

Successful Navigation
- Honestly assess whether you are engaged in your role, or whether that role needs to change.

- Communicate with staff as a way to determine whether you actually are connected, and as a way to increase your sense of engagement. Build the rapport you need to build trust with your staff.
- Recognize that leaders need encouragement, positive feedback, and development, and make a plan for fulfilling these needs.
- Be self-reflective: admit errors, and hold yourself to the standards of leaders you admire.

TEN

"Does This Doorframe Make My Head Look Big?"

Problems with Self-Absorbed Leaders

A joke has circulated around Silicon Valley for years. "What's the difference between God and Larry Ellison [founder of Oracle]? The difference is that God doesn't think he's Larry Ellison."

Well, here it is, the granddaddy mistake of them all, the biggest, which is why we saved it for last. As identified by our research, of the nine biggest mistakes that leaders can make to ruin their careers and drive their organizations over the cliff, self-absorbed leadership was the most prominent. Specifically, almost 70 percent of the leaders we talked with believed that self-absorption was the most damning mistake a leader can make. We have all worked with someone whose ego was so overinflated that they had trouble fitting their head through the door. Not surprisingly, in our interviews of high-profile leaders, self-absorbed leadership came up again and again as the biggest issue contributing to leadership failure.

What about you? Do people think you are a self-absorbed jerk? Don't try to answer this question yourself; self-absorbed leaders seldom have the ability to recognize it in themselves. And as we discussed in Chapter Nine, leaders need to be confident in order to, well, lead. But when the scale tips too far and confidence turns into grandiosity, it can result in an unexpected end to a career—or even take down an entire organization. There is a close tie between celebrity leaders and self-absorbed leaders, but remember the important difference, as well. Celebrity leaders are concerned about fame and what it can do for them—they want to live on a pedestal. In contrast, the self-absorbed leaders in this chapter have an overinflated sense of their worth, and don't really care whether they're put on a pedestal or not. Their goal isn't necessarily status, position, or promotion. Rather, their goal is to have things work the way they think they should work because, well, they are the greatest. Another important difference between the celebrity leaders of Chapter Nine and the self-absorbed leaders of Chapter Ten has to do with the symptoms: celebrity leaders' self-absorption leads to disengagement, whereas the leaders profiled in this chapter wreak havoc on their companies in entirely different ways—ways that have them in the center of the storm rather than obliviously outside of it.

Stanley Silverman, an industrial-organization psychologist at the University of Akron, completed a four-year study providing new insights into self-absorbed leaders. In a recent interview, he stated, "If you're being arrogant, you're going to derail your own career. It's just a matter of when. Nobody is irreplaceable."[1]

THE ALCHEMY OF THE SELF-ABSORBED LEADER

So, what constitutes a self-absorbed leader? Based on our interviews, three primary styles or modes of self-absorbed leadership became evident. Some self-absorbed leaders are narcissists, in love with themselves; some are arrogant, either believing or acting as if they know best or simply *are* best; some suffer from hubris, or a blind faith in their own infallibility. Some spectacularly self-absorbed leaders exhibit all of these characteristics—and do massive and often permanent damage to their organizations and their own careers. These three modes seem similar, but each may characterize a different facet of self-absorbed leadership.

Narcissism

The concept of narcissism took its name from Greek mythology: the beautiful Narcissus was so infatuated with his own reflection in a pool of water that he could not tear himself away and eventually died. According to Sigmund Freud, we are all narcissistic to some extent. It is healthy to love yourself. But a true narcissist has a personality disorder. If you are a narcissist, you don't merely love yourself; you're *infatuated* with yourself. Everything you do is right, because according to yourself, you are perfect. Moreover, for narcissists, everything is about them, and others exist to support the narcissist's self-image. Narcissists always want to be the center of attention.

Arrogance

Arrogance is similar to narcissism in that it involves an inflated sense of self, and in some cases, arrogance is actually a result of narcissism. In other cases, however, arrogance may be a result of insecurity and low self-esteem. If challenged, you will aggressively attack others to protect your ego. Unlike the narcissist, arrogant leaders don't always have to be the center of attention, but they always have to be right.

Hubris

In a leadership context, self-absorption is ultimately manifested in poor decision making. When a leader makes critical decisions while blind to his own faults and weaknesses, we say he shows hubris. The word *hubris* also has Greek roots—it originally referred to individuals who saw themselves as equal to the gods; Aristotle pointed out that one of the biggest reasons humans fail is because of this blinding pride. Hubris often is a result of too much success;

a leader may begin to feel he is "on a roll" or has the "Midas touch." He feels omnipotent, and that's when very bad things start to happen.[2]

Taking all three of these attributes together creates the perfect storm: a self-absorbed leader who is destined to fail, and in a worst-case scenario, take down his company with him.

THE PERILS OF THE SELF-ABSORBED LEADER

It is virtually impossible for a self-absorbed leader to be effective in the long term. Not only is it annoying for employees to work under them, but the entire work environment suffers. A self-absorbed leader can cut off healthy dialogue and kill motivation. Often a self-absorbed leader surrounds himself with codependents (aka "yes people") to support his ego. This often leads to poor performance as outside perspectives and ideas that challenge the leader are not tolerated. It is not uncommon for the self-absorbed to profess they are committed to supporting company values and goals. But when push comes to shove, it is all about them. Rather than using company resources to achieve organizational goals, self-absorbed leaders often use organizational resources to support their own personal goals.

Many self-absorbed leaders are trying to compensate for self-doubt and low self-esteem. These self-absorbed leaders become isolated to a degree that they cannot be trusted to act in the best interests of the company. The only people who interact with them are the politically inclined who feel the need to "play the game." For those subjected to a self-doubting and self-absorbed leader, either by choice or by their place in the organizational hierarchy, the environment can become toxic. "Here's what happens," Silverman contends. "I'm worried that other people are going to realize that I'm not very competent at my job, so I'm going to put other people down, criticize others, and belittle my employees because somehow I think I'm going to look better that way."[3]

Self-absorbed leaders deserve to be the focus of our final chapter for four reasons, which in combination mean it's simply a beastly problem.

First, self-absorbed leaders are incredibly common. When speaking to audiences, we often pose the question "Have you ever had a self-absorbed boss?" and ask for a show of hands. Inevitably, every hand in the room goes up, including ours.

Second, as we already indicated, it is difficult, if not impossible, for a self-absorbed leader to realize she is just that. One attribute of the condition is that you feel deeply that you are superior to everyone else—you even feel that you don't have any faults. Although your self-absorption is painfully obvious to everyone else, you just don't see it. Ask Darlene Darby Baldwin, president of Midtown Scientific. Early in her career, she received some unexpected feedback from a recruiter. After an interview, he asked her "Why were you so damn arrogant?" She goes on to say, "It took me eighteen years to understand what people were saying about me. When you're arrogant, you get mixed signals in business."[4] When arrogant leaders succeed, their "yes" people will enable their behavior, encouraging more arrogance.

Third, unlike hoarding, which is relatively easy to fix, trying to rid someone of self-absorption requires a great deal of work, often involving outsiders, such as a coach. But even a coach is no silver bullet. John Challenger, CEO of Challenger, Gray & Christmas, Inc. (the oldest outplacement consulting firm in the United States), told us that when one of their coaches is working with a self-absorbed leader, "If a leader is already self-absorbed, when confronted by a coach, he will think the coach is wrong!"

The final reason self-absorption is such a beastly problem is that it's so easy to fall into the trap. As you climb the corporate ladder, you may gradually develop a superiority complex. You see, power feeds ego, and inflated egos lead to self-absorption. George

Ruebenson, former president of Allstate Insurance, told us, "As a leader, often you live a charmed life. It affects how you think of yourself. I had planes, drivers, stayed in the nicest hotels, and ate at the best restaurants." He went on to say, "Early in my career, as I was aspiring to be a manager, I was stunned at how self-absorbed leaders acted. When I was younger, I committed to not being like that." Ruebenson was one of the fortunate ones. He learned early on what self-absorption looks like and, more important, what it does. When he first took on a leadership role, he vowed that he would never get sucked in. He learned from the mistakes of others to avoid becoming egotistical himself. To this day, Ruebenson remains a very humble guy, and it's hard to imagine he once had the power to affect the lives of millions of people. "If I have to tell you how important I am," he said, "then I am not."

In this chapter we cover several important topics. First, we give you some insights into how destructive self-absorbed leaders can be, not only to themselves but also to those who work for them. We then differentiate between confident leaders and self-absorbed leaders. Although they seem similar, you will learn why and how they are not the same. And finally, before sharing some strategies on how to proactively avoid falling into the trap of self-absorption, we highlight the characteristics of self-absorbed leaders and offer insights to assess your propensity to be self-absorbed.

THE SILENT VICTIMS
OF SELF-ABSORBED LEADERS

A self-absorbed leader can destroy the careers of her subordinates —or at least leave them with a very sour attitude they may take with them for the rest of their careers. Self-absorbed leaders create a culture in which being rude and demeaning is acceptable behavior for the leader. Employees in this type of environment for an extended period of time start to show signs. First comes disengagement. This is followed by apathy, low levels of job satisfaction, low self-esteem, and ultimately lower performance. The culture affects both employees' perceptions of their jobs and their perceptions of the entire organization.

It gets even worse. Self-absorbed leaders have a detrimental impact not only on their own people but on bystanders as well. Recent research has found that that "second-hand rudeness" can have long-term and devastating impacts. Two well-regarded academic researchers, Christine Porath and Amir Elez, found that simply observing inappropriate behaviors toward a coworker can have the same effects on observers as if the behavior were directed at them. It diminishes their creativity and impedes their ability to solve problems.

Wayne Hochwarter, the Jim Moran Professor of Management in the College of Business at Florida State University, recently completed a study of more than 1,200 employees to assess their perceptions of working for narcissistic leaders. He found that roughly a quarter of leaders reported by his study subjects were self-centered and had inflated egos, and a third were prone to exaggerate and brag to get recognition and praise. He concluded that "having a narcissistic boss creates a toxic environment for virtually everyone who must come in contact with this individual . . . The team perspective ceases to exist, and the work environment becomes increasingly stressful. Productivity typically plummets as well."[5] Hochwarter contends that even though research supports the assertion that under a self-absorbed leader workers are less motivated and have higher stress levels and less appreciation for their work, most organizations don't consider the negative effects that narcissists have on their employees and even on their organizations. Moreover, he says that many organizations often encourage this toxic environment because narcissists are seen as confident and outgoing. This is understandable:

without looking deeper, it is easy to attribute a surface demeanor of extroverted confidence to healthy self-esteem rather than to toxic self-absorption.

SELF-CONFIDENCE VERSUS SELF-ABSORPTION

So what are the similarities and differences between self-confidence and self-absorption? What's the point when a leader crosses the line? Self-confidence is good. It is a necessary quality of a good leader. But there can be a fine line between self-confidence and self-absorption, and many people have wondered if there is indeed a difference between them. The answer is indisputably yes.

From a cursory view, it's easy to see why some people may mistakenly view self-confidence and self-absorption as one and the same. Right or wrong, both attributes foster a sense of proven ability, a self-perception that we have certain strengths that help us to succeed.

But on closer examination, self-confidence and self-absorption are very different. Underneath the surface behavioral similarities, self-confidence is rooted in self-assurance and is characterized by an ability to perceive, value, and use the strengths of others; self-absorption, however, is rooted in low self-esteem and a feeling of insecurity, as well as a profound discomfort with or disregard for what others bring to the table.

Here's another clue: confidence usually develops over time. The more experience a leader has and the more she learns from her success and failures, the more likely she will feel sure that she will succeed in a given situation. But she also knows she is not perfect. Unlike a self-absorbed leader, she knows she has weaknesses too. Although she may be an expert some of the time, she is not an expert all of the time. Confident leaders understand that sometimes they may have to take a backseat to a subordinate who has more skill in a given task than they do. In contrast, self-absorbed leaders will never take a backseat; they need to always be in the spotlight. Their inflated egos and ensuing hubris will not allow them to accept that they have any faults at all, in any situation. They can think of other people only in relation to themselves and their own need to be the smartest, best, most infallible person in the room at all times.

Most of us think of ourselves as smarter, more dependable, and friendlier than others. As a matter of fact, according to Mark Leary, a psychology professor at Wake Forest University, nearly 80 percent of people believe they are better than average.[6] It is healthy to think of ourselves as being good. But be careful. When it comes to leadership, if the focus is always on "I am a good leader" versus "we are a good team," self-absorption has taken over. What does this mean for leaders? When a self-absorbed leader is successful on a project, he will most likely take ownership of the success. "I worked very hard to make this happen," he may say, or "My strategy was good and it really paid off." However, when a self-absorbed leader fails, rather than owning the failure, he may very well blame it on something or someone else. "Our competitors played dirty," or "We couldn't acquire the resources we needed to succeed." It is useful to think of these two positions in terms of having an internal locus of control and an external locus of control. With an *internal locus of control,* we believe that our actions resulted in the outcome. With an *external locus of control,* we believe that something beyond our control influenced the outcome.

To a degree, it's natural to congratulate ourselves when we succeed and find someone else to blame when we fail—it's part of being human. But when leading others, it's dangerous logic. Confident leaders put most of their emphasis on having an internal locus of control for *both* successes and failures. When they succeed, they know that it is due, in part, to effective leadership of their team. And when they fail, they take ownership. In contrast, because self-absorbed leaders could never fathom that their actions would lead to failure, they take advantage of an internal locus of control by overstating the impact of their own actions on successes, and they take advantage of an external locus of control for failure by overstating the impact of factors beyond their control. When cornered, they use the demons of a strong external locus: excuses and blame. It is far more important to them that they keep their sense of superiority intact than that they accurately gauge the realities of a situation or learn from both successes and failures.

In terms of how they treat subordinates, confident leaders develop their people, trying to build strengths in them. In contrast, self-absorbed leaders often brag to subordinates, belittle them in order to feel better about themselves, and take credit for their best work. The result? Subordinates want to follow confident leaders. Confidence from an effective leader has a spillover effect, where subordinates become confident as well. Conversely, subordinates do not want to follow self-absorbed leaders; they don't want to even be around them—and why would they? "We all want to work with people who are self-confident," psychologist Stanley Silverman notes. "Nurses, residents, and patients can respect physicians who are confident, and have no problem following them. People have far less respect for an arrogant person." He continues, "And they may even do things to help them fail."[7]

The big takeaway for leaders is that confidence breeds confidence, whereas self-absorption breeds arrogance and severs relationships. Confidence inspires; self-absorption discourages. It is as basic as the difference between focusing on your team versus focusing on yourself.

KNOW THE SIGNS OF
SELF-ABSORBED LEADERSHIP

There are two big benefits to understanding the characteristics of self-absorbed leaders. First, you may gain insights into how you can proactively avoid these types of behaviors yourself. Like George Ruebenson, you can then commit to avoiding these types of behaviors and their ensuing detriments. Second, maybe you already are "one of them" and don't know it. Exposure to some of the common characteristics of self-absorbed leaders may provide you some insights to turn things around. In our research, we identified eight signs that self-absorbed leaders commonly exhibit:

- Talking big
- Sense of entitlement
- Sense of infallibility
- Lack of empathy for others
- Intense desire to win at all costs
- One-upmanship
- Know-it-all attitude
- Inability to listen

In this section we examine each of these and offer examples.

Talking Big

Self-absorbed leaders see themselves as larger than life, and they want you to see them that way, too. They will "talk big," particularly about themselves and their accomplishments. They will overpromise, overcommit, and exaggerate to make themselves appear better than they really are. Often they will tell you what you want to hear, with no intent of ever doing whatever it is they are promising. Their goal is simply to appear effective.

In the last chapter we highlighted the hoarding tendencies of Jill Barad, former CEO of Mattel. Unfortunately for Barad and Mattel, she also showed a liking for celebrity-style leadership (which we discussed in Chapter Nine). According to Gretchen Morgenson, Pulitzer Prize–winning writer and financial editor for the *New York Times*, Barad "generally loves the spotlight and thrives when she is putting on a show." But perhaps the biggest contributor to Barad's downfall was her tendency to talk big. Wall Street analysts quickly learned that she "chronically overpromises and under delivers."[8]

The ultimate outcome of talking big is that people no longer trust what self-absorbed leaders have to say. A couple of clichés come to mind here: the boy who cries wolf, and once bitten, twice shy. When someone talks big to you more than once or twice, you stop believing him.

Sense of Entitlement

Self-absorbed leaders often have an invalid sense of entitlement. Because they believe they are clearly better than everyone else, they think they should be entitled to more. Self-absorbed leaders expect that accolades and perks should simply be given to them. Self-absorbed leaders expect to be treated differently and receive special privileges, and they are okay with treating others as inferior. Why not spend millions of dollars of the company's money to redecorate his office? He is worth it, of course—just ask him!

Self-absorbed leaders are the first in line to take credit, whether it is theirs to take or not. And often they will not see anything wrong with that—they truly believe they are entitled to it. Barad was not only a big talker, but she was also a huge self-promoter. She often felt entitled to take others' credit for successes, because she felt compelled to do whatever she had to do to guard her power.[9] Feeling entitled to accolades for others' successes is a common practice for self-absorbed leaders.

A Sense of Infallibility

When a self-absorbed leader is blinded by pride and arrogance, he will think he is untouchable—and maybe even invincible. And a string of successes will only exacerbate the problem. For a self-absorbed leader, once you notch a couple of victories on your bedpost, no one can beat you, right?

Remember our profile of Ken Lay at the beginning of the book? There is a reason why Bethany McLean and Peter Elkind named their best seller on the Enron debacle *The Smartest Guys in the Room.* Ken Lay, Enron president Jeffery Skilling, and Enron CFO Andrew Fastow were able to mislead the Enron board and squander billions of dollars from investors. And they continued to do so for quite some time, as they felt they were infallible. This sense of infallibility resulted in a belief that they would never get caught. McLean and Elkind describe that growing sense of infallibility as an escalation of behaviors, habits, and values that ultimately led to their demise.

Admittedly, some self-absorbed leaders have experienced great successes, but they are the exception. In his best-selling book *Steve Jobs,* Walter Isaacson described Jobs as being both "good Steve" and "bad Steve." Although good Steve was brilliant and charismatic, bad Steve was rude, arrogant, and spiteful, often described by those around him as being a "big asshole." Jobs had a feeling of invincibility—that he could do whatever he wanted, whenever he wanted. But Jobs was a rarity in that he also had an uncanny knack for understanding customer needs. From the Macintosh to the iPad, he created technology to meet those needs. Even though he was one of the most self-absorbed leaders in industry, it worked for Jobs. Best-selling business writer William Taylor points out that although Steve Jobs won the "CEO of the Decade" at the end of 2009 from *Fortune,* he was truly an oddity. "While it's hard to argue with the choice, it's even harder to reproduce his talents. The problem with trumpeting the virtues of one-of-a-kind geniuses like Steve Jobs is that—duh—there is only one of them! Memo to *The Economist:* It's not a good idea to urge CEOs to emulate leaders whose success is, almost by definition, impossible to copy."[10]

Lack of Empathy for Others

Although self-absorbed leaders want others to show them respect and even empathy, they will not reciprocate. And if they do, it is not sincere; it is done only to try to make them "look" like they care.

Consider some of the most self-absorbed leaders in industry, from Fiorina to Trump—most of them don't show much sensitivity for others. Donald Trump's lack of empathy for others has become his calling card. In his television show *The Apprentice,* he appears to savor his catch phrase "You're fired," even though it demoralizes and crushes the hopes and dreams of the "loser."

It is not surprising that corporate raiders are usually self-absorbed. Gordon Gekko, a fictional self-absorbed corporate raider portrayed by Michael Douglas in the film *Wall Street,* is based loosely on Carl Icahn, the high-profile corporate raider who has taken over numerous Fortune 500 companies, including TWA and Texaco. Icahn has often been described as self-absorbed and self-centered. It would be difficult, if not impossible to be a corporate raider and to be an empathetic leader simultaneously, as it is quite common for corporate raiders to fire thousands of employees, including leadership, when they take over resistant companies.

Intense Desire to Win at All Costs

More than anything else, self-absorbed leaders want to achieve victories, even at the expense of those around them. Games are never just games—they are *tests,* and self-absorbed leaders must ace them. These leaders will pursue victory by acting without any semblance of a conscience.[11] As a result, organizations led by self-absorbed leaders usually have a culture of intense internal and external competition, with employees often pitted against each other.

Self-absorbed leaders take the idea of competition too far. It is not uncommon for them to become paranoid, to fabricate threats that aren't really there, and, worse yet, to label others as enemies when they are actually friends. This is yet another reason why self-absorbed leaders don't have many friends. Because they are hypercompetitive, people just don't like them.

One-Upmanship

In Scott Adams's *Dilbert* cartoons, he occasionally features a character called "Topper" who one-ups everyone else. Someone will say something, and Topper will always reply with "That's nothing!" Then he goes on to one-up the other person. Dialogue is nothing but a competition to Topper. During the recession in 2009, in one cartoon Dilbert complained to a coworker that the value of his home was down 40 percent. "That's nothing!" Topper replied, "I paid a homeless 'Elbonian' family a million dollars to take my house."

Topper's claims are so outlandish they are funny. Unfortunately, in real life self-absorbed leaders engage in one-upmanship all the time. Given the combination of their belief in their own superiority and their fragile egos, they always have to be the best one, in all situations.

Know-It-All Attitude

Every self-absorbed leader believes he knows it all. He's a one-man "one-stop-shop" for all answers, great and small. And because he believes he knows it all, he is not receptive to alternative points of view, which amount to nothing more than challenges and threats to his ideas and to his sense of being. Many self-absorbed leaders tell subordinates "Just do as I say" or "I know better."

If anyone challenges such a leader, he becomes extremely sensitive. And remember, he bruises more easily than most. He cannot grasp the concept of constructive conflict. Earlier we talked about how a self-absorbed leader will surround himself with "yes men" by design. Like building a moat around a castle, he is proactively protecting himself from "attacks" or challenges from others.

Inability to Listen

Finally, self-absorbed leaders are terrible listeners. Business book author Michael Maccoby tells a story about a time he was invited to a self-absorbed leader's summer home after interviewing his subordinates. The leader asked Maccoby what the employees said about him. "They think you are very creative and courageous," Maccoby told the CEO, "but they also feel that you don't listen." Ironically, the CEO asked Maccoby to repeat what he'd said, as the CEO wasn't listening carefully.[12] When something happens that may threaten a self-absorbed leader's ego, he doesn't want to hear it. It is a self-absorbed leader's defense mechanism. Poor listening protects him from possible threats to his own self-image. This is a textbook example of selective perception. Selective perception occurs when a person subconsciously "tunes out" potentially threatening factors in his environment. It is similar to the ostrich "protecting itself" by sticking its head in the sand when danger is present (an enduring image, though it has no basis in reality). Just look the other way and pretend nothing is wrong. Maybe it will go away.

STEERING CLEAR OF SELF-ABSORBED LEADERSHIP

How do you avoid being sucked into self-absorption at some point in a successful career as a leader? It is nearly impossible to do on your own. The first thing you need to do is find an accountability partner to call you out when you start showing signs of self-absorption. If you already show signs of being a self-absorbed leader, you will also need to commit to working on yourself, as research has shown that narcissism and arrogance are hard habits to break. Bottom line: any leader will benefit by understanding the strength of humility.

Find a Truth Teller

Unfortunately, we cannot truly see ourselves by simply looking at our reflection. Mirrors don't help. The people around us must be the mirrors. Only they can provide us with the reflection we need in order to understand how self-absorbed we really are. Interestingly, in almost every interview we conducted for this book, leaders told us about the importance of what John Challenger referred to as "truth tellers." One of the best moves a leader can make to minimize the risk of using self-absorbed leadership tactics is to have a go-to person she can turn to who will be completely honest with her, *about* her.

It is important for leaders to have a person or people who can keep them connected and ground them. In the Sherlock Holmes novels of Sir Arthur Conan Doyle, Watson grounds Holmes. Without Watson, Holmes would have lost touch with reality, and he would not have been able to accomplish much. Rocker Ozzy Osbourne appears to be out of touch with, well, everything; his wife Sharon keeps him somewhat grounded. The same thing happens in business with many of today's most prominent leaders. Consider Larry Ellison. At Oracle, he is grounded by COO Ray Lane. Bill Gates? Grounded by COO Steve Ballmer.

George Ruebenson made certain that his direct reports felt comfortable enough with him that if he was off track, or needed to be redirected, his team could speak freely with him, about him. One day, Ruebenson recalls, one of his people told him "George, you've lost your mind!" He was taken aback at first, but as he was driving home that night he thought, "I am a very lucky guy to have people that will step up and reel me in when I need it."

So ask yourself, who knows me well enough to call me out when I get too grandiose? Who is it that can keep me on center? Try to keep it professional and not personal. Find someone who is not impressed by your accomplishments or titles. We all need coaching, someone we can look to for advice when things get tough. Specifically, to avoid the slow fade into self-absorption, you need someone who is willing to call you out when your head starts getting too big.

Having a truth teller or, better yet, a group of truth tellers can be invaluable. They know you well enough to understand what makes you tick; they feel comfortable enough to be honest and tell you the way it is—even when you are not being honest with yourself. Finally, they should understand your business well enough to make it all relevant. Your truth tellers could be your top management team, board members, or peers.

Be Willing to Work on Yourself

It is not enough to have someone point out to you that you are taking something too seriously, getting a big head, or acting like a jackass. What are you going to do about it?

Being a great leader takes an enormous amount of work. It takes commitment, dedication, and the willingness to work on all of these items:

- Don't be overly enamored with your own ideas.
- Give credit where credit is due.
- When things go wrong, own the responsibility.
- Be aware when you feel threatened by praise for others.
- If you find yourself getting overly competitive, ask yourself "why?"
- Don't blame others. Have a no-excuses mentality.
- Take pride in the accomplishment of your subordinates.

The more you understand the strength of humility, the less likely you'll be to fall into the trap of being a self-absorbed leader. There is tremendous power in being humble; in seeing yourself as a resource for your employees, rather than a boss. What can you do to make your subordinates succeed?

■■■

Michael Bryant, CEO of Centra Health, told us that the primary role of a leader is to make sure his people succeed. He was very clear that self-absorbed leaders will eventually fail. Bryant states, "A good leader is like a coach of a basketball team. It is not important for the leader to score the points. It is important for his team to score the points. It's not rocket science!" He continues, "So the one key to being an egoless leader is to understand the paradox. You need to build the strengths of individuals on the team, but at the same time build the strengths of your team. And when the team succeeds, you succeed. Self-absorbed leaders never get the paradox." Bottom line, self-absorbed leaders define success based on their own achievements. In contrast, great leaders define success by their team's achievements.

KEY TAKEAWAYS

Lessons Learned from Mistakes
- Self-absorption is the number one killer of effective leadership, destroyer of organizations, and ender of careers.
- Self-absorbed leadership comes from narcissism, arrogance, and hubris.
- Self-absorbed leadership is very difficult to correct, because the self-absorbed leader simply cannot see the problem.
- Not only is self-absorbed leadership damaging to subordinates, but it is also detrimental for anyone standing on the sidelines.
- Although surrounding himself with "yes" people may make a self-absorbed leader feel better in the short term, in the long run it only perpetuates the problem.

Successful Navigation
- Although confidence and self-absorption may seem similar, they are fundamentally different, and there are several signs that can help you understand the differences. Know them!
- Find a truth teller: a person or, better yet, a group that can honestly tell you the way it is, especially at times when you are not being honest with yourself.

- Understand that being a great leader is a lot of work, and commit to working on yourself.
- Understand the power of humility. Focus on what you can do to make your employees succeed.

To find out more about whether you are a self-absorbed leader, visit www.TheWisdomOfFailure.com.

Walking the Line

Gerry Shaheen, a member of the board of directors for Ford Motor Company, told us "the ability to recognize and learn from one's own mistakes is the first step to becoming a great leader." He continued, "But the ability to learn from others' mistakes is not only critical to successful leadership—it is genius." We hope that after reading this book you are convinced not only that it is important to note what leaders do well, but also that it is essential to look at the flip side—even the dark side—of leadership. You have been armed with the nine most important lessons we can learn from failure, and it is these tools that can help you walk the proverbial line without crossing to the dark side.

The line is critically important in matters of leadership. Think about it: there are times when the mistakes we have profiled in this book may actually function as strengths or even necessities. There are components of these "wrong" behaviors we have high-lighted that, when used in moderation, can actually be effective management techniques. But once you cross the line, mistakes happen. So what constitutes "crossing the line"? Mistakes are born from the *exaggeration* of these behaviors. When a leader behaves in a way that has the potential to yield good, but she overdoes it and as a result the outcome is negative, she has crossed the line. For example, a successful leader needs to be confident, but when she starts to believe she is better than everyone else, her confidence has crossed the line, turning into self-absorption and arrogance—and bad things start to happen.

The tools and insights in this book are important to keeping behavior on track. Like a checks-and-balances system, these tools can give you an important skill set to deal with leadership challenges—like developing the ability to say "no," knowing whether you have roamed too far outside the box, and recognizing when your effort to create harmony in the workplace has become dysfunctional.

But what makes it so difficult to learn from the flip side— when you have actually crossed the line—is that the prescriptions are not always black-and-white. Often what may appear to be a mistake to one leader is a success to another. What one leader— or one employee, for that matter—sees as extensively empowering his employees, another sees as being disengaged. What some may see as taking healthy risk, others may see as losing strategic direction or unbalanced orchestration. And then there's assertiveness. Some leaders follow the advice of legions of business books and proactively try to be more assertive. Yet employees may perceive this as hoarding or bullying.

So how can you, as a leader, actually tell when you have crossed the line? How can we know if we are taking things too far? Unfortunately, there is no definitive answer, no 100-percent rule, no secret. But the better you understand the lessons from the nine mistakes we highlight in this book, their causes and their signs, the more self-aware you'll become about when you may be starting to cross the line.

Though she may stray from it from time to time and need to correct course, a great leader learns how to walk the line. She is aware of the critical mistakes leaders can make, and she does what is necessary to avoid them. She also understands that balance and moderation play critical roles. For example, if a leader is concerned with hoarding and the pendulum swings too far the other way, she may become disengaged. If a leader is overly concerned about bullying her subordinates, she may go too far the other way and become overly passive. If a leader becomes too concerned with being all things to all people, she may have trouble pulling the trigger when an appropriate opportunity presents itself.

Similarly, recall in Chapter Three that synergy had a role in avoiding roaming too far outside the box. Later, in Chapter Seven, synergy was a villain in scenarios in which leaders use synergy simply for the sake of synergy.

The lessons we talk about in this book are examples of being too far toward either end of the spectrum. Deviating too far in either direction leads to failure. It is the ability to maintain balance between the lessons learned from your successes and lessons learned from your failures—the flip side—that gives you the wisdom to be a great leader.

And there you have it. Now—as we promised in Chapter One—you have the other half of the leadership story. If there is one skill that comes the closest to being the secret to success as a leader, it is balance. By knowing what to do, balanced with knowing what not to do, you now have a deeper sense of what it means to be a great leader.

NOTES

Chapter One

1. Mike Tolson, "A Life of Climbing Before Ultimate Fall: Ken Lay Rose from Poverty to Riches, and He Fell from Glory to Disgrace," *Houston Chronicle*, July 6, 2006. Retrieved from http://www.chron.com/disp/story.mpl/special/enron/4027260.html

2. James Kelleher, "Caterpillar CEO: Once Shunned, Now Celebrated," *Reuters.* Retrieved April 1, 2012, from http://www.reuters.com/article/2010/05/14/us-manufacturing-summit-owens-idUSTRE64D4JR20100514

3. Geoff Colvin, "Caterpillar Is Absolutely Crushing It," *Fortune*, May 12, 2011. Retrieved June 10, 2011, from http://management.fortune.cnn.com/2011/05/12/caterpillar-is-absolutely-crushing-it/

4. Karen Dillon, "'I Think of My Failures as a Gift.' Interview with A. G. Lafley," *Harvard Business Review*, April 2011. Retrieved June 30, 2011, from http://hbr.org/2011/04/i-think-of-my-failures-as-a-gift/ar/1

5. For examples of edited research volumes that examine learning from mistakes and failures, see Birgit Schyns and Tiffany Hansbrough, *When Leadership Goes Wrong: Destructive Leadership, Mistakes, and Ethical Failures* (Charlotte, NC: IAP, 2010); Linda Neider and Chester Schriesheim, *The "Dark" Side of Management,* in the Research

245

in Management Series (Charlotte, NC: IAP, 2010); Ricky W. Griffith, Anne O'Leary-Kelly, and Robert D. Pritchard, *The Dark Side of Organizational Behavior* (San Francisco: Jossey-Bass, 2004).

6. Max Bazerman and Ann Tenbrunsel, "Good People Often Let Bad Things Happen. Why?" *Harvard Business Review*, April 2011. Retrieved July 3, 2011, from http://hbr.org/2011/04/ethical -breakdowns/ar/1

7. Stephan M.R. Covey, *The Speed of Trust: The One Thing That Changes Everything* (New York: Free Press, 2006), 182.

8. Anita Hamilton, "Why Circuit City Busted, While Best Buy Boomed," *Time Business*, November 11, 2008. Retrieved June 5, 2012, from http://www.time.com/time/business/article/0,8599,1858079,00 .html

Chapter Two

1. Harry DeAngelo, Linda DeAngelo, and Karen Wruck, "Asset Liquidity, Debt Covenants, and Managerial Discretion in Financial Distress: The Collapse of L.A. Gear," *Journal of Financial Economics* 64 (2002): 3–34.

2. Cindy LaFarre Yorks. "Fashion: Shoe Business' Star-Studded Sneaker Wars," *Los Angeles Times*, June 13, 1990. Retrieved June 5, 2012, from http://articles.latimes.com/1990-06-13/news/vw-173 _1_celebrity-endorsement

3. Kruti Trivedi, "Trying a New Shoe for Size; Can Owners of Skechers Learn from Their Mistakes?" *New York Times*, July 18, 2000. Retrieved July 15, 2011, from http://www.nytimes.com/2000/07/18/business /trying-a-new-shoe-on-for-size-can-owners-of-skechers-learn-from -their-mistakes.html?pagewanted=all&src=pm

4. Barry M. Staw, "Knee-Deep in the Big Muddy: A Study of Escalating Commitment to a Chosen Course of Action," *Organizational Behavior and Human Performance* 16(1) (1976): 27–44.

5. Ryan Nakashima, "MySpace CEO Owen Van Natta Resigns After Less Than a Year," *Huffington Post*, February 10, 2010. Retrieved July 25, 2011, from http://www.huffingtonpost.com/2010/02/10 /myspace-ceo-owen-van-natt_n_457732.html

6. Adam Ostrow, "You Can Now Login to MySpace with Facebook," *Mashable*, November 18, 2010. Retrieved July 20, 2011, from http://mashable.com/2010/11/18/you-can-now-login-to-myspace-with-facebook/

7. Evann Gastaldo, "MySpace to Ax Up to Half Its Workers – Downsizing Could Be Announced This Month, Sources Say," *Newser*, January 4, 2011. Retrieved July 18, 2011, from http://www.newser.com/story/108947/myspace-to-ax-up-to-half-its-workers.html

8. For examples of blog sites that discuss Mercedes-Benz USA brand dilution, see Sam Abuelsamid, "Report: Mercedes-Benz C-Class Lineup Set to Expand in U.S.," Autoblog. May 24, 2010. Retrieved June 5, 2012, from http://www.autoblog.com/2010/05/24/report-mercedes-benz-c-class-lineup-set-to-expand-in-u-s/; Michael C., "Mercedes Sets High Goals – Expands C-Class Lineup in the US," BenzInsider. May 25, 2012. Retrieved June 5, 2012, from http://www.benzinsider.com/2010/05/mercedes-sets-high-goals-expands-c-class-lineup-in-the-us/; "2012 Mercedes B-Class Tuned by Brabus," Autoevolution. Retrieved June 5, 2012, from http://www.autoevolution.com/news/2012-mercedes-b-class-tuned-by-brabus-photo-gallery-42442.html

9. Andreas Cremer, "Audi Outsells Mercedes-Benz in First Quarter on Demand from Chinese Buyers," Bloomberg, April 7, 2011. Retrieved July 16, 2011, from http://www.bloomberg.com/news/2011-04-07/audi-outsells-mercedes-benz-in-first-quarter-on-demand-from-chinese-buyers.html

10. Michael E. Porter, "What Is Strategy?" *Harvard Business Review*, November 1996. Retrieved August 2, 2011, from http://hbr.org/1996/11/what-is-strategy/ar/1

11. "Wall St. Ten Brands That Will Disappear in 2012," *24/7 Wall St.*, June 22, 2011. Retrieved July 10, 2011, from http://247wallst.com/2011/06/22/247-wall-st-ten-brands-that-will-disappear-in-2012/#ixzz1Qj5NUVX3http://www.crunchgear.com/tag/rants/

12. IBS Center for Management Research, "Restructuring at Sears Roebuck & Co. (1992–03)," *ICMR*, 2004. Retrieved July 9, 2011, from http://www.icmrindia.org/casestudies/catalogue/Business%20Strategy2/Restructuring%20at%20Sears%20Roebuck.htm

Chapter Three

1. Jacob Leibenluft, "Why Do Trains Go off the Tracks? Faulty Brakes, Hairline Cracks, and Rock 'n' Roll," *Slate*, May 19, 2008. Retrieved July 28, 2011, from http://www.slate.com/articles/news_and _politics/explainer/2008/05/why_do_trains_go_off_the_tracks .html

2. Terry Pratchett, "Top Terry Pratchett Quotes," InfoBarrel. August 26, 2010. Retrieved May 24, 2012, from http://www.infobarrel .com/Top_Terry_Pratchett_Quotes

3. Kirk Cheyfitz, *Thinking Inside the Box: The 12 Timeless Rules for Managing a Successful Business* (New York: Simon & Schuster, 2003), 3.

4. Vivek Kaul, "Why Does Maverick Thinker Seth Godin Advise You Not to Think Outside the Square?" *Economic Times*, September 16, 2011. Retrieved July 23, 2011, from http://articles.economictimes.indiatimes .com/2011-09-16/news/30165308_1_seth-godin-iphone-business -model

5. Michael E. Ross, "It Seemed Like a Good Idea at the Time: New Coke, 20 Years Later, and Other Marketing Fiascoes," *MSNBC*, April 22, 2005. Retrieved July 21, 2011, from http://www.msnbc.msn .com/id/7209828/ns/us_news/t/it-seemed-good-idea-time/

6. Steve Strauss, "New Coke, Business Mistakes, and You," *American Express Open Forum, Powering Small Business Success*, August 30, 2010. Retrieved August 1, 2011, from http://www.openforum.com/idea -hub/topics/managing/article/new-coke-business-mistakes -and-you-steve-strauss

7. Constance Hays, *The Real Thing: Truth and Power at the Coca-Cola Company* (New York: Random House, 2004), 106.

8. Malcolm Gladwell, *Blink: The Power of Thinking Without Thinking* (New York: Little, Brown, 2005).

9. Barbara Mikkelson, "New Coke," Snopes.com. May 19, 2011. Retrieved May 24, 2012, from http://www.snopes.com/cokelore /newcoke.asp

10. Earl Nightingale, *Lead the Field* (abridged audio book) (New York: Simon & Schuster Audio/Nightingale-Conant, 2002).

11. David Yoffie and Michael Cusumano, "Building a Company on Internet Time: Lessons from Netscape," *Harvard Business Review* 41(3) (1999): 8–28.

12. Marcel Proust, "The Quotations Page." Retrieved May 24, 2012, from http://www.quotationspage.com/quote/31288.html

Chapter Four

1. Michael Dell, "Maximum Speed," *Executive Excellence* 16(1) (1999): 15–16.

2. Douglas McGill, "Smokeless Cigarette's Hapless Start," *New York Times*, November 19, 1988.

3. Tony Hsieh, *Delivering Happiness: A Path to Profits, Passion, and Purpose* (New York: Business Plus, 2010), 108.

4. Ted Thornhill, "Pee Before You Fly Policy of Japanese Airline," *Metro*, October 2, 2009. Retrieved May 24, 2012, from http://www.metro.co.uk/weird/747254-pee-before-you-fly-policy-of-japanese-airline

5. Troy Wolverton, "Pet Sites Bark Up the Net Tree," *CNET*, November 3, 1999. Retrieved September 10, 2011, from http://news.cnet.com/Pet-sites-bark-up-the-Net-tree/2100-1040_3-232410.html

6. Cheyfitz, *Thinking Inside the Box* (ch. 3, n. 3), 30–32.

7. Nate Lanxon, "The Greatest Defunct Websites and Dotcom Disasters," *CNET*, June 5, 2008. Retrieved September 22, 2011, from http://crave.cnet.co.uk/gadgets/the-greatest-defunct-web-sites-and-dotcom-disasters-49296926/

8. Kent German, "Top 10 Dot-Com Flops," *CNET*. Retrieved May 24, 2012, from http://www.cnet.com/1990-11136_1-627837-1.html

9. Linda Himelstein, "Louis Borders," *Business Week Online*, September 27, 1999. Retrieved October 12, 2011, from http://www.businessweek.com/1999/99_39/b3648010.htm

10. Jennifer Bott, "Quality, Service Drive Online Grocer Webvan," *Detroit Free Press*, September 14, 2000. Retrieved October 23, 2011, from http://www.frep.com/money/tech/webvan14_20000914.htm

11.   Randall Stross, *eBoys: The First Inside Account of Venture Capitalists at Work* (New York: Crown, 2000).

12.   "Webvan Shuts Down," CNN Money.com, July 9, 2001. Retrieved October 3, 2011, from http://money.cnn.com/2001/07/09 /technology/webvan/

Chapter Five

1.   Joseph R. Marone, "Tom Coughlin: Management Style Analysis," NJ.com, February 5, 2008. Retrieved March 3, 2012, from http://www .nj.com/business/index.ssf/2008/02/tom_coughlin_management _style.html

2.   Laura Rowley, "The Financial Toll of Workplace Bullies," *Yahoo! Finance*, May 5, 2011. Retrieved March 29, 2012, from http://www .workplacebullying.org/2011/05/06/yahoo/

3.   Ellen Cobb, "Workplace Bullying: A Global Overview," Management -Issues Ltd. Online, July 8, 2011. Retrieved March 29, 2012, from http://www.management-issues.com/2011/7/8/opinion/workplace -bullying-a-global-overview.asp

4.   Adam L. Penenberg, "Workplace Bullying: A Management Primer," *CBSNEWS.com*, October 20, 2008. Retrieved February 15, 2012, from http://www.cbsnews.com/8301-505125_162-51242718/workplace -bullying-a-management-primer/

5.   Andrew Garber and Jim Brunner, "GOP Caucus Bans State Sen. Pam Roach, Tells Her to Get Anger Counseling," *Seattle Times*, January 9, 2010. Retrieved January 14, 2012, from http://seattletimes .nwsource.com/html/politics/2010932705_roach30.html

6.   Ibid.

7.   Ibid.

8.   John A. Byrne, "Chainsaw," *Businessweek*, October 18, 1999. Retrieved November 12, 2011, from http://www.businessweek.com/1999/99 _42/b3651099.htm

9.   "Ex-Employee Sues Warner Bros. for Harassment and Discrimination," *ebossWatch*, August 8, 2010. Retrieved September 12, 2011, from http://blog.cbosswatch.com/2010/08/ex-employee-sues-warner -bros-for-harassment-and-discrimination/

10. Mark Abramson, Katharine Crnko, and Andrea Useem, video interview with Ford CEO Alan Mulally, "On Leadership: Ford CEO Alan Mulally on Catching Mistakes," *Washington Post*, July 15, 2011. Retrieved November 6, 2011, from http://www.washingtonpost.com/national/on-leadership-ford-ceo-alan-mulally-on-catching-mistakes/2011/07/15/gIQAnfVAGI_video.html

11. Ibid.

12. Penenberg, "Workplace Bullying."

13. Byrne, "Chainsaw."

14. Penenberg, "Workplace Bullying."

15. Rowley, "The Financial Toll of Workplace Bullies."

16. Penenberg, "Workplace Bullying."

17. Dillon, " 'I Think of My Failures as a Gift' " (ch. 1, n. 4).

18. Michael Maccoby, "Leadership and the Fear Factor," *MIT Sloan Management Review* 45(2) (Winter 2004): 14–18.

19. Rowley, "The Financial Toll of Workplace Bullies."

20. John Baldoni, "Warren Buffett: Why Did He Enable a Bullying Exec?" *CBSNEWS.com*, April 28, 2011. Retrieved March 29, 2012, from http://www.cbsnews.com/8301-505125_162-40144240/warren-buffett-why-did-he-enable-a-bullying-exec/

21. Ray Sanchez, "Did Depression or an Alleged Bully Boss Prompt Editor's Suicide?" *ABC News*, August 19, 2010. Retrieved May 24, 2012, from http://abcnews.go.com/Business/MindMood ResourceCenter/editors-suicide-draws-attention-workplace-bullying/story?id=11421810

22. Internal Audit Department Audit Report of the Virginia Quarterly Review, *Virginia Quarterly Review*, October 20, 2010. Retrieved June 5, 2012, from http://www.virginia.edu/president/documents/20OctoberReport.pdf

23. Cobb, "Workplace Bullying: A Global Overview."

Chapter Six

1. "Conflict: Constructive or Destructive?" Retrieved October 25, 2011, from http://www.consultpivotal.com/conflict.htm

2. James Larsen, Ph.D., "Constructive Conflict," *Business Psychology— Latest Findings*, article No. 135. Retrieved March 29, 2011, from http://www.businesspsych.org/articles/135.html

3. W.C.H. Prentice, "Understanding Leadership," *Harvard Business Review*, January 2004 (originally published 1961), pp. 102–109.

4. Gary L. Neilson, Bruce A. Pasternack, and Karen E. Van Nuys, "The Passive-Aggressive Organization," *Harvard Business Review*, October 2005. Retrieved February 12, 2012, from http://hbr.org/2005/10 /the-passive-aggressive-organization/ar/1

5. Ibid.

6. DeAnne M. Aguirre, Lloyd W. Howell, Jr., David B. Kletter, and Gary L. Neison, "A Global Check-Up: Diagnosing the Health of Today's Organizations," Booz Allen Hamilton, 2005. Retrieved May 24, 2012, from www.boozallen.com/media/file/missiondna-global -research.pdf

7. "Putting People Before Profits: Classic PR Case Study, But Without the Fairytale Ending," WordPress. Retrieved March 29, 2012, from http://toughsledding.wordpress.com/2010/03/05/putting -people-before-profits-classic-pr-case-study-but-without-the -fairytale-ending/

8. Ibid.

9. Al Gini and Alexei M. Marcoux, "Malden Mills: When Being a Good Company Isn't Good Enough," Loyola University. Retrieved March 31, 2012, from http://www.stthomas.edu/cathstudies/cst /conferences/thegoodcompany/finalpapers/gini%20and%20 marcoux%20fin.pdf

10. Radley Balko, "Altruism? Bah, Humbug," *Daily Apple*, December 22, 2004. Retrieved May 24, 2012, from http://www.cato.org /publications/commentary/altruism-bah-humbug

11. "French People Expect No Economic Prosperity in 2011," *Business Forum*, April 1, 2011. Retrieved on March 16, 2012, from http:// euvietnam.com/en/newdetail/1794/22681/french_people _expect_no_economic_prosperity_in_2011.vcci

12. Prentice, "Understanding Leadership."

13. *View from the Top*, documentary written by Tom Scott, produced by Jack Perkins, published by Radio New Zealand, 1997.

14. Prentice, "Understanding Leadership."

15. "Did I Stutter?" *The Office*, National Broadcast Company, Deedle-Dee Productions, April 24, 2008.

Chapter Seven

1. Avery M. Henderson, Ph.D., M.P.H., "Overcoming Inappropriate Competition in the Workplace," *Avid Articles*. Retrieved March 28, 2012, from http://www.avidarticles.com/Article/Overcoming-Inappropriate-Competition-in-the-Workplace/26400

2. Joann S. Lublin, *Wall Street Journal*, January 2, 2001.

3. "Playing Favorites—Romantic or Otherwise—Is a Messy Game in the Workplace," *Knowledge@Wharton*, August 8, 2007. Retrieved March 29, 2012, from http://knowledge.wharton.upenn.edu/article.cfm?articleid=1785

4. Ibid.

5. "Top Five Tips for Leveraging Strengths and Supporting Weaknesses," *Careerbuilder*. Retrieved March 29, 2012, from http://www.careerbuilder.com/jobposter/small-business/article.aspx?articleid=ATL_0194LEVERAGESTRENGTHS_s

6. Michael Goold and Andrew Campbell, "Desperately Seeking Synergy," *Harvard Business Review*, September 1998. Retrieved March 28, 2012, from http://hbr.org/1998/09/desperately-seeking-synergy/ar/1

7. Ibid.

8. Henderson, "Overcoming Inappropriate Competition in the Workplace."

9. Melissa Korn, "Playing Favorites," *Wall Street Journal*, August 29, 2011. Retrieved May 24, 2012, from http://online.wsj.com/article/SB10001424053111904009304576532352522029520.html

10. Robert T. Whipple, "How to Avoid Playing Favorites," *Leadergrow*. Retrieved March 28, 2012, from http://leadergrow.com/articles/63-how-to-avoid-playing-favorites

11. Korn, "Playing Favorites."

12. Goold and Campbell, "Desperately Seeking Synergy."

13. Ibid.

14. Ibid.

Chapter Eight

1. Robert F. Hurley and James Ryman, "Making the Transition from Micromanager to Leader," working paper, Fordham University, 2003.

2. Paul R. Bernthal and Richard S. Wellins, "Leadership Forecast: A Benchmarking Study," *Development Dimensions International*, November 2003. Retrieved October 17, 2011, from http://www.ddiworld .com/DDIWorld/media/trend-research/leadershipforecast2003 -2004_fullreport_ddi.pdf

3. Estienne de Beer, "The Menace of Micromanagement," *Accountancy SA*, posted October 2006. Retrieved October 17, 2011, from http://www.accountancysa.org.za/resources/ShowItemArticle.asp ?Article=Menace+of+Micromanagement&ArticleId=956&Issue =640

4. Kathleen Morris, "The Rise of Jill Barad," *Businessweek*, posted May 25, 1998. Retrieved November 7, 2011, from http://www.businessweek .com/archives/1998/b3579001.arc.htm

5. Ibid.

6. David L. Dotlich and Peter C. Cairo, *Why CEOs Fail: The 11 Behaviors That Can Derail Your Climb to the Top—and How to Manage Them* (San Francisco: Jossey-Bass, 2003).

7. Ibid.

8. Gretchen Morgenson, "Barbie's Guru Stumbles; Critics Say Chief's Flaws Weigh Heavy on Mattel," *New York Times*, Business Day, posted November 7, 1999. Retrieved November 7, 2011, from http://www .nytimes.com/1999/11/07/business/barbie-s-guru-stumbles -critics-say-chief-s-flaws-weigh-heavily-on-mattel.html?pagewanted =all&src=pm

9. Douglas M. Branson, *The Last Male Bastion: Gender and the CEO Suite in America's Public Companies* (New York: Routledge, 2010).

10. Laura Stack, "How to Handle a Micromanager," *Washington Women's Weekly*, updated February 28, 2011. Retrieved September 17, 2011, from http://www.womensweekly-wdc.com/2011/02/office-productivity -how-to-handle-a-micromanager/

11. Ralph Nader, "Ralph Nader Quotes," Brainy Quotes. Retrieved June 5, 2012, from http://www.brainyquote.com/quotes/authors /r/ralph_nader.html

12. Robert Rosenthal and Lenore Jacobson, *Pygmalion in the Classroom: Teacher Expectation and Pupils' Intellectual Development* (New York: Irvington, 1992).

13. Sydney Finkelstein, "The Seven Habits of Spectacularly Unsuccessful Executives," *Ivey Business Journal*, January/February 2004. Retrieved November 29, 2011, from http://www.jacksonleadership .com/pdfs/7Habits_IveyBusinessJournal.pdf

Chapter Nine

1. Jonathan Stein, "Rudy Pulls a George Bush Moment on the Price of Bread, Milk," *Mother Jones*, posted April 11, 2007. Retrieved March 29, 2012, from http://motherjones.com/mojo/2007/04 /rudy-pulls-george-bush-sr-moment-price-bread-milk

2. Amy Barrett, "Inside the Mind of a Runaway CEO," *Inc.*, November 2011. Retrieved November 29, 2011, from http://byliner.com /amy-barrett/stories/inside-the-mind-of-a-runaway-ceo

3. Ibid.

4. James V. Grimaldi and Jacqueline Trescott, "Controversial CEO to Leave Smithsonian Business Ventures," *Washington Post*, posted May 17, 2007. Retrieved March 29, 2012, from http://www .washingtonpost.com/wp-dyn/content/article/2007/05/16 /AR2007051601964.html

5. "Chainsaw Al: He Anointed Himself America's Best CEO. But Al Dunlap Drove Sunbeam into the Ground," *BusinessWeek*, posted October 18, 1999. Retrieved December 8, 2011, from http://www .businessweek.com/1999/99_42/b3651099.htm

6. Jim Collins, "The Misguided Mix-Up of Celebrity and Leadership," Conference Board Annual Report, Annual Feature Essay,

September/October 2001. Retrieved March 29, 2012, from http://www.jimcollins.com/article_topics/articles/the-misguided-mixup.html

7. Branson, *The Last Male Bastion* (ch. 8, n. 9).

8. Ibid.

9. "Why Carly Fiorina Should NOT be Elected to the United States Senate, Carly-Fiorina.com. Retrieved December 19, 2011, from http://www.carly-fiorina.com/hp-employees-on-carly-fiorina/gbook.php

10. Richard Rapaport, "How Carly Fiorina Wrecked Hewlett-Packard," posted September 29, 2010. Retrieved December 19, 2011, from http://realityframe.blogspot.com/2010/10/how-carly-fiorina-wrecked-hewlett.html

11. David Mendell, "What About Me? The United States of America v. Rod Blagojevich," *New Yorker,* posted July 26, 2010. Retrieved March 19, 2012, from http://www.newyorker.com/reporting/2010/07/26/100726fa_fact_mendell

12. Ibid.

13. Ibid.

14. Ibid.

15. Corporate Leadership Council, "Driving Performance and Retention Through Employee Engagement: A Quantitative Analysis of Effective Engagement Strategies," Corporate Executive Board, 2004. Retrieved December 15, 2011, from http://www.mckpeople.com.au/SiteMedia/w3svc161/Uploads/Documents/760af459-93b3-43c7-b52a-2a74e984c1a0.pdf

16. Del Jones, "Besides Being Lonely at the Top, It Can Be 'Disengaging' as Well," *USA Today,* posted June 21, 2005. Retrieved December 19, 2011, from http://www.usatoday.com/educate/college/business/articles/20050626.htm

17. Scott Robinson, "Make the Open Door Policy Work for You," *TechRepublic,* posted November 26, 2002. Retrieved December 19, 2011, from http://www.techrepublic.com/article/make-the-open-door-policy-work-for-you/1049854

18. Jones, "Besides Being Lonely at the Top."

19. "Darwin E. Smith 2004 Inductee – Leadership," Paper Industry International Hall of Fame, posted 2004. Retrieved March 15, 2012, from http://www.paperhall.org/inductees/bios/2004/darwin_smith.php

20. Collins, "The Misguided Mix-Up of Celebrity and Leadership."

21. Peter Lattman and Geraldine Fabrikant, "A Conspicuous Absence at Berkshire Meeting," *New York Times,* Business Day, posted April 26, 2011. Retrieved January 19, 2012, from http://www.nytimes.com/2011/04/27/business/27sokol.html?pagewanted=all

Chapter Ten

1. Marcia Pledger, "Some Call Arrogant People Leaders in the Workplace; Others Prefer 'Jerk,'" *Cleveland.com,* posted December 4, 2011. Retrieved January 26, 2012, from http://www.cleveland.com/business/index.ssf/2011/12/some_call_arrogant_people_lead.html

2. Christine L. Porath and Amir Erez, "Overlooked But Not Untouched: How Incivility Reduces Onlookers' Performance on Routine and Creative Tasks," *Organizational Behavior and Human Decision Processes* 109 (2009): 29–44.

3. Pledger, "Some Call Arrogant People Leaders in the Workplace."

4. Ibid.

5. "Researcher: Narcissistic Bosses Destroy Morale, Drive Down Bottom Line," *Florida State 24/7, The News Site of Florida State University,* posted August 7, 2009. Retrieved March 1, 2012, from http://news.fsu.edu/More-FSU-News/News-Archive/2009/August/Researcher-Narcissistic-Bosses-Destroy-Morale-Drive-Down-Bottom-Line

6. Carl Vogel, "A Field Guide to Narcissism," *Psychology Today,* posted January 1, 2006. Retrieved March 1, 2012, from http://www.psychologytoday.com/articles/200512/field-guide-narcissism

7. Pledger, "Some Call Arrogant People Leaders in the Workplace."

8. Morgenson, "Barbie's Guru Stumbles" (ch. 8, n. 8).

9. Ibid.

10. William C. Taylor, "Leadership Isn't Infallibility," *Bloomberg Business-Week,* posted November 24, 2009. Retrieved March 1, 2012, from

http://www.businessweek.com/managing/content/nov2009/ca20091124_021126.htm

11. Michael Maccoby, "Narcissistic Leaders: The Incredible Pros, the Inevitable Cons," *Harvard Business Review,* January-February 2000. Retrieved March 1, 2012, from http://www.maccoby.com/Articles/NarLeaders.shtml

12. Ibid.

ACKNOWLEDGMENTS

We have been extremely fortunate to work with some of the brightest minds in business leadership. This book is truly the culmination of our interactions with clients, colleagues, and executives over the last decade. The strength of this book is a reflection of these people.

This project has been a major undertaking. It is a combination of ideas from active leaders supported with results from academic research. We are grateful to the many people who interviewed with us. The CEOs and leaders who were so generous with their time created the context and stories that make this book so real. They shared their insights with us, in both formal interviews as well as personal conversations. These leaders believe in learning from mistakes, and they worked with us because they felt they could improve other leaders' lives by way of example.

This book would not have been possible without the outstanding team that so generously shared their talents with us. First, we would like to thank Genoveva Llosa for her guidance and direction. She took the ideas from our research and framed them into a book that appeals to a broad audience. We would also like thank Jenna Free, as she was more than collaborator—she was truly a thought partner throughout this project. Finally, we would like to thank Jennifer Robin for providing the impetus to initiate this project. We have benefitted from her insights and perspectives.

We would also like to thank Natalie Reames for the in-depth research she provided to identify the difficult stories that no one likes to talk about. Chris Francis, Eric Michel, and Candace Esken provided the attention to detail necessary to prepare this book for publication. Thanks to Carolyn Monaco and Alicia Simons for creating an outstanding platform to launch this book. Additionally, we would like to thank Katie Sowa for leveraging her network of CEOs.

A special thanks to Kelsey Wright, who helped coordinate interviews with numerous leaders throughout the country.

We would also like to thank Bradley University and the Heartland Partnership for their support throughout this project. We are proud to work with two outstanding organizations.

Finally, we would like to thank our families for their encouragement, support, and understanding. Often, in the middle of writing chapters, we would ask ourselves how our children could benefit from ideas in this book. So, as we help them to grow and develop, we want our kids to know that making mistakes is part of life and embracing these experiences will make them better people.

INDEX

ABOUT THE AUTHORS

Laurence G. Weinzimmer is an internationally recognized thought leader in organizational strategy and leadership. He is a sought-after business advisor to numerous Fortune 100 companies, the Caterpillar Inc. Professor of Management in the Foster College of Business Administration at Bradley University, and author of three books, including the best seller *Fast Growth*.

Along with advising and teaching, Larry regularly addresses audiences across the United States and abroad on the topics of balanced leadership and creating and sustaining high-performance organizations. He has frequently been featured in leading business magazines, including *Fortune, Executive Excellence,* and *Entrepreneur,* and has been interviewed by leading national news networks, including FNN, CNN, ABC, and *NBC Nightly News*.

Larry is also a highly recognized researcher. His work appears in over fifteen languages, and he has been widely honored for his research accomplishments by many prestigious organizations, including the Academy of Management.

Larry also offers his expertise to a number of not-for-profit organizations, including the United Way, the American Red Cross, and Local Initiatives Support Corporation.

Jim McConoughey is a sought after business development and community leadership expert. He is an active fund manager for venture and early-stage capital investments and is an in-demand advisor to a vast number of small to mid-size businesses and economic organizations. Jim's particular focus is working with organizations to identify and evaluate strategic growth opportunities. He is the recent CEO of the Heartland Partnership, a Peoria-based management company that focuses on business development in the Central Illinois region, and also managed the Center for Economic Development Excellence, a research group affiliated with the Economic Development Council for Central Illinois.

Along with extensive client work, Jim lends his expertise to multiple private and public boards and charitable organizations throughout the region and across the country. He has been featured in *Money, Fortune Small Business, Crain's Chicago, Chicago Tribune, Reuters, Economist,* and numerous other national and international publications. He has also appeared on CNN, *NBC Nightly News,* NPR, *Fox News,* Bloomberg, *Voice of America,* and other television and radio programs.

For more information about *The Wisdom of Failure,* please visit www.TheWisdomOfFailure.com.

Introducing the Wisdom of Failure Keynote

Talking about failure is difficult, if not taboo. Our business cultures are designed to reward short-term success and penalize failure. This fresh keynote tackles the issue head on by showing how insights learned from failure are indispensable in creating great leaders—that when we take the time to examine failure, we can proactively avoid making the same mistakes ourselves. Audiences walk away with the ability to recognize the most common causes of leadership failure and clearly outlined strategies for navigating toward success.

Larry and Jim are also available for additional keynotes:

Larry Weinzimmer: *Designing High-Performance Organizations*. In this keynote, Dr. Weinzimmer addresses what differentiates those who lead the pack from those in the middle. He shares findings from his groundbreaking research that identifies three catalysts of high-performance organizations: the unique ability to identify critical market opportunities, a culture based on common sense, and designing a value-focused top-management team.

To learn more about speaking and consulting opportunities with Larry, contact him at Larry@TheWisdomofFailure.com.

Jim McConoughey: *Smart Investing for Start-Up and High Growth Companies*. In this session, Jim talks about the reality that you need to do many things right to succeed—but only a few things wrong to fail. Jim applies his extensive knowledge of early-stage capital investing so audiences walk away with a new understanding of how to invest wisely, avoid potential minefields, and keep moving forward on the path to success.

To learn more about speaking and consulting opportunities with Jim, contact him at Jim@TheWisdomofFailure.com.

Take Advantage of Free Wisdom of Failure Assessment Tools on the Web

Visit www.TheWisdomofFailure.com

- Find out more about what kind of thinker you are—a "coarse-grained thinker" or a "fine-grained thinker."

- Assess whether your company is characterized by "dysfunctional harmony."

- Learn more about your intrinsic motivators: How do you benchmark against different leadership styles?